AF873537

Through the Waters

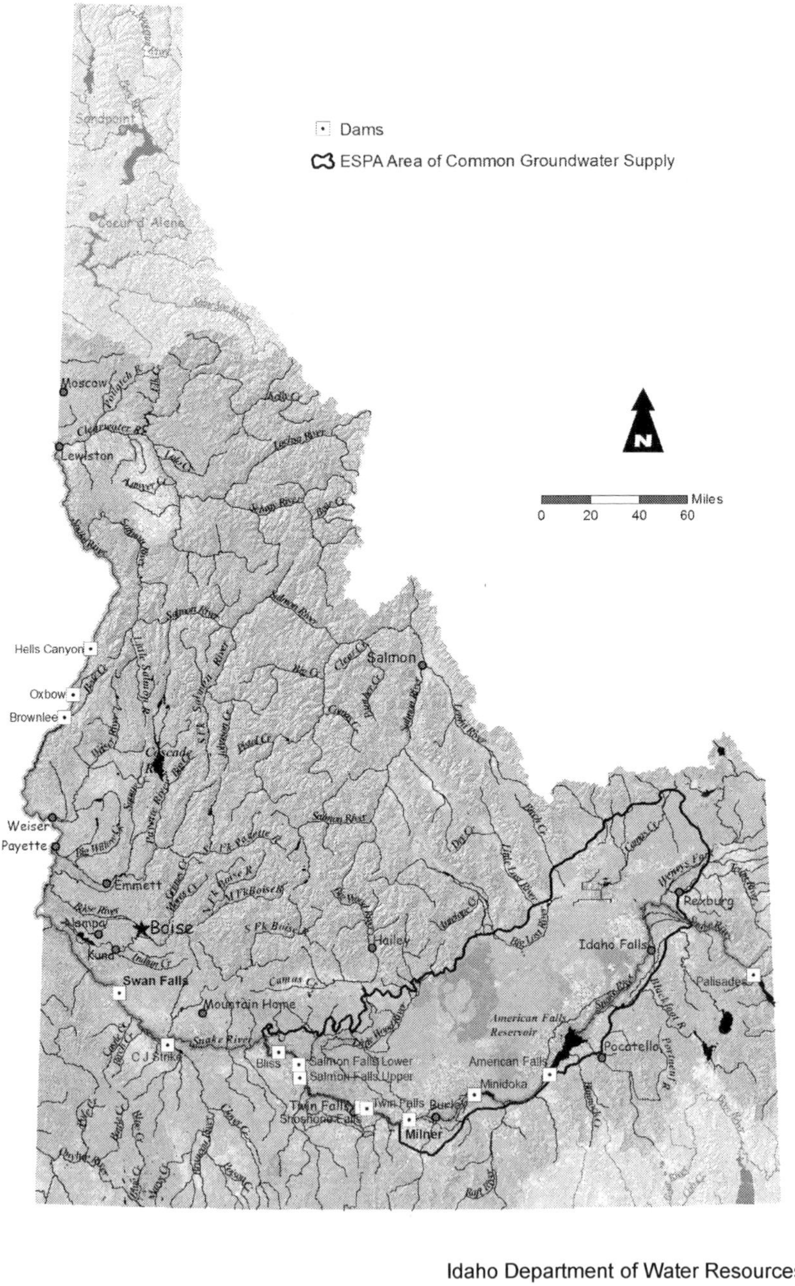

Idaho Department of Water Resources

Through the Waters

An Oral History of the Snake River Basin Adjudication

edited by
The Water Law Section of
The Idaho State Bar
and Randy Stapilus

Ridenbaugh Press
Carlton, Oregon
2014

THROUGH THE WATERS An Oral History of the Snake River Basin Adjudication

For more information, contact Ridenbaugh Press, P.O. Box 834, Carlton OR 97111.
Printed and bound in the United States of America.
First edition September 2014
10 9 8 7 6 5 4 3 2 1

Library of Congress Cataloging in Publication Data

[editors] Idaho State Barr Water Law Section; Randy Stapilus

Title

Bibliography

1. Idaho Politics and Government. 2. Idaho-Law. 3. Idaho-History.

I. Idaho State Bar Water Law Section. II. Title.

ISBN-10 978-0-945648-19-2 (softbound)

Cover photo: The Tetons and the Snake River, by Ansel Adams (1941), commissioned by the U.S. Department of the Interior.

Ridenbaugh Press

P.O. Box 834, Carlton OR 97111

Phone (503) 852-0010

www.ridenbaugh.com

stapilus@ridenbaugh.com

Contents

Dedication

This book is dedicated to former Attorney General Jim Jones and to the memory of Governor John Evans and Idaho Power Company CEO Jim Bruce. These individuals had the foresight and courage to look beyond their differences to chart a course for water policy into the 21st century, and recognized that a general adjudication would be the cornerstone for effective management of the waters of the Snake River. Their foresight, along with the dedication of many individuals, has led to the milestone this book is commemorating.

Participants

VINCE ALBERDI General manager of the Twin Falls Canal Company from 1992 to 2008, and previously an engineer for the TWCC and the Northside Canal Company. He is a member of the Idaho Water Resources Board. *Interviewed August 1, 2014, by telephone, by Randy Stapilus.*

BRIGETTE BILYEU Special master in the SRBA; she was one of the first three appointed, in 1993. She was born in Pocatello, where both of her parents (C.E. "Chick" and Diane Bilyeu) served as state senators. She worked as a reporter for KPVI-TV and KIFI-TV in Idaho. After graduating from Harvard University and receiving her law degree at the University of Idaho, she practiced law with the Elam, Burke & Boyd law firm in Boise before her appointment at the SRBA. *Interviewed July 1, 2014, in Twin Falls, by Emmi Blades.*

TED BOOTH Special master in the SRBA. After receiving his law degree from the University of Utah College of Law, he worked as a law clerk for two future SRBA judges, Barry Wood and Roger Burdick. He also worked in private practice in Gooding before his appointment to the SRBA position in 2004, replacing Tom Cushman, who had retired. *Interviewed July 1, 2014, in Twin Falls, by Emmi Blades.*

JAMES BRUCE President and CEO of Idaho Power Company, he grew up in Boise and lived there most of his life. He attended the College of Idaho, the University of Portland and Georgetown University. As an attorney he joined Idaho Power in 1951 and was active in its legal cases for many years. He was named president of the company in 1971 and CEO in 1976; he retired in 1985. He was centrally involved in the Swan Falls negotiations that led to the SRBA. He died at Boise on February 20, 2014. *Interview from a deposition in the SRBA, taken November 15, 1990.*

ROGER BURDICK He was the third SRBA presiding judge and later a justice of the Idaho Supreme Court. He received his law degree from the University of Idaho in 1974 and entered private practice in Boise and Jerome, also serving as a deputy prosecuting attorney at Ada County, and a public defender in the Magic Valley. Appointed a magistrate judge in 1981 at Jerome County, he was appointed to the district bench in 1993. Burdick was assigned the SRBA in 2001, while also serving as administrative judge for the Fifth District. In August 2003 he was named to the Idaho Supreme Court, and in 2011 began a four-year term as chief justice. *Interviewed July 2, 2014, in Boise, by Dylan B. Lawrence.*

VERN CASE A farmer and water user near Wilder (about a mile from the Snake River), and a director of the Wilder Irrigation District, a director for Riverside Irrigation District and a director of the Idaho Water Users Association. *Interviewed August 1, 2014, on telephone, by Randy Stapilus.*

PATRICK COSTELLO Legal counsel to Governor John Evans, he was one of the negotiators of the Swan Falls Agreement that resulted in the SRBA. After receiving degrees from Kansas University and the Boston University School of Law, he worked as a television reporter at Boston and in Boise. He became staff attorney for the Idaho Office of Energy in 1980, then counsel to the governor from 1981-86. He then co-founded the Park Costello and Burkett firm in 1989. He was a magistrate judge at Clearwater County from 1992-99, and later served as a law professor at the University of Idaho. *Interview from a deposition in the SRBA, taken November 14, 1990.*

TERRENCE DOLAN Special master in the SRBA; he was one of the first three appointed in 1993. Previously, he served for seven years as the Special Master in the Big Horn River General Adjudication and Hot Springs County District Court Commissioner in Thermopolis, Wyoming. He practiced law in Arizona and Wyoming. *Interviewed July 1, 2014, in Twin Falls, by Emmi Blades.*

KARL DREHER Director of the Idaho Department of Water Resources (from 1996-2006) during the mid-period of the SRBA. A veteran Colorado water manager, he led the Idaho department as the volume of work in the SRBA was picking up. He has since consulted on groundwater issues in the Republican River Basin and served as general manager of the Edwards Aquifer Authority. He lives in Colorado. *Interviewed July 31, 2014 by telephone, by Andrea Courtney.*

KEN DUNN A director of the Idaho Department of Water Resources, he led the agency (from 1981-87) as the SRBA was being launched. He received a B.S. (Civil Engineering) from California State University at Sacramento. A civil engineer since 1962, he worked for the Bureau of Reclamation before going to work for the state of Idaho in 1967. *Interview from a deposition in the SRBA, taken November 7, 1990.*

CARTER FRITSCHLE Long-time water rights technician and manager at the Idaho Department of Water Resources, currently Adjudication Section manager. He started with the department in 1986 examining water rights, became the first water resource agent specifically assigned to the SRBA, and more recently has managed the adjudication section. *Interviewed July 18, 2014, by response to written questions.*

HOWARD FUNKE Attorney representing, among others, the Shoshone-Bannock Tribes in the SRBA and in other matters. He now is based in Coeur d'Alene, and his clients include the Coeur d'Alene Tribe. *Interviewed August 1, 2014, in Coeur d'Alene, by Dylan Hedden-Nicely.*

DANIEL HURLBUTT He was the first presiding judge in the SRBA, from 1987-98, and set up many of its processes and procedures. A native of the Chicago area, he attended Colorado College and the University of Denver College of Law. He practiced antitrust litigation in Chicago with the firm Chadwell Kayser Ruggles McGee and Hasting. Moving to Idaho, he was appointed a magistrate judge in Lincoln County in 1980 and a district judge in the 5th District in 1984. He was assigned the SRBA in 1987.

Hurlbutt resigned from the bench in 1998. He is a senior judge, mediator and arbitrator based in Ketchum. *Interviewed June 25, 2014, in Ketchum, by Dylan B. Lawrence.*

JIM JONES An Idaho Supreme Court justice and former state attorney general. A legislative aide to former Senator Len Jordan, he engaged in a private law practice in the Magic Valley until his election as attorney general in 1982; he was re-elected in 1986. While there, he played a central role in the Swan Falls settlement and establishment of the SRBA. In 2004 he was elected to the Idaho Supreme Court. *Interviewed June 23, 2014, in Boise, by Candice McHugh.*

JOHN KEYS A former regional director of the U.S. Bureau of Reclamation, he became Commissioner of the agency from 2001-06. An Alabama native who studied at the Georgia Institute of Technology, Brigham Young University and Colorado State University, he started work with the USBR in 1964 and in 1986 was named Northwest regional director. He died in a plane crash in Utah on May 30, 2008. *Interview from a deposition in the SRBA taken November 9, 1990.*

PAT KOLE A former deputy attorney general, he was one of the negotiators of the Swan Falls Agreement. As an attorney he worked at the Ada County prosecutor's office (1976-79), at the Caldwell firm of Gigray Miller Downen and Weston (1979-83), then at the Idaho Attorney General's office (1983-89). He then joined the Boise firm Moffatt Thomas Barrett Rock & Fields, and is a vice president at the Idaho Potato Commission. *Interview from a deposition in the SRBA taken November 14, 1990.*

FRANCIS McGOVERN A law professor at Duke University who served as court-appointed mediator in the Nez Perce tribal negotiations in the SRBA. His web page at Duke notes, "As a court-appointed special master or neutral expert, he has developed solutions in most of the significant mass claim litigation in the U.S., including the DDT toxic exposure litigation in Alabama, the Dalkon-Shield controversy, and his current work involving the silicone gel breast implant litigation." *Interviewed July 29, 2014, by telephone, by Ann Vonde.*

DUANE MECHAM After growing up on farms and ranches in the Northwest (including one near Emmett), he received his law degree from Brigham Young University and in 1986 became an attorney for the U.S. Department of Interior. He worked first at Washington, D.C., then in 1996 transferred to the Portland, Oregon, office of the regional solicitor, where he still works. *Interviewed July 23, 2014, in Portland, Oregon, by Randy Stapilus.*

JOHN MELANSON The fourth presiding judge in the SRBA. The Connecticut native served in the Army and received his law degree from the University of Idaho School of Law. After private law practice in Buhl, he was appointed a magistrate judge in Lincoln County in 1995 and then to the 5th District bench in 2000. In 2003 he became the fourth presiding judge of the SRBA. He was appointed to the Idaho Court of Appeals in 2009, where he still serves. *Interviewed on June 5, 2014, in Boise, by Ann Vonde.*

REBECCA MILES Executive director of the Nez Perce Tribe, formerly a member of the tribal council. She was a central figure in the tribe's discussions about signing the Snake River Water Rights Agreement of 2004. *Interviewed July 18, 2014, in Lapwai by Candice McHugh.*

PETER MONSON Trial Attorney and Assistant Section Chief with the Indian Resources Section at the U.S. Department of Justice, active in the SRBA from 1985 until his retirement in 2012. Until the early 1990s he was the sole Department of Justice attorney active in the SRBA, and he was the lead federal attorney in all of the SRBA Indian Water settlements (Sho-Ban, Nez Perce, and Sho-Pai). He received several awards for his work on the SRBA including two John Marshall Awards from the Attorney General (1995 and 2004) and a Citation of Commendation from the Solicitor, U.S. Department of the Interior, in February 2001. *Interviewed July 24 and August 2, 2014, by telephone, by Randy Stapilus.*

TOM NELSON He was Idaho Power Company counsel and negotiated the Swan Falls Agreement, which led to the Snake River Basin Adjudication. An Idaho Falls native, he served as a deputy state attorney general from 1963-65, he moved to private practice at

Twin Falls, which he continued for 25 years; Idaho Power was a primary client during much of that time. He was confirmed to the bench of the U.S. Court of Appeals for the 9th Circuit in 1990. He took senior status in 2003, and died in 2011. *Interview from a deposition in the SRBA taken October 31, 1990.*

BRUCE NEWCOMB He is a former speaker of the Idaho House of Representatives and the legislator perhaps most active in working on legislation and funding for the SRBA. A native of the Declo area, he managed his family's farming operations. After becoming active in the political battles emerging from the Swan Falls decision, he ran for and won a seat in the Idaho House in 1986. He rose through the ranks of leadership, becoming speaker in 1998, serving in that position eight years, longer than anyone else. Since retiring from the legislature in 2006, he has worked in government relations for Boise State University. *Interviewed June 19, 2014, in Boise, by Candice McHugh.*

LAIRD NOH He was a state senator and chairman of the Senate Resources and Environment Committee from 1983 through 2004. He was a leader in the effort to resolve the Swan Falls conflict and took an active role the SRBA throughout his tenure in the Idaho Legislature. A native of the Twin Falls area, he studied at the University of Idaho and the University of Chicago before returning to help manage his family's sheep ranching operations. Noh was elected to the Idaho Senate in 1980 and retired from the position in 2004. *Interview by Travis Thompson and Paul Arrington, at Twin Falls, on July 9, 2014.*

GREG PANTER He was a state lobbyist for Idaho Power Company during the years of conflict and negotiation of the Swan Falls Agreement, which led to the SRBA. *Interview from a deposition in the SRBA taken October 23, 1990.*

JEFF RAYBOULD A farmer at the Rexburg-St. Anthony area (in the Raybould Brothers family farm operations), chairman of the Fremont-Madison Irrigation District and a member of the Idaho Water Resource Board. *Interviewed August 1, 2014, on telephone, by Randy Stapilus.*

RAY RIGBY A leading water law attorney in Idaho, he led development of key settlement terms in the Swan Falls dispute. A native of the Rexburg area, he received his law degree from the University of Idaho College of Law. He entered private practice, with water law as a major emphasis, in Rexburg. He was elected Madison County prosecutor and later to the state Senate, and ran unsuccessfully for lieutenant governor in 1974. *Interviewed June 20, 2014, in Rexburg, by Jerry Rigby.*

JOHN ROSHOLT One of the leading water attorneys in Idaho. He was highly active through both the Swan Falls conflicgt and Snake River Basin Adjudication. After earning his law degree at the University of Idaho College of Law (where his fraternity brothers included Tom Nelson), he served as a deputy in the Idaho Attorney General's office. He moved to Twin Falls in 1964 and entered private practice, with a focus on water law. *Interviewed June 30, 2014, in Twin Falls, by Travis L. Thompson and Paul L. Arrington.*

DAVID SHAW He was a veteran of the IDWR and the first chief of its adjudication bureau. Raised on a family farm near Emmett, he received a degree in agricultural engineering from the University of Idaho and started work with the IDWR in 1973. He began work on the Snake River Basin Adjudication on July 1, 1985, one of the first people specifically assigned to it. He left the agency in 1996, and is a consultant with ERO Resources Corp. *Interviewed June 20, 2014, in Boise, by Meghan Carter.*

DEAN STEVENSON A farmer in the Paul-Kimama area for the past 24 years, he has lived in the area all of his life. Currently he is chairman of the Magic Valley groundwater District. *Interviewed July 31, 2014 by telephone,by Candice McHugh.*

CLIVE STRONG Joined the Idaho Attorney General's Office in 1983. He became Chief of the Natural Resources Division in 1985. He has been a leading figure in Idaho water law for three decades. Raised in the Wendell area, he studied forestry at the University of Idaho and obtained law degrees from there and the University of Michigan. He practiced (at Moscow, Idaho) and taught (at the University of Puget Sound Law School) before joining the Idaho Attorney General's Office; he was assigned the Swan Falls cases his third day there. He assisted with the negotiation of the Swan Falls Agreement, and has represented the State of Idaho throughout the Snake River Basin Adjudication, filing the petition to commence the adjudication in 1987. *Interviewed July 3, 2014, in Boise, by Ann Vonde.*

DAVID TUTHILL He was the second chief of the water adjudication bureau at the IDWR, and later became director of that department. He joined the Department of Water Resources in 1976 as an engineer, became manager of its western regional office, and was named chief of the adjudication bureau in 1996. He was named director of the department in 2007, and retired from the agency in 2009. He then founded Idaho Water Engineering, a consulting firm where he continues to work. *Interviewed May 21, 2014, in Boise, by Randy Stapilus.*

ERIC WILDMAN Judge Wildman is a general jurisdiction judge for the state of Idaho. He was appointed to the bench in 2009. Following his appointment, the Idaho Supreme Court assigned him to preside over the Snake River Basin Adjudication and the Coeur d'Alene-Spokane River Basin Adjudication and to hear statewide all administrative appeals from the Idaho Department of Water Resources. Judge Wildman received his Bachelor of Science degree in economics from the University of Utah and his Juris Doctorate from the University of Idaho College of Law. Thereafter, Judge Wildman clerked for a district court judge and later worked in private general practice in Gooding, Idaho. In 1999, Judge Wildman became the staff attorney for the Snake River Basin Adjudication until his appointment to the bench in 2009. *Interviewed June 10, 2014, in Twin Falls, by Chris Bromley.*

BARRY WOOD The second presiding judge at the SRBA, in 1999 and 2000. A native of Owyhee County, he grew up on a farm and studied at the University of Wyoming and earned his law degree at the University of Idaho College of Law. After practicing in Homedale, he was named a magistrate judge in Lincoln County, then was appointed to the 5th District Court bench. He was assigned the Snake River Basin Adjudication with the departure of the first presiding judge, DANIel Hurlbutt. He retired from the bench at the end of 2009. *Interview by Andrea Courtney, in Boise, on June 9, 2014.*

NORM YOUNG He was administrator of the Water Management Division, IIDWR. After obtaining a degree in agricultural engineering from the University of Idaho, he started work at the IDWR in 1969 (primarily as a groundwater hydrologist), and stayed until his retirement in 2003. He currently is a private consultant with ERO Resources. *Interviewed June 30, 2014, in Boise, by Shelley Davis.*

A basin-wide disclaimer

A number of the interviewees in this book are attorneys who, for the most part, represented various parties in the adjudication. The interviews in this book, however, are personal: They are speaking only on behalf of themselves, not on behalf of clients or employers.

Interview transcription

A great deal of time was donated or discounted by court reporters, and court reporting firms, around the state. They included:

Bilyeu: Sabrina Vasquez.
Booth: Sabrina Vasquez.
Burdick: Lori Pulsifer, QnA Court Reporting, LLC.
Dolan: Sabrina Vasquez.
Hurlbutt: Diana Kilpatrick, M&M Court Reporting.
Jones: Ann K. Wardwell, M&M Court Reporting.
Melanson: Colleen P. Zeimantz of M & M Court Reporting.
Newcomb: Jeff LaMar, M&M Court Reporting.
Rigby: Shantae Miller, T&T Reporting.
Rosholt: Catherine Pavkov, M&M Court Reporting.
Shaw: Jeff LaMar, M&M Court Reporting.
Strong: Diana Durland, M&M Court Reporting.
Tuthill: Barbara Burke, M&M Court Reporting.
Wildman: Sabrina Vasquez.

SRBA Presiding Judges

1987-1998	Daniel Hurlbutt
1999-2000	Barry Wood
2000-2003	Roger Burdick
2003-2008	John Melanson
2008-	Eric Wildman

Directors, Department of Water Resources

1974-1977	Keith Higginson
1977-1981	Steve Allred
1981-1987	Ken Dunn
1987-1995	Keith Higginson
1995-2006	Karl Dreher
2007-2009	David Tuthill
2012-	Gary Spackman

Available for the First Time in Your State!

COMMEMORATIVE TEE SHIRTS:

I RETIRED ON THE SNAKE RIVER ADJUDICATION

\$\$

\$\$

1987 - 1997

****

ORDER FORM

Name:________________________
Address________________________
____
Size: S M L XL No:____

Make Check or Money Order Payable to:
ADVOCATE RELIEF FUND
IDAHO STATE BAR
(No phone orders please!)

Also Available: I BOUGHT MY BMW THROUGH THE SNAKE RIVER ADJUDICATION;
I SENT MY KIDS THROUGH COLLEGE ON THE SNAKE RIVER ADJUDICATION.

For each shirt send a flat fee of $100.00 plus a variable fee of $3.50 per kilowatt of capacity.

Page 16 April 1988

From the April 1988 edition of the Idaho State Bar *Advocate*.
Reprinted with permission.

The River

When the early travelers along the Oregon Trail reached what is now Idaho, they encountered what seemed to them two treacherous and difficult obstacles.

One was the desert itself, a couple of hundred miles of it.

The other, ironically, was the big river – which would be called the Snake – flowing near their trails, which in places they were obliged to cross, often at great difficulty.

Some of the survivors of those treks may have been astonished at what happened a generation and more down the line: The two obstacles were merged to advantage, creating a whole new region of human settlement.

Many of the waterways in Idaho have become renowned for their fishing or whitewater or scenic opportunities. The Snake River, which draws most of its water from the plains and mountains around it in Idaho, has come to be known as a working river, its water turned into the tap root of the southern Idaho community and economy.

The water was put to use for many things, but two have dominated through most of Idaho's history.

The first is irrigated farming, which began almost as soon as mining brought prospectors to the hills and farmers broke ground to grow food for feeding them.

The second is hydropower, which began in earnest a few decades after irrigated agriculture as demand for electricity picked up toward the end of the 1800s.

Around the turn of the century (the 19th into the 20th), and ever since, those two uses became deeply intertwined. Across much of southern Idaho, the Snake River and some of its tributaries had cut canyons far below the desert surface, and moving water for irrigation out of the river and onto the desert required pumping, which required electricity, and a lot of it, at low price. Hydropower could supply that need.

For decades these uses worked, economically, logistically and naturally, in some harmony – as long as enough water flowed through the Snake to meet everyone's needs. Eventually, however, the margins began to close. In the 1950s vast tracts came to be irrigated through pumped groundwater, which depleted the aquifers that helped feed the Snake River. Electric power demands grew along with the size of Idaho's communities and with varied manufacturing – of everything from frozen potatoes to microchips – began to place new demands on electric power in the area. Hydropower was inexpensive compared with power produced from most other means, such as coal-fired plants, but with an end to major dam construction on the Snake and its tributaries in the early 1970s (the last was the ill-fated Teton Dam), hydropower resources on the river seem to have been capped.

The river remained important as a power resource, however. And because the ability to produce hydropower depends on substantial flows of water through the rivers, the region was headed toward a collision between the demands for hydropower and the demands for other uses, such as irrigation, manufacturing and domestic uses.

That day arrived in 1982, in the form of a decision by the Idaho Supreme Court.

CLIVE STRONG The Swan Falls case is a seminal water law case in Idaho. The heart of the controversy is the relationship between hydropower and agricultural development.

In order to understand Swan Falls, it's important to understand the geography of the state.

The Snake River – from the Wyoming border to Milner Dam largely runs along the surface and is easily accessible for agricultural development. So, from the late 1800s through the early 1900s, there was a heavy emphasis on developing the water of the Snake River above Milner Dam.

Below Milner Dam the river enters into a very deep and incised canyon. So, in the early 1900s the water in this reach of the Snake River was not accessible for agricultural development, but was ideal for hydropower development.

In the early 1900s Idaho Power Company acquired the Swan Falls Dam, which was originally constructed to provide power for mining in Owyhee County. Idaho Power then began acquiring other dams along the river, the American Falls Dam, as well as constructing dams in the stretch of the Snake River from Milner Dam to Swan Falls Dam, which is located south of Kuna.

As the development began, obviously taking water out of the Snake River above Milner Dam was reducing [flow] in the reach of the Snake River below the dam, which was impacting hydropower generation. But in the early 1900s there was kind of a symbiotic relationship between the power company and the irrigators because irrigators were the customers for the power. So, the company viewed irrigation as beneficial to its long-term interest and implicitly subordinated its water rights to upstream development. Under the prior appropriation doctrine, water rights are allocated based upon when they're first put to beneficial use. Under a subordination agreement, a senior water right holder with an earlier priority agrees not to exercise the priority of the senior water right against junior water rights.

So in this instance, the power company essentially agreed not to exercise its senior priority water rights against the junior water rights that were being developed.

That became really important because most of the hydropower plants are designed to use the entire flow of the river. The Swan Falls water rights have priority dates between 1901 and 1917. These priority dates predate a lot of the agricultural development. The water rights were licensed at a flow rate of a little over 9,000 cfs*, which if exercised would have precluded upstream development.

A plan was developed in 1920 between the Bureau of Reclamation, the State of Idaho and irrigation interests, which was designed for optimum use of the waters of the Snake River above Milner Dam. The central premise of the Board of Engineers report was that the optimum use of the river was to develop the water supply above Milner Dam and to allow the water below Milner Dam to be used by the power company.

Some might ask why the power company would agree to allow juniors to infringe upon its senior surface water rights. The reason was that in the early 1900s most lands were irrigated by gravity irrigation. Large volumes of water were diverted onto the Eastern Snake Plan Aquifer, which encompasses an 11,000 square mile area from basically the Hagerman Valley all the way up to Rexburg.

The aquifer is hydraulically connected to the river, and a large portion of its water empties into the Snake River in the Thousand Springs reach.

So, the thought was that water developed above Milner would percolate into the aquifer and then be available for hydropower development below Milner. There was a trade off in that the company might lose some of its production capacity at the Shoshone Falls and Twin Falls plants and some of the ones in Hagerman Valley; but, increased spring flows would be available for the downstream use in the company's other hydropower plants.

The symbiotic relationship existed up through the 1950s when the company decided to build what is called the Hells Canyon Complex. At the the infancy of the Hells Canyon Complex, there was a large controversy. The federal government was actively seeking to develop the waters of the west through large reclamation projects.

The Bureau of Reclamation sought to develop a federal Hells Canyon project. The company opposed the federal project because it would interfere with its interest in developing hydropower in the basin. The company sought Idaho's support for private hydropower. Governor Jordan agreed to support the company on the condition that the company subordinate its hydropower water rights. In the Hells Canyon FERC license, a provision was included that expressly documented the subordination. Unfortunately that documentation wasn't carried forward into many of the state water right licenses,

---

* cubic feet per second, a common measure of water flow.

particularly in earlier upstream water rights. So the seed of the Swan Falls controversy was the failure to document the understanding regarding the subordination of hydropower water rights.

The other element that led to the Swan Falls controversy was a fundamental change in technology in the 1950s. Groundwater pumping became feasible, which led to the development of the groundwater of the Eastern Snake Plain Aquifer. The consequence was the reduction of the flows in Thousand Springs that had been part of the the 1920s trade off for subordination of hydropower water rights.

As spring flows began to decline in the 1970s, the power company observed a need for additional power production. So, it proposed developing a coal-fired plant called the Pioneer Plant, near Boise.

That elicited a lot of concern from rate payers, some irrigators, and some environmental interests. In 1977 they filed a petition with the PUC [Public Utilities Commission] arguing that the company should not be able to rate base the Swan Falls Power Plant.

The effort by the group of aligned interests to deny the company's ability to rate base Swan Falls hydropower plant forced the company into a position of asserting its water rights for Swan Falls. The company asserted that its water rights were not subordinated to upstream uses contrary to the long-held belief of the state and irrigators.

The Swan Falls lawsuit precipitated a lot of controversy. The company felt that it was in a real dilemma. In a memorandum from Tom Nelson, who was the company's attorney at the time, to Jim Bruce, who was chairman of Idaho Power Company at the time, Tom recounted the company’s past history of subordination of its water rights to upstream uses and acknowledged that the position it was king was contrary to its past practices.

Tom's conclusion was that the company was unlikely to win on the subordination issue with respect to past development but that the company had an opportunity to preclude future development in the Snake River Basin.

Swan Falls 1980-1983

LAIRD NOH The immediate predecessors to this case involved the Orchard coal fired plant which Idaho Power proposed, and the strong pushback which was led by a fellow sheep rancher, state Senator John Peavey.

> The seeds of Swan Falls

It is well known that they brought suit against Idaho Power for failing to defend their water rights at Swan Falls. But some of the interesting politics behind that aren't well known, and had to do with the Desert Land Entry Act and the aggressiveness of Idaho Power to promote high lift pumping.

There was a large block of very important winter-early spring grazing land in the Bell Rapids area from Glenns Ferry to Castleford, and those were key grazing privileges, mostly on BLM [Bureau of Land Management] land, for both cattle and sheep. And as the Desert Entry Act came on, many of these grazing areas were turned into desert entry, pump-irrigated farms. Legally, the holders of the associated grazing permits were just out of luck. Senator Peavey was savvy enough that he convinced many of the livestock permittees – some very prominent ranchers, such as the Purdys from the Wood River Valley and the Faulkners, from Gooding, to join in the litigation to try to block Idaho Power from continuing to encourage more agricultural development of those key grazing areas along the river.

NORM YOUNG The belief being that the price of electricity was going to go up or there was going to have to be coal-fired power plants, if the water was taken away from the hydropower plants if you had another 800,000 acres or even some big portion of that developed.

JAMES BRUCE I was employed by the Idaho Power Company from September 1951, and before that, I was in the prosecutor's office and the attorney general's office and had a private law practice for a couple of years.

I guess I was the head cheese. I had the responsibility of overseeing the activities of the company, generally overseeing it, and I was elected as – or appointed by the board. I was elected as a director of the company. And so I had just overall oversight duties to see that the Idaho Power Company was progressing.

TOM NELSON Informal but thorough, Mr. Bruce was a very hands-on sort of guy, and was not big on staff. He knew more about Idaho Power Company than anybody I was ever around. And you could find him anywhere in the company at any time, and he tended to manage by knowing what was going on. But it was informal. I mean, he didn't have a big staff meeting where all kinds of issues were discussed every third Tuesday, and all that sort of thing.

Idaho Power Company was a major player in the Swan Falls controversy from its inception, and I represented Idaho Power Company, I believe as lead counsel, if not sole counsel, in all stages of the controversy.

LAIRD NOH When I was elected [to the Senate] I did represent Twin Falls County, water was all we had and I was associated with agriculture and understood water. I was college friends with John Rosholt and Tom Nelson, so I really felt my primary responsibility was to learn all I could about water. I was active in the water issues, and took every opportunity I could to learn more about it.

PAT KOLE When I was hired [at the attorney general's office] in 1983, I had met and worked with Jim Jones prior to 1983, and when we were talking in 1982, he had talked about my joining the staff so that a more aggressive posture in that [Swan Falls] litigation might be assumed. And after he was inaugurated, he called and asked if I wanted to come on board primarily to work on that and other natural resource issues. . . .

In 1984 I believe I spent the majority of my time working on the Swan Falls case.

LAIRD NOH Another key element, as least in my approach, was that the Twin Falls Canal Company's water right was one of the very few which was senior to the Swan Falls water right. So that maybe put me in a little more of a neutral position. I always came down pretty heavily against Idaho Power.

NORM YOUNG Look at the drought, for example. Everybody wanted a backup well, a supplemental well. I shouldn't say everybody, but it seemed like everybody did. And so well drillers were busy.

Again, my sequence may be wrong, but there had been protests filed by the spring users, fish propagation people in particular, and they'd not gotten very far in terms of the department saying groundwater shouldn't be approved. So the lower Snake River Recharge District – I believe that legislation was about that time in which the fish propagation folks in the Hagerman Valley tried to solve the problem themselves by putting in some recharge in the Shoshone area.

TOM NELSON The issue started to take shape actually during the Pioneer Power Plant proceeding, which took place in the early and mid 70s. As part of gaining a certificate of public convenience and necessity for this major coal-fired generating plant, Idaho Power Company had to show a need for the capacity of energy the plant would produce. In doing so, it had to show what the capability of its existing existing system was, and they did what they call a depletion study. And that demonstrated that if the prediction that Idaho Power made were accurate, that river flows would continue to decline as a result of new agricultural production.

And there was another leg to that also, in that to the extent new agriculture production went in, an Idaho Power Company serviced territory, it also contributed to the load. So it was a kind of double barreled hit. And the company's load analysis, needs analysis showed this depletion and increased load, which gave rise to some adverse testimony, as I recall, in the Pioneer proceeding itself, but in one of the succeeding rate cases of the Idaho Power Company, then we had specific testimony concerning this depletion and the company's failure to protect its water rights.

The thrust of the testimony was that the new agricultural depletions were much junior to the company's water rights on the Snake River, and the company should go out and assert those water rights in an attempt to block that new agricultural production. And since the company had failed to do so, then there should be some punitive action taken against them at the PUC.

TOM NELSON The company had some questions internally.

First, for years it had encouraged new agricultural production, and I think there is probably half a room full of documents that could be produced about the company's support of new agricultural production. This all came at a time when there was an economy of scale in building larger and more power plants. In fact, up until recently, I think Idaho Power Company had had more rate reduction proceedings in its history than rate increase proceedings.

So it was a mutual back scratch. If you put more ground in production and increased the load to the company, everybody's rates went down. That happy combination of circumstances ended in the '60s when economies of scale no longer existed, or at least to the degree it had. So, new power plants were a major detriment, if you will, to the rate structure of the company.

But the company wasn't sure where it stood in this shift, and also knew that it had encouraged new agricultural production for many years. Plus the company had agreed to a subordination condition at its Hells Canyon plant in the mid '50s, and the company wasn't sure of the legal effect of that subordination on the upstream plant. So frankly, the company didn't really know the status of its water rights at the time this really started to surface.

After the Pioneer proceedings, the first stage of them were completed, John Rosholt and I were directed by the company to start preparing a lawsuit to raise the issue of the protectability of the company's water rights above Hells Canyon. We had that lawsuit in preparation at the time of the filing of the complaint with the PUC by a number of Idaho Power Company ratepayers in '76 or '77. So the response of the company was to go to the courthouse to attempt to establish the protectability of its water rights. The ratepayers beat us to the courthouse, in the sense they got to the PUC before we got to the district.

In '76 or '77 a group of 20, say, Idaho Power Company ratepayers filed a complaint with the PUC paralleling the testimony which had been submitted in a previous rate case to the effect that the company was not protecting its water rights, and that there should be some punitive action taken against the company by reduction of rate base or otherwise, because of its failure to protect its water rights.

Senator John Peavey was in it.* I'm not sure if he was in the state senate at the time, because there was a period in there when he had been in the Senate and was not in the Senate and went back to the Senate. And some environmental and consumer activists located I guess mostly in the western part of the state, when I think about it, and they joined together as a the complainants in the PUC.

[They contended] that the company's failure to protect its water rights from depletion by new agricultural development should result in some punitive damage by the PUC.

We attempted to get the PUC to dismiss the proceeding. But external to that, we also then did file the first Swan Falls litigation in district court [in Ada County].

That was against the state of Idaho by and through the Department of Water Resources. I think we named the water resource board. We had a question of the effectiveness of the state water plan, and whether the state water plan was itself taking of the power company's water rights, and then selected water users in various reaches of the Snake River above Swan Falls.

Basically we contended that the company had valid and protectable water rights at Swan Falls and at certain projects above Swan Falls. And that the defendants were depleting or had depleted the river to the detriment of the company's water rights.

The ruling of the district court was that since the company's whole system is coordinated for operation, that the subordination of the Hells Canyon project had had the effect of subordinating the effect of the entire hydro system. Therefore, all the company's rights above Hells Canyon were subordinated.

KEN DUNN [Subordination] means the holder of the water right cannot retain his right to adversely affect future upstream

* John Peavey, a sheep rancher in the Carey area, served in the Idaho Senate from 1970-76 and 1980-94.

appropriators. The power company was maintaining that they had an unsubordinated right at Swan Falls, and within the limits of their water right, could prohibit any subsequent diversions of water to their date of priority that would reduce the flow through their turbines below the maximum amount of their water right.

Our position was that the Swan Falls water right was subordinated and that subordination was based on their acceptance of a license in the Hells Canyon project and their prior actions in encouraging development upstream from Swan Falls from the time they obtained that right through the 1960's. It was important to the department because we administered state water law and because it would have precluded any further development of the state's water resources above Swan Falls.

If Idaho Power's water right at Swan Falls was held not to be subordinated, would that mean the Snake River would be over-appropriated – more water claimed under water rights than was available?

KEN DUNN Substantially over-appropriated. I mean there's not – there would not be sufficient water in the river during the – during a substantial portion of the year to meet the full right at Swan Falls.

The Supreme Court decides Swan Falls

CLIVE STRONG In a real surprise to everyone, the Idaho Supreme Court reversed the district court in 1982 and held that in fact Paragraph 43 of the FERC license for Hells Canyon only subordinated the company's water rights at the Hells Canyon facility, not at Swan Falls.

The case was remanded back to the district court for the purposes of determining whether the company had lost its water rights through other equitable doctrines such as forfeiture, abandonment, or estoppel.

JOHN ROSHOLT The fact was that at the time of Hells Canyon, the state had become a little more sophisticated and had written the subordination provision on the licenses that they gave the power company, the water right licenses. And they had failed to do that on most of the power company's other projects above Hells Canyon up through our region of the state. It was a clerical oversight, or whatever. . . .

But I thought [4th District] Judge [Jesse] Walters did a wonderful job of reading my complaint. And, unfortunately, the case then went on appeal . . . And Jim Bruce, who was then the CEO of the power company, said, we've got to have the court of last resort in our state affirm this, so that we can be secure in continuing what we're doing. And so it was appealed to the Supreme Court.

And the five people then on the Court, an interesting group. But the guy elected to write the opinion on the Swan Falls appeal was Alan Shepard, the guy that had hired me years ago. And I won't mention who his law clerk was. But it now happens to be the senior partner in this firm.

And the Court looked at it and they said, these guys – you know, this isn't right. These guys are – they're supposed to protect their water rights at Swan Falls. And if they do that, it will be good for the State of Idaho and the rate payers and everybody else. And they turned the case around a hundred percent by a five-to-zip ruling. End of story. No appeal from it.

That put Bruce in a position, then – or Mr. Bruce as the president, or CEO of the power company, of having to go out and attempt to protect all of this – or this position. So he then filed a case, which we all called Bruce versus The World, where he named every water right applicant, every guy that was in the licensing process or had not made substantial expenditures in his project as defendants. I think there was 7,500 of them. We geared up and we served every one of them.

JIM JONES I just got elected as attorney general in early November of 1982. Later that month the Idaho Supreme Court issued the Swan Falls decision, which essentially shocked and outraged a large part of the water community. I don't think it bothered Idaho Power too much because they got a bonanza that they had not been expecting. In fact, their attorney, who was at that time Tom Nelson, had told them back in 1976 that there wasn't a real possibility that they could use the Swan Falls water right to essentially unsubordinate the Snake River. And apparently they didn't heed his advice.

They claim that they were forced into it by a proceeding in the Public Utilities Commission that essentially said Idaho Power is not protecting its property rights by not asserting its Swan Falls water right, which at the time was, I think, 9,450 cfs, although they had never really actually used more than 8,400.

In any event, the District Court, I think, got it right. It said, "Well, when the Hells Canyon deal was made with the State back in the '50s, Idaho Power had agreed to subordinate its water rights all up and down the Snake River." And that deal, by the way, was brokered by my former employer and mentor, I guess you'd call him, Senator Len Jordan, who in the '50s, at the time the question arose as to whether there would be one federal dam, a high federal dam, or three privately-owned dams had brokered a deal, okay, the State will support the three private dams by Idaho Power on the Hells Canyon if you'll agree to subordinate.

BRUCE NEWCOMB We have a ranch and farm in Declo. And we were some of the first groundwater appropriators pressurized in the state of Idaho. And my dad always raised me that water is worth more than gold. And we would see that. I think he recognized that for a lot of people that water was a finite resource, not infinite like most people thought.

But anyway, then they had the lawsuit that came forth that was by John Peavey, who was then a state senator, and some other folks that said that Idaho Power had a priority date that preempted a lot of the groundwater diversions.

Everybody always thought that they had subordinated Hells Canyon Dam complex. And in the court case it was – and Idaho Power really wasn't a friendly person. You know, they didn't really want to pursue that at the time because Bob O'Connor was the CEO. He had interests with my Uncle Bud on Bell Rapids, he and his son did. And, so they had desert land up there.

Anyway, they weren't necessarily friendly to that lawsuit.

PAT COSTELLO November 1982 was when the State Supreme Court decision was first announced, which was an unexpected development that kind of caught everyone by surprise, and we had several meetings after that to discuss what to do about it, which ultimately led to the decision to draft the subordination legislation to try to pass it during the 1983 session.

TOM NELSON Idaho Power Company appealed, and I'm not sure that the PUC didn't appeal also, but at least Idaho Power Company did appeal. And there was also an appeal involving the effectiveness of the state water plan, and that ran on a parallel track. I think we had precipitated the argument, but we didn't really participate in that appeal directly as I recall.

The water plan decision was that the state water plan was effective independent of action by the state legislature given the Court's reading of the constitution.

The decision in the other case, the Swan Falls case, was that the FPC subordination provision in the Hells Canyon license did not have the effect of subordinating upstream projects, and therefore the company's water rights were valid. The trial court had not reached the issues of abandonment, forfeiture, estoppel and so on. And those were remanded to the district court for further action.

PAT KOLE The Supreme Court issued its opinion . . . that essentially overturned Judge Walter's district court decision. At that point we had to begin preparing the case for trial. Mr. Jones wasn't, I guess, particularly pleased with the way the case had been progressing with the Department of Water Resources attorneys handling the case, so he wanted to move the case into the central office.

My recollection would have been May of 1983 or thereabouts.

He asked me to oversee it in conjunction with the Department of Water Resource attorneys and to begin the process of looking to bring another attorney into the central office to assist.

Right after I got assigned to that case, I ended up spending two and a half months in Orofino, and that case concluded in September of '83. I came back to the office on weekends and tried to monitor it and take files with me. So during the summer I would say I was primarily getting up to speed on the legal issues that were involved. We then began the process of trying to find additional staff, and beginning in October of '83, we started preparing on two fronts, the legislative front and on the judicial front, to try and do what we could to resolve the Swan Falls case.

At some point in there we hired Clive Strong.

CLIVE STRONG I started with the Office of Attorney General on August 1, 1983. My third day in the office I was assigned the

Swan Falls case, which I'm pleased to say we finally resolved after 30-plus years.

LAIRD NOH My sense was that none of the attorneys involved, Idaho Power's – John, Tom – really thought Idaho Power was going to win that case. And I remember the director of the department Ken Dunn coming into my office late one day, flushed in the face. Can you believe what happened? Idaho Power won the case!

JEFF RAYBOULD I was farming at the time, and I was well aware of Swan Falls. When the whole things came up about the Swan Falls water right it became very clear it was going to impact almost every water user in the state, especially those with more junior rights, especially those involved with storage. It was important to a lot of us that we find a resolution to that problem that the other water right holder and Idaho power could live with.

NORM YOUNG If it wasn't that afternoon, it was the next morning that Ken Dunn announced his unwritten moratorium on processing of applications. So the processing [of applications] ceased immediately.

TOM NELSON One of the other things that the company did as part of the initial filing with the district court was to file a blanket protest on new appropriations with the Department of Water Resources. We had some fairly hot struggles, as I recall, about whether or not we could do a blanket protest. Our response was, fine, we'll do a separate protest in each filing then, and that was a tremendous amount of paperwork. So the department finally accepted that blanket protest and the filings.

The company – after the district court decision, after the Supreme Court decision imposed an embargo tariff we call it - refused to hook up new users in what became the trust water area. And the state then imposed a moratorium on processing of new water rights applications above Swan Falls until we got it all sorted out.

TOM NELSON The first [Supreme Court Swan Falls] decision was November 19, 1982. We petitioned for rehearing because we thought the court had used a little loose language in describing the Swan Falls water rights. And they issued a second opinion in March of 83, as I recall, which I think is the opinion that's actually in the book. . . .

We named pending applications, ending permits, all tributaries above Swan Falls. And we also named certain licenses on the theory that during the time that the district court decision was outstanding before the 82 decision of the Supreme Court, the company really had no forum in which to protect its water rights without being accused of bad faith. And there was some authority for the position that the statute of limitations doesn't operate when you have no forum in which to protect your rights. So we had actually named some license holders in the complaint.

As best I can tell, and the records are sketchy to nonexistent, but the records I could find would indicate we served something over 2,000.

First, of course, you have the problem of finding people, number one, because oftentimes the department's records didn't reflect the actual ownership of the paper rights. And there was a lot of hostility generated by the whole process. And our processors were not warmly received as they went around the state serving people. So it was a fairly tricky time to be in.

JOHN KEYS Up until the Swan Falls case, all of the water resource agencies that I know of presumed that the Hells Canyon Complex and Swan Falls were subordinated to upstream development of water resources. That court case turned that around. And the ultimate adjudication that resulted from that will have an effect on future development in the basin.

If you look at the majority of our claims, which are for – they are storage claims. There is not a lot of effect. But in those projects that we were working on for project sponsors, the Swan Falls decision eliminated the water supply for those studies. So a profound effect on those projects.

PAT COSTELLO [Governor Evans] was for subordination; strongly for subordination. His concern was that the impact of the first Swan Falls decision was that suddenly overnight we had a fully appropriated river system unless on remand the power company would have been found to have forfeited or abandoned part of its right. That meant there could be no new development, primarily agricultural development in the Snake River Basin above Swan Falls without having to purchase water. And at that time the way he viewed it was that people would have to go hat in hand to the power company to beg them to sell them some water to put another 40 acres under cultivation.

The Idaho political response

He was primarily concerned about family farmers and ranchers like himself that had children that they would want to bring into the operation, and would want to expand their operation and bring them in, and would not be able to get the water rights to break new ground. That had been part of not only his family history, but southern Idaho history since statehood and before.

NORM YOUNG The next two legislative sessions, the solution was simply going to be for the legislature to subordinate Idaho Power's water rights. And they were heated sessions.

I know there was a lot of effort put in to trying to get those bills drafted and passed, and how much of a role the department played, I don't recall. But the end result was that the simple subordination bills never passed.

PAT KOLE The Swan Falls controversy, when the Supreme Court handed down its decision, provoked a lot of community response throughout southeastern Idaho, and many legislators contacted our office asking if there wasn't a legislative solution that could be advanced to the problem. We did a lot of research for those legislators trying to figure out if a state statute could be passed to help solve the problem.

Initially the major thrust was to do the legal research on subordination issues, to determine whether or not the 1982 constitutional amendment that had been adopted was self-executing such that the water rights of Idaho Power Company could now be legislatively subordinated without compensation being due.

I believe it was an informal guideline that concluded that the legislature did have the power . . . to subordinate Idaho Power's right without compensation being due.

TOM NELSON It depends a little bit on the area, but the farther east you went, the more heated the response. And it was basically a political response fanned a little bit by the Department of Water Resources to the effect that Idaho Power Company can't be the water master of the state's rivers, and we've got to put the state back in control of its own destiny, and we can't be in the position of going to the power company for water rights, and that sort of thing, which resulted in a legislative attempt in the 83 session to subordinate legislatively the company's water rights.

Basically the state itself responded mostly politically, as I recall. I remember there was a lot of breast beating and doomsaying about the disastrous effect this had on the water rights framework of the state of Idaho. But beyond that, I don't recall a specific initial state response. It was mostly the political one.

LAIRD NOH That sparked a round of very intensive hearings around the state in 1983, and the governor allowed the joint committee made up of members of the House and Senate Resources Committees, to use the state airplane to conduct and attend the hearings. Vard Chatburn,* who chaired the House Committee, a very wise, savvy, experienced individual, was a great mentor for me. We had hearings in Idaho Falls, Pocatello, Twin Falls and Boise. The crowds were very large, the witnesses many, and the hearings ran late. As I recall, the Boise hearing began at 6:00 p.m, and lasted until 2:00 a.m., without a recess, the longest hearing I attended in 24 years in the Idaho Senate. Out of this came the legislative proposal to subordinate Idaho Power's water rights at Swan Falls.

TOM NELSON A lot of emphasis [was] from eastern Idaho legislators representing the agricultural community over there, where they had a lot of exposure to problems if the company's water rights were to block agricultural development. There were a lot of well applications pending in that area. I think the state Department of Water Resources played a role also.

PAT COSTELLO In the legislature I can say that one of the main arguments against subordination was, the power company said

---

* J. Vard Chatburn, a farmer from Albion who was one of the longest-serving Idaho legislators (1956-86), was for many years up to his retirement chair of the House Resources & Conservation Committee and the chamber's leading figure on water policy. He died April 9, 1995.

if this legislation passes, we will seek compensation because this is the taking of vested property without just compensation, and they raised the spectre of liability in the tens if not hundreds of millions of dollars that the state was facing. It was one of their most potent arguments against subordination legislation, in my estimation.

I don't recall the attorney general getting involved in this during the 1983 session. He got actively involved in it either at the end of that session or later that year, and then from that point on was very actively involved in it.

I think Kent Foster, to tell you the truth, he is the one I first recall bringing up the proposal to draft subordination legislation. I think that was his idea and he's the one that recommended it to the governor. Then we did have a meeting that he attended, and I believe Ray Rigby and the PUC – or not the whole PUC, but one of the PUC commissioners.

Senate Bill 1180

GREG PANTER Quite frankly, that was the overriding concern that I had at the time as far as a lobbyist for Idaho Power Company, is trying to protect Idaho Power's water rights from having the legislature subordinate them.

I would characterize the environmental community as having been allies of Idaho Power Company. I would characterize various irrigation interests as being adverse to the interests of the power company, although that's not entirely correct because there were at least one or two individuals from the irrigation community who spoke out in our behalf. I might also say there was one other major industrial user who was also involved; that was FMC. Their interest would have been, you know, any adverse effect on Idaho Power Company's rates would obviously [harm] them economically because they're a large user of power.

TOM NELSON In addition, the company was successful in getting – and the company didn't act alone, I might say – what was known as Senate Bill 1180 passed in the 83 session of the legislature. Concurrently the company had filed the second lawsuit, which became known as the "7,500 lawsuit", because that was my estimate of how many water rights were involved in the filing. I think the title was 200 pages long or something like that, and I counted the defendants on several pages and multiplied by the total, and it came out to be 7,500. So it became known as the 7,500 lawsuit.

The Senate Bill 1180 was an attempt [to] allow the company to release people who actually had existing uses or major investments in support of a proposed use from that lawsuit without incurring penalty from the PUC.

The Public Utilities Commission had been critical of the company's position throughout Swan Falls I, the first case, believing that it should renege on the agreement structure and the subordination of the Hells Canyon project. So we knew that the PUC was going to be looking over the power company's shoulder. We also know that naming existing water rights and people with major investments to initiate new water rights was going to be a pretty dynamite thing to be undertaking.

In '83, as I said, we were successful in getting the bill passed which essentially stripped the PUC of jurisdiction to contest the action of the power company if it chose to dismiss that kind of water user from the 7,500 lawsuit. There was some concern in the legislature that the power company would take the benefits of the act, but not release the people. So second section was added which required a contract to implement that release and benefit, and was actually negotiated then in 83.

CLIVE STRONG Ultimately, there was a bill passed, Senate Bill 1180, that provided the company would agree to recognize all existing uses but did not provide for subordination to any future uses.

NORM YOUNG Senate Bill 1180 passed, which I think gave Idaho Power some cover, some protection when combined with the concessions received in the Swan Falls Agreement that went with that so that Idaho Power was able to protect itself from the ratepayers, of lawsuits.

I don't know that I ever viewed Idaho Power as attempting to make a water grab. I don't think I ever saw it that way. Maybe I was naive. But from my view, they were simply trying to protect themselves as a company from having to pay ratepayers or others for not having protected their water. They couldn't afford to have that happen.

JIM JONES Essentially the state would make a deal whereby the power company would release its claims against those people. And they wouldn't have any ability to say yea or nay. And I think the idea was that the power company, when it proposed the legislation, didn't want people to be weighing in on it. And, quite frankly, the people that were substantially invested saw it as being a solution, at least to their immediate problem. And the governor, I think, indicated that he wasn't too keen on it.

There were quite a few water users that expressed the concern, "Okay. That's fine for the 5,000, but what about control of the river going forward?"

But, there was not a lot of vocal opposition to the legislation, although Chatburn and Noh were leading the charge, you know. It was a murky situation. And so it looked like at least a first step toward getting things kind of sorted out.

PAT KOLE Senate Bill 1180 was a – I think it had two components, one to relieve the Public Utilities Commission of jurisdiction, and the second one to direct the governor to enter into a contract that would have released certain people from the threat of a lawsuit by Idaho Power Company.

JIM JONES The power company's legislation got approved, sent to the governor, he signed it, and the legislature adjourned.

The legislature appointed an interim study committee to look at the thing and come back with recommendations. The Water Resources Board was considering what they could do. And one of the things that they looked at was whether they could purchase the power company's presumptive rights. And the power company said, "Well, we're really not wanting to sell them," and, "You maybe condemn them, but we're not going to be just, happy with that."

The governor also appointed a task force, a Swan Falls task force, to look at the situation and make recommendations. And Ray Rigby was appointed as chair of that committee.

TOM NELSON It depends on who you talk to, I guess. It was our view that [the contract] was not signed as a political effort by the governor to keep pressure on the power company to give up, or to otherwise compromise its position on Swan Falls.

PAT COSTELLO I have to say we did not have much in the way of the face to face negotiations over the SB 1180 contract. That was primarily exchanging drafts. The power company put forward a proposed agreement. We marked up our objections to it and then we had a meeting or two to resolve those, but there wasn't more than maybe two or three face to face meetings over that contract.

JIM JONES The task force [related to Senate Bill 1180] came out with a study September 1st of 1983. They said, "Governor, do not sign the contract," because during the summer the contract had been negotiated back and forth between the power company and the state. The governor had given it to the task force to look at, and they said, "Please do not sign it."

Some of the concerns were that no individual water right holder has been able to weigh in on this, and they may have different views, and you're essentially forcing it down their throat, even though it looks like it's probably to their benefit. The contract may be unconstitutional, partly because of that and for other reasons. And shouldn't sign it unless you get an opinion from the attorney general's office, and a variety of other things.

One of the things I brought with me was a memo that I got from Clive on September 1st. He was at the meeting and documented what they said. I think the meeting was an eye opener for Clive, and it was certainly an eye opener for me.

After the meeting Ray Rigby pulled Clive aside and he said, "You know, you really need to step up your litigation effort." I mean the power company had high priced lawyers, as many as they needed. The state was just swamped. They had a young attorney who did not have a lot of experience working on the case, backed up by Phil Rassier, who was a very savvy lawyer, is not probably your typical litigator. I think he liked to be behind the scenes a little bit. But they were just essentially overpowered. And he said, "You guys really need to step up your game."

And so as a result of that meeting, I became actively involved in the thing. Clive did say that the power company had a slick presentation that they were going around showing to anybody, and a lot of people had been convinced that maybe this contract was the way to go because it would protect, 5,000 of the people that had the most at stake, give the rest of them a chance to make a case and maybe get eliminated from the suit. But that didn't do anything with regard to the communities or any future farmers or anybody that wanted to develop later on. . . .

So at that point we took over the case at the central office level. Pat Kole, who was then Natural Resources Division chief was ostensibly in charge of the litigation from that point on, but Clive was essentially the driving force behind the state's litigation strategy.

The governor did on the 11th of September follow the recommendation by the task force to ask for an attorney general's opinion. Strangely enough, that very same day, I think it was probably on the 12th, that that appeared in the paper, the governor is asking the attorney general for an opinion on the constitutionality of the 1180 contract, I'll be darned if Logan Lanham, the chief lobbyist for the power company, didn't call up, "Jim, I've got to see you today."

I can remember the meeting.

I walked in and Logan was very gracious, like he always was, and said, "Jim, do you remember we supported you in the election, gave you a contribution?" I remembered it was 500 bucks. And he said, "I guess you're going to be issuing an opinion." He says, "I hope your opinion is fair minded and even-handed."

And, you know, I might not have been born that long ago, but it didn't take much to read into that, you know, we're going to squash you if it doesn't come out in our favor.

Logan was very – I had known him since the early '70s when I worked for Senator Jordan. Just a nice, fine, courtly gentleman. He had this lilac flavored aftershave. The first time you walked into the office – this guy has a commanding presence. He practically scared me to death. But that aftershave somehow did not fit in, but woe to the person who ever made a comment. He'd squash you. Anyway, Logan made it pretty apparent that they were hoping that the opinion would come out right. And I said, "Well, we'll do what's right."

So anyway, that very same day, or shortly after that, this letter goes out to all of the 5,000 people who are going to be released under the 1180 contract.

Idaho Power Company, strangely enough, sent this letter to all the people saying, "Hey, there's a way that your problem can be solved. Urge the governor to sign the contract and all your troubles will be over."

So anyway, things moved along, and there was some rumbling that some of the attorneys were not happy, some of the water folks were not happy with the contract. Kent Foster says, "Maybe somebody ought to file a lawsuit to challenge the legislation."

And lo and behold on the 10th of November, 1984, such a lawsuit was filed by the Williams family over, I think, in Blackfoot challenging the constitutionality of Senate Bill 1180.

And on the 14th of November, I had no alternative but to send a letter to the governor saying, "Governor, we better put this thing on hold. We don't think that we should issue our opinion on the contract because it's under constitutional challenge and the state will be in the position of having to step forward in this lawsuit and defend." . . .

So anyway, I informed the governor – or I publicly announced that there would be no opinion, no signing of the contract.

On the 16th the governor said, "Yeah, I'm not going to sign the contract."

So everybody started preparing for the 1984 legislative session. The power company came in with a proposal that would alleviate the need for a contract. It would just be a legislative enactment that says these 5,000 people are released from the lawsuit, the PUC gets off, the power company's back, and everything is copacetic and fine and dandy.

1984: The subordination battle builds

JIM JONES On the 23rd of January of 1984, the governor and I launched our subordination bill. And I think that was really a – well, compared to the way things go nowadays, where if you're Republican you hate the Democrats, and if you're a Democrat you hate the Republicans and you won't work with either side, I thought it was interesting that here the governor and I had a joint proposal as a Democrat governor, a Republican AG, to do something.

And so I brought a copy of a press release. Incidentally, I didn't have a public relations guy in the office. I did all my own press releases, so that's all my own work.

So anyway, we launched our subordination legislation. And also on the 27th there was a symposium in American Falls to discuss the Swan Falls controversy, and I was invited to attend. I think the power company was there and a number of other people that had something to say.

And I didn't do a press release for it, but there's the announcement for the meeting. There were a whole lot of people there. And it was interesting because my presentation was on the issue of the 1180 contract, why it wasn't a very good idea, why we needed to have subordination. And going into the meeting, we had gotten a lot of feedback from people, particularly defendants, who thought that the contract was the way to go, because it would protect them.

And at the start of the meeting I got a lot of that kind of question, "Well, isn't this what we ought to do? I mean why are you and the governor stirring up trouble?"

But it was interesting because at the end of the meeting you could almost sense a change in attitude, I mean a fairly wide ranging change in attitude. And to me, I regarded that as a bit of a turning point in the thing because from that point on we picked up steam until I think everybody to the east of Boise was on board, with a few notable exceptions, some of the legislators and some of the public officials. But it was just like there was a massive change in attitude from that point on.

CLIVE STRONG In the 1984 legislative session there was a fierce battle over subordination. Jim Jones and, interestingly enough, Governor Evans, who was a Democrat, were aligned together on the issue. Both of them worked with Senator Laird Noh and Representative Vard Chatburn to pass legislation fully subordinating the company's water rights.

I was working with – my boss at the time was Pat Kole. He was the chief of the Natural Resource Division. We were drafting subordination bills as fast as Idaho Power Company was killing them.

JIM JONES In the meantime I got to thinking, well, if the power company had its federal licenses subordinated at the request of the Department of Interior, maybe we ought to meet with the Department of Interior and see if we could get them to weigh in on this and get involved in the two pending – or the three pending FERC proceedings.

So we contacted Senator McClure's office to see if we could meet with the official in charge of water and power policy in the

Department of Interior. And it just seemed like it took forever to get the appointment. It took about three weeks to get the appointment.

But anyway, Ken Dunn, who was then the head of the Department of Water Resources, and I traveled back to Washington. And we go into this guy's office. His name is Hal Furman. I think he was from Alabama.

Didn't know much about water or power, either one. He was a political appointee.

But anyway, we were fairly optimistic that DOI would carry through with its longstanding policy of supporting subordination. Walked into Mr. Furman's office, and he says, "You guys are from Idaho." He says, "I have a good friend from Idaho. Just was playing golf with him last week. Yeah, let's see. Logan Lanham, works for the power company out there. We had a great time."

I told Ken, I said, "We're screwed." And we were.

LAIRD NOH House Bill 489 passed the House comfortably and moved to the Senate, where it was struck by instant, parliamentary lightening!

And the reason – I have a full page devoted to this in my diary – oh, I was upset! The entry for February 13, reads, in part, "Idaho Power struck swiftly this morning, moving to table the subordination bill, 17-16." My seat mate to the right was David Little, Emmett, and David was very close with Idaho Power. Parliamentary rules require that in order for a legislative body to take action on a piece of legislation, it must be at the desk of the presiding officer. The normal, very routine procedure is for legislation arriving from the other body, to be referred by the presiding officer to the germane committee for hearings and a committee vote. This occurs during the first items of business for the day. The list of bills arriving from the House was read, including HB 489. Senator Jim Risch, highly skilled in parliamentary procedures, was in the chair, because the lieutenant governor was absent. Senator Little immediately jumped up, confirmed that HB 489 was at the desk, and moved to "lay it on the table". Instantly, there was a second.

That is a non-debatable motion. Senator Risch immediately called for a voice vote, so that no one would be recorded as voting aye or nay, and he could announce the result. A senator, much more experienced than I, immediately called for a division of the house, which requires a standing vote, but which still is not recorded, but it at least allows for a chance to see and remember who is standing and who isn't. The presiding officer counts and announces the result. Senator Risch declared that the motion had passed, and we were on to the next order of business. It was all over in less than three minutes.

The Idaho Power forces had gotten to Senator Dane Watkins, Idaho Falls. Instead of coming on to the floor, he had remained in his office, "taking a walk", so to speak. He was the only member absent for the vote, and he had many irrigators in his district. Had he been present to support his irrigators, the motion would have failed on a tie.

I was in shock.

It was a well-planned move. Idaho Power could count their votes.

TOM NELSON It never did get through. It would pass the House and be killed in the Senate. So no subordination bill ever passed the state legislature.

BRUCE NEWCOMB I became a real activist. So I started a PAC [political action committee] after this all settled. And, I went after John Peavey – let's see, and a couple other representatives. One of them was from Jerome and one was from Gooding – Johnny Brooks and Gordon Hollifield. And John Peavey. Hollifield used to ride around with the lobbyists from Idaho Power all the time. They were just in their pocket.

So, you know, at Idaho Power's behest, even though they weren't friendly to the lawsuit in the beginning, it was their fiduciary responsibility when the court came down to defend that water right.

JIM JONES I had a former client, Gary Robbins, from Dietrich, who had expressed an interest in running against John Brooks. And I got ahold of Gary, and I said, "Whatever you need, I'm there to help." And I encouraged him to run, and he did.

I went to somebody I had worked with on the Jerome County Central Committee, I had been the chairman of the Central Committee, the Republican Central Committee in Jerome, and there was this lady that worked with me on the Central Committee. Her name was Maxine Bell. I said, "Maxine, you ought to run." She said, "No, I've got too many commitments. And besides, I don't think I could do that job."

I said, “Well, I think you could.”

And she said, “Well, I wish I could, but I can't do it.”

So I called my second cousin, Waldo Martens. “Waldo, you need to run for the legislature.”

He said, “What? I never thought about that. I don't think I could do it.”

I said, “Waldo, I think the people need you.”

So he said, “Well, I'll think about it.”

And then later he got ahold of me: “Sure, I'll run.”

So Waldo was running against Gordon Hollifield. And Gary Robbins was running against John Brooks. And lo and behold they both won in the primary.

And this was in light of this – I think it was like a $100,000 advertising campaign that the power company had saying how people's rates were going to skyrocket if subordination went through and how terrible it was going to be. I mean there were full-page or half-page ads in every paper in the southern part of the state, plus there were these ads on TV and showed some guy's pocketbook, a picture of a guy's posterior, and he had his hand on his pocketbook. And it said that “It's going to hit you in the pocketbook.”

BRUCE NEWCOMB Well, Hollifield and Johnny Brooks and Peavey were kind of – they're fair-haired children, and so I went after them. And we had groups of – I mean it was an easy PAC to form because I mean I had the Burley High School auditorium completely full of water users from all over the Magic Valley.

. . . Johnny Brooks and Gordon Hollifield were in the House, and Peavey was in the Senate. And so we did knock off or helped knock off Hollifield and Johnny Brooks. But we couldn't get Peavey.

Searching for Armistice 1984-1986

Idaho Power and its supporters still remained at loggerheads with the state government and others who sought subordination. The time for direct negotiations seemed to have arrived.

JAMES BRUCE I think the attorney general in '84 had come to the conclusion by that time, as had all of us, that it was necessary to get it settled and we should settle it in the best manner possible. And again, I can't say dates specifically or anything, but certainly when we had the meetings, it was decided that – it wasn't decided.

But it was obvious that we needed to come to some kind of conclusion because the state of Idaho, with the lawsuits and everything else that was going on, were really causing a lot of tension, a lot of problems for people. So I think it was the general consensus that we needed to go on and see what we could do.

Any time you have a settlement, you have to have a give-and-take and come to an amicable agreement, and that's what we were trying to do and that's what the negotiators were doing and that's what we were striving for. I don't think I wanted to take anything. I was only trying to find out what the rights of Idaho Power Company were. Obviously, sometimes the rights that you see on the one side and the right that somebody else sees on the other side will be different. That's why we have a lot of lawyers and courts and everything else.

KEN DUNN Originally representatives of Idaho Power Company met with me to get my approval to enter into negotiations with them to try to solve the Swan Falls issue, and I advised them that I was not in a position to negotiate with them.

Because as the administrator of the state water rights, I merely administered them. I did not have authority to modify those water rights. Subsequent to that, negotiations were entered into at the request of the governor, Governor Evans, between the state and Idaho Power Company, and I participated in that.

CLIVE STRONG After the legislative standoff, Governor Evans wrote a letter to Jim Bruce, chairman of Idaho Power Company, and suggested the parties sit down and see if they could reach a resolution.

Big Three negotiations begin

The company responded favorably to that overture.

PAT KOLE My recollection is that in May or June of 1984 as the legislative session had wound down the size and scope of the litigation became increasingly clear, that I walked down to the governor's office, sat down with Pat Costello and said maybe we ought to try to talk this one out. And about that same time, the governor had been sent a letter by Idaho Power Company asking him to sign the 1180 contract. And Pat and I drafted a letter for the governor's signature back to Idaho Power Company saying before we talk about signing the 1180 contract, why don't we get together and talk and see if we can't resolve the case.

I think the letter actually went out in June or early July.

At this point the only thing I had done was obtain authority from Mr. Jones to go down and talk to the governor's staff. And I believe I brought back the draft of the letter and had him okay it before it was mailed to Idaho Power.

I believe that they responded in writing, but I'm not too positive on that, and I believe that a meeting was arranged shortly thereafter.

PAT COSTELLO It started when Jim Bruce sent the governor a letter, once again proposing that the governor sign the 1180 contract. The governor replied saying he would prefer to enter into negotiations over total settlement of the Swan Falls – all of the pending Swan Falls litigation. And the power company agreed to meet and talk about that and the first meeting was held the first week of July of 1984. And the governor and Jim Bruce and Jim Jones met at that time.

They agreed that their three negotiators, Tom Nelson for the power company, Pat Kole for Jim Jones and me for the governor, would meet and see if we could come up with a number for the flow at Swan Falls, that the power company would agree to compromise its right, and what other conditions would have to be met in order for the power company to agree to settle the litigation.

. . . Immediately after that, that was it basically the three of us, Tom, Pat and I, proceeded to meet and have discussions among ourselves and then reported back to the three principals in two or three weeks' time.

I had the impression at the first meeting that the three principals viewed this as basically a problem of coming up with a number, and that the three of us were to try to come up with the right number. It quickly became apparent in talking at the staff level that it was a lot more complicated than that. Their only marching orders were to see if we could come up with terms of a settlement, basically.

TOM NELSON The process really got started by a meeting among Jim Bruce, who was the CEO of Idaho Power, the governor, Jim Jones, Pat and myself. [Subsequent meetings were attended by Kole, Costello and Nelson], or, Pat, Pat and Tom as it became known, and perhaps somebody from IDWR gathered in the governor's office in the summer of '84 to explore among the principals whether there was any reason to make a real effort to resolve the issue. And from that came this Pat, Pat and Tom group as the negotiators. So we had the involvement of the principals at that meeting, which kicked off the process.

PAT KOLE My recollection is it would have been myself, Mr. Jones, Mr. Costello, the Governor, Mr. Bruce, Tom Nelson and Logan Lanham.

In general it was Idaho Power Company's position that they wanted to have the state of Idaho execute the 1180 contract, and the state of Idaho saying to Idaho Power Company, before we sign this, we want to talk about all of the issues, and Idaho Power Company saying, if you want to talk, we'll talk.

These were discussions primarily between the principals, and though it kind of had an atmosphere that there had been enough groundwork laid that everybody knew what the principals were going to be saying.

NORM YOUNG Again, the principals were the president of Idaho Power, Jim Bruce; and Jim Jones, the attorney general; and John Evans, the governor. So that's why we called it the Jimmy-Jimmy-John? show, okay?

Developing the framework

PAT COSTELLO Eventually after talking, we had come down to the six primary points. I eventually put together the first draft of the framework and then we circulated that back and forth and did some wordsmithing on it. Then once we got that done, then obviously we did drafts on the main agreements.

CLIVE STRONG The essence of the framework was – a classic split-the-baby kind of approach. The state water plan at the time allowed for depleting the flows at Swan Falls down to 3,300 CFS. Typically, the low flow occurs in the summer because of irrigation diversions. In early July we typically see the low flows at Swan Falls Dam. The historic low flow was 4,500 CFS.

The negotiators agreed, first, that all existing uses would be protected. Essentially the Senate Bill 1180 approach.

Both Governor Evans and Attorney General Jim Jones, however, insisted upon some opportunity for future development. So the compromise reached by the negotiators was to split the difference between 4,500 CFS and 3,300 CFS. The state agreed to move its minimum flow from 3,300 CFS to 3,900 CFS during the summer and 5,600 CFS in the winter and to protect that flow for power generation. Flows in excess of 3,900/5,600 CFS were made available for future development. The parties also agreed to pursue a suite of executive and legislative policy changes, including amendment of the state water plan and commencement of a general stream adjudication.

That's really the essence of the Swan Falls Framework. The parties then proceeded with drafting a final agreement.

PAT COSTELLO We probably met once a week through July and then there was another meeting of principals and we reported our progress and there had been progress at that point.

At that meeting they agreed that there was enough progress being made that the parties would hold off, keep their powder dry as far as the legislative elections that were underway, and agreed they would try to come to – basically, the truce was in effect until Labor Day and that they would try to resolve this agreement by Labor Day, but after that, both parties would go out and try to campaign for pro or anti-subordination candidates. Both sides though they could make enough changes in the Senate to prevail instead of having the deadlock we had. There had already been some supercharged rhetoric going on during the primaries. That's when Jim Jones became visibly active as far as supporting subordination. He went out and campaigned for some pro subordination candidates in the primary and the power company and some of its supporters were launching attacks back against him. And we agreed in July that there was no way we could negotiate this thing if they were going to continue name calling, so there was this truce that was agreed to that was supposed to extend until Labor Day.

Then we were really under the gun to try to come up with something and our meetings became much more frequent. Eventually it became a daily thing, where we were meeting every day.

PAT KOLE Somebody mentioned to the press that these meetings were going on. I think from that point forward, it became pretty difficult to keep things under wraps.

I don't recall them ever coming. I remember walking out of a meeting and staring into TV cameras one day, but that's about it.

CLIVE STRONG From, I think, approximately May of 1984 until October they met on a regular basis. My role was the scrivener. As they came up with ideas, I was asked to draft the relevant documents.

Were the negotiations friendly?

TOM NELSON Not particularly. In fact, they were coldly professional in a lot of respects.

NORM YOUNG I wouldn't say that I was at every meeting, but I was at a number of them. And very good-faith negotiations. I think there was a firm recognition on everybody's side of the importance of water to growth in Idaho but also the importance of stream flows for Idaho Power, for fish, for every other use in the river.

And I think that represented an incremental growth period in the thinking of many Idahoans. Before that time, there weren't very many people that viewed the water in the river as being very valuable. It was valuable when it was taken out for beneficial use.

Well, I think it got hashed out enough in that process that people started to see the tension between taking it out and having beneficial use versus having beneficial use in the river. Pretty healthy.

NORM YOUNG One [study] was to try to figure out where we were in terms of the impact of the present development, of the existing development, on river flows when fully felt. That was not an easy concept. That was starting to sink in to the hydrologists and others' understanding that it might be decades before the full effect of a well quite a ways away from the river would be felt on the flow at Swan Falls.

So a "present condition" study was attempted. It may have been in process even before the Swan Falls Agreement, but it was important to know because you had to know where you were at before you knew what you had to divide up.

The water board had put a 3,300 CFS minimum flow at Murphy in the first water plan back in '76, I guess it was; '74. Well, was there anything above 3,300, or had that already been allocated?

The best guess was it was – 4,500 was what was left once the full impact of present development was felt. So they thought there was a 1,200-CFS difference.

PAT KOLE The deadline that we were all concerned about was putting something in place so that the possibility of there being political fallout candidates who were running for the state legislature would be less. So the goal was to find out if there was a possibility of an accommodation as soon as possible, but in no event the beginning of October.

It became clear to me very early on in the negotiations that the problems that were identified by the parties in the way that they had approached the issue were not inconsistent, not contradictory. They just needed to be expanded so they could see where they met. I think within a very short period of time, by September, perhaps even August, it was clear to me that we would be able to come up with an agreement.

The principal issue was who would run the river, whether it would be a private utility or whether it would be public ownership. And the state had always wanted to make it clear that this was their job to be the water master, and not a private utility. And once both sides agreed that the state should be in charge, that it just then became a question of protecting everybody's water rights throughout the system and making sure that everybody was treated fairly and equitably.

Whether they [Idaho Power] wanted to [run the river] or not, they were as a result of the court decision de facto in charge of the river because of the way they could assert their water right or not assert their water right against different uses that would give them the ability to manage the resource. From the state's point of view that was untenable.

I think the other issues were, if the state's going to manage the river, how it is going to be done? If we're going to try to come up with a comprehensive plan for managing the river, what interests are going to be balanced?

PAT KOLE Probably the biggest area of controversy would have been the difference between a subordinated water right and a subordinatable water right. Idaho Power Company flat out took the position that they were not going to subordinate their water right, but they would create a subordinatable water right. I guess I'm just a little bit of a stubborn individual; I really felt like they ought to subordinate their water right. But eventually I became convinced that given the history and the other constraints we put in, trust water and trust concept, that we would be as well protected with the subordinatable water right as subordinated water right.

Did it become public?

Boy, it seems to me that it did. It seems to me that Jim Jones went after Pat Costello; I recall Jim Jones giving a speech someplace and I believe he labeled Mr. Costello as a loose cannon. And somebody in the governor's office thought it was kind of humorous and they went out and there was a cannon in front of the capitol and they put a sign on the cannon, "S.S. Costello," as I recall.

The trust water solution

PAT COSTELLO The main one – and this became public – was a dispute over how to characterize the water that was being freed up from the power company's right to be available for future appropriation. The attorney general's position was that they were holding out for an immediate transconveyance of those rights to the state from the power company for distribution to these future uses. The governor's position and my position on it as a legal matter was that they were better off not doing that and we were better off doing it incrementally because it preserved this argument that the river was fully appropriated. If they conveyed the way back to the state, then we were admitting that we had a block of water that was not appropriated, and so that was where the disagreement was.

And the other thing was the power company was not going to agree to a simple no strings attached conveyance of that water to the state and the deal was not going to come together. We didn't think what the power company was asking for was a concession on our part, so that was the disagreement. The attorney general viewed that as being a concession and that was the disagreement. The attorney general called a press conference and made it public, is how it became public.

CLIVE STRONG As the negotiators were drafting the final agreement – this was really the 11th hour – a conflict arose between the company and Attorney General Jim Jones. The company was willing to agree to recognize future uses approved pursuant to state law, but insisted upon the water right being subordinatable.

Subordinatable means that once the state issued a new water right, then the company would, at that time, agree to subordinate to the water right.

That position was unacceptable to Attorney General Jim Jones. Jim did not trust the company, and he threatened to pull his support from the agreement unless the company agreed to fully subordinate its water right down to the Murphy minimum flow.

It looked like the agreement was going to fall apart. Governor Evans, trying to find a solution to the problem, convened a kitchen cabinet to look at the issue, which included an attorney by the name of Ray Rigby, a well-respected attorney in water law.

They met, I believe on a Sunday. Governor Evans had a meeting in eastern Idaho to talk about the conflict and how it could be resolved.

Ray suggested that the water rights [be] put in trust. He analogized the situation to a child guardianship.

So that idea was broached with the power company. The power company didn't like the idea, but ultimately acceded to it. The agreement was signed on October 25, 1984.

PAT COSTELLO The danger was, if he [Jim Jones] wasn't on board. I mean, the thing had to be passed by the legislature and the Republicans controlled the legislature. If the Republican attorney general opposed the agreement, we probably would have had great resistance in the legislature to get it through. Whether that resistance would have been enough to kill it, I don't know. That's something we wondered about.

RAY RIGBY In other words, the power company eventually made concessions that they could go ahead and use so much of this water, and it was kind of what our committee and what the governor and Department of Water Resources of the state had agreed it would probably take care of the needs of agriculture for the foreseeable future with all of the development that was going on.

And then there was an awful lot of drilling of wells for water which was practically nonexistent before World War II, and now they were drilling wells all over the area, central Idaho mostly.

And, of course, that benefited the power company because they sold power to the pumps, and the farmers got the water and reclaimed hundreds of acres. There were even several plots put up north of Rupert for drawings by returned soldiers. And so that seemed to work, but the question again is: Who would hold that water right until that happened?

And I had an idea, why don't we put it in trust? And what was interesting was: Well, who is going to be the trustee?

And I had had a case where we had, in this county as county attorney, taken some children away from some parents who had really done a horrible job. Those three little kids could have been just absolutely lost. And so we asked the state to take custody of those children and hold it in trust, hold them in trust. And then through the years we found the right people and those three little kids were placed in some lovely homes. And that's a whole beautiful story that I could tell you of, but it proved to be the right thing.

But the theory of the trust came out of that. And when I proposed that to the power company people, their attorneys, and to our people, everybody seemed to be in accord. And so they said, "For heaven's sake, let's get it signed."

And so that's just what happened and that agreement was signed, and it put that water in trust. So now we call it "Trust Waters".

LAIRD NOH I remember getting a call, I think it was Sunday morning. I don't remember who the call was from, I believe it was someone from the governor's office, who said, can you come to Pocatello? I believe it was 4 o'clock in the afternoon. The governor had been at his ranch south of Pocatello gathering cattle or moving cattle and he was going to be on his way back to Boise, and he was going to be at this room at the courthouse at Pocatello. And the attorney general is going to be there, and a number of the other players, Tom Nelson was there, Ray Rigby from Rexburg was at many of these meetings, and Ray has an idea we want to try out. Can you get over there?

And so I did. That was when Ray pitched the idea of trust, placing the water in trust. I recall that he likened this to the standard idea of trust – the party still owns the assets, but the trust has certain objectives and responsibilities to the parties. The state would own the water in trust, for the benefit of the citizens. ...

PAT COSTELLO It was lurking in the background then. We papered over the difference in the framework because we didn't have to get into the detail as to how this extra water was going to made available. But when it came to writing the actual legal documents, we had to confront the issue, and we reached basically an impasse over it. Things were falling apart and that's why he called the press conference. I mean, that was the point in time when he called the press conference.

We reached kind of a middle ground where we split the title between legal and equitable title and created a trust. The power company maintained – or let's see. The power company maintained equitable title and the state took legal title and it preserved our ability to argue the river was fully appropriated, but at the same time assuaged Jim Jones' concern that the power company was irrevocably giving up this argument that they owned the river.

The idea of an adjudication arose early. One of the early proposals for it came from Idaho Power attorney Tom Nelson.

Enter the adjudication

PAT COSTELLO Initially, no position at all for or against [Nelson's proposal]. It had not been something to my knowledge that had been suggested to the governor until that time. But after consulting with Water Resources about it, we agreed that would be in the state's interest as well as in the power company's interest.

KEN DUNN I'd been a proponent of the adjudication probably at the start. My recollection is that we had begun an adjudication of a reach of the Snake River called 02, which is just department terminology of a reach from the south central area of the Snake River. It just seemed logical to me that we should have continued that into a general adjudication.

It was necessary in order to properly administer the waters of the Snake River, and one of the items of decision in the Swan Falls decision was the flows to pass Swan Falls. And if I was to administer water rights to assure that those flows were maintained, I had to know the nature and extent of water rights in the system.

KARL DREHER You can't manage something you haven't defined.

LAIRD NOH One of the background motivations for the general adjudication came even before that period when the Water Resources Board was established, and it was established as I recall primarily because someone discovered – that would have been I'd guess in the early 70s – that the Los Angeles city council had on their desk plans to move water from the Snake River at Hagerman, pump it out and take it down to southern California. And then there was the federal McCarran Act which as I understand it has a provision that if the state wants maximum leverage to protect the water rights of their state from out of state appropriation, they have to know what water rights they have, and be using that water relatively efficiently. I've aways felt that was one of the motivating factors.

RAY RIGBY The governor was concerned about the adjudication of the water rights in Idaho and the claims that were being made by the Idaho Power Company. And their attitude was when they were granted the rights to install power generating plants at three locations, one right next to another in the Hells Canyon area, that's over on the Oregon/Idaho border, that the power company would be in a position of taking all of the water that comes down that river to that point and keeping everybody else out of it. . . .

And so as a result of that, Governor Evans and Attorney General Jim Jones asked me to chair this committee to help resolve this dispute.

PAT KOLE Back in 1976 when I was first with the attorney general's office, I handled cases for the Department of Water Resources. One of the first trips I ever took was with Ken Dunn to Idaho Falls, to a court hearing in Blackfoot. If you've traveled along that road, you go along the Snake River, crisscrossing it at several points. Back at that time the Department of Water Resources indicated a need for adjudication in the Snake River in order to effectively assure water users that they had a certain water right. In the back of my mind I knew that. I arrived at the negotiations with a belief that a general adjudication with the Snake River was a good idea. I mentioned earlier the pressures that existed to divert Idaho water out of the state. Once again, a general adjudication is necessary in order to prevent that kind of water exportation. There was a widespread belief throughout the state that the initial court decrees defining water rights in the state wouldn't meet the requirements of a modern adjudication decree, and so there was a belief that a general adjudication would help resolve that problem.

PAT KOLE In one of the first meetings between the negotiators, Tom Nelson brought in all the pending applications for appropriation within the Snake River drainage, and convincingly pointed out that there was too many to ever result in a well-managed water basin. And I remember Mr. Costello expressing some dismay and disbelief. After that I think Mr. Nelson left and I believe I told Mr. Costello about my earlier experiences working with the Department of Water Resources, and probably the comments made by Mr. Nelson were not only accurate, but the state really did not have a good management system in place. I think we set up a meeting with Ken Dunn and very quickly verified that independent of the Swan Falls controversy, there was a need for a general adjudication.

PAT COSTELLO [That was in Idaho Power's interest] because there was no other way that any agreement as to the flows they would get at Swan Falls could be enforced. We could give them a paper right saying they are entitled to 45 csf, but if we could not regulate the upstream uses in a meaningful way, we couldn't deliver 4,500 – or excuse me, 3,900, whatever number we agreed to.

PAT KOLE It provides a lot of benefits to all the other water users through the basin. Anybody who is going to be asserting a right, it provides certainty and it provides enforceability.

There's, as I mentioned, this fear that somebody could come along and acquire all the shares of stock in Idaho Power and transfer the water out of the state. And it was the belief of some of the individuals in the water user community that this would put one more impediment into that process.

I believe there had been a perception in the Department [of Water Resources] for a number of years that there was a need for adjudication. Not because of the Swan Falls situation, but because we were simply reaching a point where with the finite resource there was a need to have more efficient management.

PAT COSTELLO As far as a tentative agreement, [we reached one] within a matter of a couple of weeks, I think. The only reservation about it at all was that we were afraid that if the overall settlement was contingent on that [adjudication], it might be very difficult to get it through the legislature and it might be a deal killer. But as far as the merits of the idea of adjudicating the river, the governor didn't have any problem with that once he had consulted with Ken Dunn and the Water Resource Board.

Two primary things. One – well, there are several things. There were a number of paper rights on the river that we had no idea how much of those rights were actually being used, and adjudication would require people to come in and prove what they had. If you looked at the paper rights on record, the river was over-appropriated by several times, at least according to what Water Resources was telling us, but we knew that there was more water in the river than the paper rights would lead you to believe. So we wanted to bring some certainty to what rights people actually had. We wanted to be able to have a water master deliver water. We wanted to liquidate federal reserve water right claims – primarily the Sho-Bans – and just bring some certainty overall to what everyone had then to be able to plan the state's water policy with knowledge of what rights were out there and how much water was available.

CLIVE STRONG Another factor that weighed in favor of an adjudication was quantifying the federal reserved water rights.

In Idaho, and generally in the west, we follow the prior appropriation doctrine. In order to obtain a water right, a water user must obtain it through a state process. But, there's an exception to that; when the federal government reserves lands for an expressed federal purpose, the federal government can create an implied or express reserved water right.

The most significant federal reserved water rights are Indian reserved water rights, water necessary for tribes to develop trust lands.

The Shoshone-Bannock tribes reside on the Fort Hall Indian Reservation in Eastern Idaho. We knew they had reserved water rights and that the exercise of those rights could have a tremendous impact on our ability to manage the river.

Federal reserved water rights carry a priority date as of the date of the reservation. So, with regard to Fort Hall, the reserved rights date back to to 1867. They are some of the earliest water rights on the river.

So, the reasons for the adjudication was a combination of water management, federal reserved water rights, and also just getting a handle on the amount of water available for future development.

TOM NELSON One of the political clubs that was being swung, particularly in eastern Idaho, was that Idaho Power cannot be allowed to be the water master of the Snake River. And all the protestations of Idaho Power to the effect that it's not the water master, it's simply a water right holder like anybody else, didn't really dampen that argument down. So it was partly in response to that argument that if you want to be the water master, then you better give yourself the tools to be the water master. Also, the state had recognized for a number of years that an adjudication of the Snake was required, and so it made no sense to establish a flow at Murphy and not have a management system in effect which could make sure the river met that minimum.

RAY RIGBY [The adjudication] was one of the other conditions. Well, I don't know whether it was a condition, but it was strongly urged by both sides. In other words, "What waters are we subordinating to," says the power company.

And we say, "Yes, we should know. We've wanted to know anyway. As a practitioner of law, the disputes between water users right here in our own area, particularly when the pioneers settled here, what about the Indians down on the reservation?"

And that was a real big issue that started everybody thinking we better have this adjudicated. And so the upper valley water users actually lost a little priority, but it solved the problem, at least until we had the question that you've been involved with with those water users in that area.

So our people up here took some changes in their priorities, not the date of their water right, but how it fit in the list of priorities.

JEFF RAYBOULD It was in the early 90s when I became involved on the board of the Fremont Madison Irrigation District. I think people were supportive of having an adjudication. I don't think anyone realized at the time it started the complexity and all the issues that would have to be resolved. I don't know anyone who was opposed t the process.

JOHN ROSHOLT Once that was together – and as part of that agreement, the requirement was that we have to get a handle on all the water rights. And the only way that you could get a handle on all the water rights in Idaho where the federal government owned 70 percent of the real estate was to bring in the McCarran Act of Adjudication. And it's the only federal law I know of that allows the United States to go into state court. And it actually requires it. As long as it's a basin-wide adjudication.

CLIVE STRONG When we finished the Swan Falls Agreement, it was apparent that we did not have a good record of water rights. There were beneficial use claims, the ones established by use, that had never been documented. Many of the water rights had changed over time and there were a lot of pending applications. The records simply weren't adequate for administration of the water rights.

I think that's the real reason that both the company and the state supported the adjudication– it wasn't a requirement of the Swan Falls agreement.

LAIRD NOH I wasn't an attorney, I just thought it was going to take a long time. Everybody said forever, no state has ever completed a general adjudication. It's going to be a long situation.

NORM YOUNG You had the Committee of Nine, the water board, other water user gurus, probably Sheryl Chapman and those folks saying, "Yeah, this has got to happen."

And without those kinds of encouragements, it would never have happened. But there had to be that sort of reason like getting your water right firmed up, recognizing your existing use even though it's bigger than it was when it was originally licensed or decreed. So there was something in it for the water user, and it sold. And I'm glad it did. It's very important.

DANIEL HURLBUTT It was a very significant issue in the state, and there was a lot of heated litigation about it. And the whole notion of whose rights prevailed under what circumstances, and when and under what circumstances significant rights, like Idaho Power's hydropower rights, could be forfeited. I think there was a lot of concern about how, in the future, the system could be managed without those kinds of litigation matters cropping up continually.

JIM JONES Number one, there had been some partial decrees here and there for discrete areas. And how do you fit those together?

And I think everybody was starting to see that this whole basin both the surface water and the groundwater, was interconnected.

And there was the question of how do you assure that the power company gets its summer and winter flows. And people were starting to think about potential challenges, not by just the power company, but others, of upstream users' projects, this, that, and the other.

And I think they're looking at this situation where Len Jordan had worked a deal with the power company, and somehow that was not documented in a fashion where it could be enforced. And so there's just so many imponderables, I think everybody agreed that we needed to get an adjudication so everybody would sort of know where they stood and how everybody's rights meshed with others up and down the stream and how you would enforce this thing. So it just looked like the right thing to do.

There were a lot of people out in the water community that were concerned about it because they had the impression that it might end up infringing on their rights, but I think we tried to give them comfort. And I, quite frankly, had some concerns myself, just how are you going to be able to sell this to the people. But most people understood what was the object of the thing.

The Swan Falls framework was signed on October 1, 1984.

TOM NELSON As soon as we got to the point where we thought we could put the framework together, as I remember, we had a meeting of the principals to endorse the idea and say, yes, let's do that. And of course they had to meet to sign it. I think there was a big fanfare in there and all this sort of thing. And in fact, I have the pen that the parties used to sign the agreements.

TOM NELSON We had to have the whole package, or it wasn't going to go.

NORM YOUNG Just from my own viewpoint, the workload that immediately came out of the Swan Falls Agreement was adopting, drafting, and getting promulgated the water appropriation rules so we knew how to apply those standards. And so those got adopted in 1986. The agreement called for reprocessing permits, permits that had already been issued if they hadn't already been developed. So you needed to find out what the extent of development was on the permits and then reprocess those. Again, you had to have the rules.

The actual processing of new applications and actually of the reprocessing of the permits couldn't get started until the Swan Falls Agreement was fully in effect. And I don't think that happened until, what, '87, '88.

Implementing the framework

NORM YOUNG It was sort of viewed that the water that was made available by the subordination of the power rights ought to be treated differently, that it was an asset that was different than unappropriated water, and as such, it ought to be subject to term permits in order to be sure that, number one, who really knew whether the 4,500 baseline was really right, was it really there or was it something less than 600 CFS? And then when you looked at the public interest criterion, could you really look out beyond some term and say it was still going to be in the public interest?

And that flew. Whether it should have or shouldn't have, the permits that were issued for the subordinated water had a term of 20 years. Those now have come around and are subject to reprocessing.

The other idea then was that in order to be able to provide some assurance that that unsubordinated water was going to be available and those permits were going to be good, the water board needed to be able to acquire storage water either in existing reservoirs or construct reservoirs or do something so that when the minimum stream flow of 3,900 or 5,600 was being encountered, there was something immediate that could be done.

So the idea of attaching a fee, an annual fee to the use of the water under a term permit, was to buy that water in the upper Snake some way.

But I think cooler heads said, "If you're going to adopt a rule, Department, you have to have some statutory basis," and we didn't have one. And the legislature really never did give us those kinds of fee authorities. So that didn't fly. Although, I think permits issued did that that in the future you may be subject to an annual fee. At least we started off that way.

PAT COSTELLO [The big obstacle to the adjudication was] money, or at least that was our perception at that time, that would be the thing that would make it hard to get it through. We were in the midst of several years of budget shortfalls and a recession and money was very scarce for anything in state government, and the idea of something of this magnitude being lodged was – we knew that it would have trouble being accepted by the legislature.

We asked Water Resources to give us that number. I had my recollection refreshed last night. It was 19 and a fraction million dollars, I believe.

I don't know if we were just talking from Swan Falls upstream or from Lewiston upstream at that point. Eventually we were talking about Lewiston upstream. I don't know if the 19 million included the whole river or not.

There was no general fund money. All of the general fund money was over committed. We were having holdbacks; we were having across the board percentage holdbacks in budgets that were funded by the general fund, so there was no question about even asking for general fund money to fund it. We knew that it would have to be a self-supporting effort and the the resistance in the legislature would be to be politically bear the political heat of imposing substantial fees on the water users and their districts. Not a politically popular thing to do to ask people to pay fees. We couldn't see initially – it was difficult for us to see a great constituency in favor of the adjudication, and all it would take would be a significant number of waster users coming in and objecting to having to pay the fees. And we felt that would be enough to derail the adjudication legislation. So that was why we were concerned about having the whole agreement contingent on getting passage of that because we thought that would have problems.

PAT COSTELLO After the agreement was entered into and before the start of the legislative session or – in any event, by January of 1985, the documents had been out for public review, and one of the comments we got back was from the city of Idaho Falls, Mayor Tom Campbell, I believe, objecting to the way that we were charging fees for hydropower because the city of Idaho Falls operated some hydropower facilities, and their contention was the mainplate rating was a more equitable way to measure the value of the hydropower right than the volume of water going through the dam, going through the turbines. And as a result, the proposed adjudication statute, the bill, was revised to go from csf to a nameplate rating to measure.

We were committed by the terms of the agreement itself to use our best efforts to get the whole legislative package passed. We also discouraged the legislature from making any changes in any of the legislation except those that got agreed to by the parties in advance, because all of the pieces were contingent on each other. And the parties were concerned that either one of them might go to their champions in the legislature and say go ahead and pass the good stuff here and don't pass the others, and then we would go back to the other side and say, gee, we did the best we could and it wouldn't pass. The parties, I think, all three remained very faithful to their commitment that they would push for all of the parts – passage of all the parts, even the ones they weren't as excited about as the others.

Paying for the adjudication

Economist Richard Gardner was asked to chair a committee related to SRBA financing.

KEN DUNN His role was – one of the roles was to determine a fee system to pay for the expenses of the Department of Water Resources in conducting a general adjudication.

There had been earlier adjudications in which the expenses were paid after the fact by the court requiring the participants to pay their share. The laws have changed in the state over time.

There was a discussion on this, and neither one of them was accepted because they had not proved successful in the past. Both of them required a general fund appropriation, one on a reimbursement basis, which was extremely difficult. And given the ten-year duration of this, it was felt that it would be impossible to come back ten years later and try to recover those expenses by the court. And given the size of the adjudication, it was felt that if the state paid for it, then other beneficiaries of the adjudication would not be participating in the expenses.

PAT COSTELLO Tom and Pat and I came up with a list of the different categories of water users and people who could sit at the table to represent those groups. So we asked those people to serve as an ad hoc committee on funding the adjudication. And I asked Dick

Gardner from the Division of Financial Management to serve as the staff person and facilitator for that group. So he coordinated those meetings and crunched numbers for them.

It was obvious that you had to have irrigated agriculture represented, and hydropower interests. And we needed the cities and municipalities, municipal users. And we felt that there needed to be a representative of the public at large, sort of a consumer type.

TOM NELSON My recollection is that we used the Water Resource Board, asked them to take the framework out to the public and explain it to them, which the board did. And I can recall attending public information meetings that the board set up in Idaho Falls, Pocatello, Burley, Boise, and Lewiston, and I think maybe Twin Falls, but I'm not sure about that.

I don't recall that there was really a lot of opposition that was voiced. I know there were some in the community at large that believed that until Idaho Power was drawn and quartered, the state hadn't done a good job, but that was kind of fringe extreme position. Most of it, they had some questions. We answered questions, and that really seemed to satisfy the people that came to the hearing.

PAT COSTELLO First of all, we did a road show on the framework, which included the fee structure. In fact, we probably got more questions at the public meetings on the Swan Falls agreement about the adjudication fees than we did the overall agreement, which was surprising. We thought there would be a lot of concern about the subordination provisions and the amount of water right that Idaho Power was getting, but people were interested to know how much they were going to be expected to pay for the adjudication and the fee schedule for was disseminated at the – we had a meeting in Idaho Falls, Pocatello, Burley, Twin Falls, Boise and Lewiston, and there were press releases put out in each of those communities in advance of those meetings, and those took place in the latter part of October, very early November of 1989. Then, of course, there were legislative committee meetings on the adjudication statute including the fee provisions. Those bills were printed and given statewide distribution as well and were covered by the news media.

Will the feds pay filing fees?

CLIVE STRONG If you're going to do an adjudication, there's always a question of how to pay for it.

My recollection was that there was an initial estimate that the adjudication would cost about $28 million. There was a feeling that the water users should pay for the adjudication. So, Tom Nelson, Pat Costello, and departmental representatives began a process of working with the stakeholders to develop a process for funding the adjudication.

The idea of filing fees was controversial. Everybody wanted everyone else to pay for the adjudication. Ultimately, an agreement was reached on an allocation of costs between hydropower, irrigation, domestic, commercial, municipal and industrial users. There was an expectation the United States would pay a fee as well.

The funding formula was expected to generate about $21 million. Interest on the fees was expected to result in a total fund of $28 million – the estimated cost of the adjudication.

PAT COSTELLO I was aware that there was an issue whether or not the feds would agree to pay the fees or whether they could be legally required to. I didn't know. I had never done any research on it and I didn't really know the contours of what the controversy was over that. Since it wasn't clear that they would have to pay any fees at all, and since we were working on very short timeline, my feeling at least was that it wasn't necessary to include any federal representatives.

PAT KOLE We wanted to make sure that we did nothing that would jeopardize the ability of the state to assess fees against the United States.

I myself never did any research on that topic. I don't recall if any written memorandums were ever prepared on that. I do recollect at some point entering or hearing discussions on that issue, and I believe that there was a fellow named John Keys, who, I believe worked for the Bureau of Reclamation, who had some legal research done on that topic. And it seems to me that there may have been a written memorandum prepared on that at one point that was disseminated or circulated, but I can't recall in my mind whether or not I ever got a copy of that or just saw it in a meeting or heard about it.

KEN DUNN It was generally as to whether the Bureau of Reclamation would pay the fees if they were established by the legislature to conduct the general adjudication of the Snake River. He [Regional Director John Keys] said that they would pay them. He said that they could pay them.

JOHN KEYS My opinion at that time was that we would pay those fees. I would emphasize, *at that time*.

PETER MONSON There were some early discussion when the idea of having an adjudication came up and the question came up about how to pay foe it, I gather they thought well just have the parties pay for it through filing fees. I think some federal people said they thought that it was okay, not recognizing the nuances of that.

KEN DUNN The letter was framed as a question as to whether the bureau could pay the fees to cover state expenses of the adjudication for water rights, and the solicitor's response was yes, the bureau could pay those fees. It was consistent with past actions, as I recall.

JOHN KEYS After, it was brought to my attention that the opinion that we had received from our field solicitor did not consider the McCarran Amendment.

Did you tell Ken Dunn about your change of mind?

Not that I remember. Because it was a legal question, and the opinions that I had given him were strictly my own opinions.

And if I recall even at that time, we cautioned him that they were my opinions, and they were not legal opinions, that the final determination of who pays is a legal question. And certainly my opinion was only my own.

The agreement needed legislative approval, and a range of political actions ensued to implement the settlement.

The Legislature considers the framework

TOM NELSON We got support from the Water Users Association. I believe the canal companies that had opposed subordination in the legislative wars came over and testified for it. The governor's office, the attorney general's office, obviously Idaho Power Company, testified in support of it. I believe the PUC even came over and testified in support of it. So there was a great deal of support. There may have been some adverse comment, but none comes to mind.

There is a consumer organization known as Idaho Consumer Affairs, which has been active in a lot of public utility matters for the PUC since about the time of Pioneer, I guess. One of the active members of that group is a man from Nampa by the name of Harold Miles. Harold filed a suit in district court in Ada County challenging the constitutionality of the portion of the legislative package which took jurisdiction away from the PUC to effectively take punitive action against the company for entering into the agreement.

A decision adverse to Mr. Miles was appealed by him to the Supreme Court. And the district court decision was upheld on different grounds in an early opinion. I think we had a change of personnel at the court. . . . And after some delay, the court again affirmed the district court decision.

JIM JONES I had some old dude from down at Jerome who was kind of a gadfly. His name was Fred Stewart. And Fred was up in the legislature arguing against everything. No adjudication. No settlement. No concession to the power company. And he was dogging everybody. He was pestering the heck out of me. And we had a lot of people like that who were just raising every problem they could come up with.

PAT KOLE I remember during the legislative hearings there was this giant map of the United States that was located in the state capitol, and an individual by the name of Fred Stewart somehow talked some of the custodians and maintenance people in the capitol into carting the map from the basement, and it was on a huge display, kind of a board, up in the rotunda. He had taken tape and shown proposed pipelines to California. That was the kind of thing that was out in the public eye that needed to be addressed.

LAIRD NOH In those days many of the committee secretaries taped the committee hearings, it helped them putting the minutes together, which are often pretty sketchy. In this case I asked the secretary to preserve all of the tapes on the Swan Falls hearings, thinking it was likely to wind up in court. She did that, and I took them down to the legislative council that provides all the bill drafting services for legislators, and asked them to put those in safe preservation, which they did. Of course that proved to be very useful. ...

Legislating zero flow at Milner

CLIVE STRONG The zero flow at Milner and the two rivers concept really goes back to the 1920 Board of Engineers. The Report set forth a plan for treating the Snake River as two rivers. The plan proposed to fully use the flow of the river for development of the Snake River Plain. But, the effect of this development on hydropower would be offset by replenishing the spring flows in the Thousand Springs reach by return flows from the irrigation seeping into the aquifer.

The zero flow at Milner is an article of faith in Idaho. Indeed, after the Swan Falls Agreement was signed in 1984 the Department caused a consternation in Eastern Idaho when it proposed rules that would have included the surface water of the Snake River above Milner Dam in the trust water area.

The water users above Milner Dam basically came unglued and felt they had been betrayed. The legislature resolved this controversy in 1986 by amending Idaho Code Section 42-203B(2) to make clear that, for purposes of administration, the the Snake River, and surface and groundwater tributaries to the Snake River upstream of Milner Dam, are not within the trust water area and are not to be considered for purposes of administration of the hydropower water rights.

NORM YOUNG If you've noticed the line that goes across below American Falls and up to the west of Blackfoot and on up towards Rexburg, it stairsteps.

Our hydrologists were asked to make that line as to where the groundwater table – based upon mass measurement of wells, where the water would be tributary above and where it would then be tributary below Milner. And complicating it was the perched aquifer at Burley and up at Ashton or Rexburg.

But throwing that aside, there was this point at which if you drew the lines perpendicular to the groundwater contours, the flow lines would go above or below Milner. And that's where that line came from.

But the hydrologists in the department were most reluctant to draw that line because as they rightly pointed out, if you, the next day, put a well in on one side or the other, that new well moves the line or if you pump an existing well harder than you did. And so they didn't want to draw the line. But that was pre-model days, groundwater model days or at least any sophisticated model. So that's where that came from

And a similar line was drawn at the lower end across the Mountain Home Basin, and there's been interesting debates about whether that's right or not.

JIM JONES I can tell you that the Swan Falls deal was not fully laid to rest in 1984 or 1985 or even in 1986.

There was kind of an interesting postscript.

You know, everything went pretty well. The legislature passed the legislation, the adjudication was filed. But as part of the agreement, it was pretty apparent that you needed to nail down everything you could. Had to have the Public Utilities Commission sign off. They did. Water Resources Board. They did.

But it required sign-off by the Federal Energy Regulatory Commission. And nothing ever seems to get done there. I mean it took them a year to consider our petition for getting into the relicensing for Swan Falls.

And so you're sitting there through '85, nothing happened, into '86, nothing happened. So we get this bright idea, Well, why don't we get legislation through the Congress to approve the Swan Falls agreement, since FERC doesn't seem to want to deal with it.

So I called Senator McClure's office and said, "We'd like to get some Swan Falls legislation through." I actually went back to meet with him.

"No. We settled it."

So he says, "Well, okay. We'll take a look at some legislation."

So we got some legislation put together to give approval to the Swan Falls agreement in lieu of FERC action. And I think this was in 1986. And everything was going hunky-dory.

A bill came through – and I can't tell you what bill it was right now just right off the top of my head because I haven't made it part of my little presentation, but Senator McClure found this big bill, he attached the little Swan Falls approval to it. The bill goes over to the House. They approve it. It goes to the president. He didn't like something in the big bill. So he vetoed it, President Reagan. So we were back to square one.

This time I think they started the legislation in the House -- or maybe it got started in the Senate. I can't recall. I'd have to take a look at that.

But anyway, it gets over to the House. I think it got approval in the Senate as a stand-alone bill. Then it goes over to the house. And Congressman Dingell is looking at it, and he's thinking, Well, there's no environmental concerns being addressed in here.

So we had a call for some environmental studies. And Richard Stallings was the Second District congressman at that time. And he didn't think that that was a bad idea. We said, "No. If you allow FERC to do environmental studies with regard to, you know, the subordination issue, that could be a roadmap to unsubordination."

And of course Clive was jumping up and down. He says, "We can't do that. We can't allow that to happen."

So anyway, I had to get really nasty with Stallings. I sent out several press releases saying that he was selling Idaho out, allowing people to get a foothold to upset the agreement.

But nevertheless, it passed the House. It goes to the Senate, and it's just pending agreement with the Senate. You know, they're having a conference committee to determine the fate of the legislation. I called Senator McClure and told him I'd just as soon have no legislation.

I said, "Kill it if you can't amend it."

He says, "Well, it looks like it's going to go."

And I said, "Well, then you've got to knock that provision out of it, the studies." I said, "If you don't, it could undo the whole deal.

He says, "It can't be done."

And I very undiplomatically said, "If it doesn't get done, then tomorrow morning I'm going to hold a press conference, and I'm going to blast you from heck to breakfast."

And I'll be darned, the conference committee approved the bill, striking the studies provision.

Motivation for settlement

TOM NELSON Anybody who has negotiated a complex agreement recognizes that at a certain point the parties are committed to settlement. Even though they're not fully in agreement on the details, they are committed to settlement, and it takes something major to derail it at that point.

[Idaho Power negotiated] for much the same reason as you negotiate any issue. With a negotiated settlement, you can isolate, define and limit the risks. And clearly there were a lot of risks involved in proceeding with the Swan Falls controversy the way it was getting structured. There was a risk of an adverse outcome. There was a political risk. And there was certainly a financial risk. So basically I think the company's interests were much the same as the state's and the others, was to get the risks down to an acceptable level.

Number one, it could have lost – it could have gotten a court decision that said that its conduct throughout the years had resulted in a complete estoppel to protest future development of agricultural land. It could have had an erosion of this political base in the legislature to the point where it got a subordination bill passed, which would have shifted the focus then from the case as structured to a probably long-running issue in the courts on the constitutionality of the subordination legislation. It had the attendant financial risks that would follow from complete subordination of its water rights in the depletion of the river, together with the costs of the litigation.

CLIVE STRONG If they hadn't found a compromise, we faced the distinct possibility that a large part of the Eastern Snake Plain

Aquifer could be shut down. It was uncertain how the litigation would turn out.

I was reasonably confident we would win on the equitable theories, but the consequence if the state lost was huge. I think that kept the irrigators at the table.

From the power company's perspective, it was clear they weren't going to win the political battle. Shutting down a large part of the economy of the state of Idaho wasn't in the company's interest.

VINCE ALBERDI I think that sometimes it takes something like a Swan Falls to kind of wake us up and really determine the future of where we're going in water.

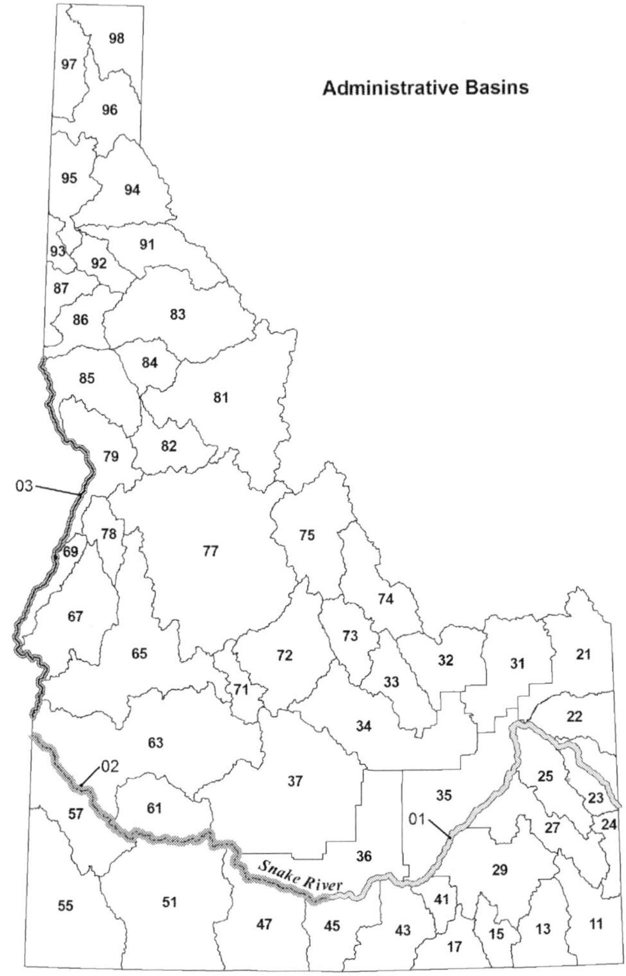

The water basins of Idaho, as numbered by the Idaho Department of Water Resources. (map courtesy Idaho Department of Water Resources)

Forming an adjudication 1986-1989

Now that the settlement was being approved, the adjudication had to follow. The outline was there, but a mass of details had to be filled in.

DAVID SHAW Nobody knew what that was, but it needed to be done. The only way to protect water rights in Idaho is with a water district and to have a water district you have to have an adjudication. *Nettleton versus Higginson* is the case that says that.

So the die was cast, so to speak, in 1985.

There were concerns about doing an adjudication because of the horror stories from all the states around, and even the Payette adjudication itself had been going on since the mid-'60s. And there were concerns about what's it going to do. You know, "There's some people diverting water illegally, and we've got to stop those people, but not me and my neighbor. We're good guys. You got to leave us alone."

So also enacted in 1985 was something called the Amnesty Statute that basically gave people a free pass if they didn't fully comply with the historical process of developing water rights. So that's kind of the background for getting this going.

The state decided the way to fund the adjudication was through filing fees. So when people filed claims for their water rights, they would pay a fee based on the kind of water use they had.

Finding the (first) judge

DANIEL HURLBUTT I went from antitrust litigation that was really world-wide in scope, to cases like pigs at large in Lincoln County. So it was a pretty radical change.

As a district judge in Twin Falls, and I'd only been involved in a couple of smaller water cases that were just local to the Twin Falls area.

I volunteered as one would volunteer in the army.

One day the Supreme Court was sitting in Twin Falls as they do as part of their constitutional duties. And I was in my chambers, and during one of their recesses in walked then Chief Justice Allan Shepard, and he sat down in my office and loosened his tie, pulled out a cigarette, and was chatting and looked at me, and said: Well now, the state just filed this adjudication before the Supreme Court, which under statute the Snake River Adjudication was to be initially filed in front of the Supreme Court, and they were then to select the presiding judge and county and venue. And he said – I don't know whether this is truly what happened, but he said, Well, we had to pick a presiding judge, so I went around to all the other justices and had them put a name in a hat, and when I got back to my chambers I pulled out ballots, and you were on each one of them. Would you like to take the case? It was a little difficult to tell the chief, no, I didn't want the case.

And so I think, as he explained it, they knew my background in complex litigation, and he thought that that would be important in the Snake River Adjudication, so I accepted the case.

I laughed only because he's from Massachusetts. I was originally from Chicago, and I said, "You know, Chief, you've given me a case that provides the opportunity of angering more registered voters in the state of Idaho than any other case that's probably ever been filed." He laughed and understood what I was saying.

So away we went.

LAIRD NOH Personally, I knew Dan, in fact my wife had worked for him, he was a district judge in Twin Falls. There was litigation challenging the validity of the jury selection process and he ruled against it, and he hired my wife to put a legal system in place which she did, and tried to get her to move on to other things, which she didn't.

So I knew him quite well, and highly respected him. I knew he knew nothing about water law. But I really think he was a genius when it came to organizing and understanding technology. I've always felt, and I think others shared that, that was maybe one of the key fortunate strokes, that it was the ability to organize those masses of water rights and papers and cases that he put in place, that served the process very well.

DANIEL HURLBUTT Then the Supreme Court had to designate a county of venue. They considered several different counties, but it was important to the Supreme Court that it not be in Ada County, that it be out where more water users were located, and Twin Falls was pretty centrally located. It appeared as though we had initially the court clerk's office in a position to handle this until we could put together a more comprehensive system.

I was told that they wanted to first select the judge, and then they'd worry about the county. So that's the order in which the selection went, as far as I understood it.

DANIEL HURLBUTT It made news, but I don't think it was controversial. I think it became clear at least to most that the process was needed. The specifics of how it might work were somewhat controversial, but were initially pretty unclear, but I think that there were concerns by different parties, because of past adjudications and what effect those might have on this new adjudication, and there were concerns certainly about the expense, and to do a comprehensive adjudication of the entire system, it had to be done consistent with federal law, the McCarran Amendment.

There were concerns about what happens when you include the United States, whose presence in Idaho is so significant, and what kind of complexity that might add to the process. But I think that the then Attorney General, Jim Jones, now on the Idaho Supreme Court, and the Department of Water Resources, the legislature felt that the time had come when this was really not just something that should be done, but something that was an absolute necessity.

CLIVE STRONG The people in the Boise River basin in particular didn't want to participate in the lawsuit. They viewed this as an eastern Idaho problem, because the Boise River enters the Snake River below the Swan Falls Dam. They had been through an adjudication called the Bryan adjudication in the early 1900s. So they didn't feel a need to have their water rights adjudicated, and wanted to be excluded from the adjudication.

We were concerned that the United States would not agree to that narrow of an adjudication or it would put us at risk of not having jurisdiction under the McCarran Amendment.

At the time, Donald Olowinski represented the Boise Project Board of Control, and we ultimately negotiated an agreement in which the statute provided we would commence the adjudication upstream from where the Snake River – I believe it's where the Snake River exits Idaho. And the rest of the Snake River Basin would not be included unless it was necessary for purposes of obtaining jurisdiction over the United States under the McCarran Amendment.

When we filed the petition, the United States took the position that the entire Snake River Basin needed to be included in the adjudication. And so our first round of litigation was, what does the McCarran Amendment require for purposes of obtaining jurisdiction over the United States for the general adjudication?

The district court held that the entire river needed to be included. That decision was appealed to the Idaho Supreme Court. The Idaho Supreme Court affirmed the geographic scope of the adjudication. The first SRBA decision appears in Volume 115 of the Idaho Reports at page one. The Boise/Kuna Irrigation District sought cert* with the United States Supreme Court, which was denied. So the scope of the adjudication was established by that order. It was going to include the entirety of the Snake River Basin.

PAT COSTELLO There was an amendment to the adjudication statute to preserve the Boise River water users' ability to argue that – well, we included a provision there that said we would only have to go below Adrian [Oregon] if it was necessary to bring the U.S. in, and in the event we didn't we would leave them out. There was language put in there to make it easier to exclude the lower portions of the Snake so that the Payette and the Boise wouldn't have to be re-adjudicated unless we had to do it to bring the U.S. in. We signed off on that.

* Shorthand for a writ of certiorari, which is issued by a superior court (in this case the U.S. Supreme Court) to bring before it proceedings from lower courts. Of the many requests by participants in legal cases for issuance of "cert" by the U.S. Supreme Court, only a relative few are granted.

PETER MONSON We first learned about the SRBA in 1985, after there had been litigation between Idaho Power and other water users. We were approached, the Department of Justice was, by Clive Strong I believe, who came to a meeting with us and laid out the groundwork. They told us, we're thinking about doing this adjudication, and we wanted to see if you see any issues ... we had some conversations about the scope of the adjudication of the Snake River. There were two proposals at the time. One idea was to end it where the river leaves Idaho at Farewell Bend, and the there was the idea of adjudicating the full basin. There was also discussion about whether to include certain river systems that had been recently adjudicated ...

Making it a McCarran adjudication

JOHN ROSHOLT McCarran was the senator from Nevada for whom the Las Vegas airport is named. And he was a very prominent senator. But for the 30 years before the McCarran Act was passed, and I think it was in the late '40s, the western water interests had been lobbying for a McCarran Act to force the feds into state courts, which allegedly knew more about state waters than the federal courts would have known; even though there were water decrees in both courts all over the west. But this – every time they'd get down to it, the feds would say, well, you know, we're the sovereign, you can't force us into state court and we're not coming. And then when the McCarran Act was passed, and there were a bunch of really prominent western lawyers that participated in getting that done.

CLIVE STRONG Most importantly, we wanted the adjudication to be what is called a general stream adjudication. A general stream adjudication is one in which all rights are determined. And it's important, because under federal law, there's a virtually unique statute called the McCarran Amendment.

Under the McCarran Amendment, the United States has agreed to waive its sovereign immunity to participate in a general stream adjudication under state law. Typically the United States is immune to suit in state court absent a waiver of sovereign immunity. So we needed to make sure this adjudication met the terms of the McCarran Amendment.

GREG PANTER As I recall from memory, it was principally the Boise Valley water users in the Lucky Peak Boise River system. And I think that they – I believe it was the Payette River water users were somewhat concerned about the adjudication. I should add I don't know they were concerned about the adjudication per se. But their contention at that time was that their systems had already been adjudicated. And to the extent that they had gone through and shared in that expense, they didn't see the need to have to go back through and re-adjudicate those rights.

BRUCE NEWCOMB Vard Chatburn got macular degeneration. And so he called me up. I used to run cattle up across the fence from him up an Albion, and so he said, "I want you to consider running for my position." And he didn't tell me then he had macular degeneration.

So anyway, I always had a really bad taste in my mouth for the legislature because of the whole controversy. And anyway, so then he called me back up and wanted me to come up to his house so I did.

I told him I really didn't want to do this, you know, because I really didn't like that process at all. And he said, "Well, I got macular degeneration, and I'd like you to take my place."

Well, I had run once as a Democrat. And so I had never gone through the hoops from the Republicans. But I had changed, you know, because I went to the state convention and I came back and told my dad, he was an FDR Democrat, and I said, "Your party is a figment of your imagination."

And he started laughing and he said, "Well, I voted for a lot more Republicans than I ever did Democrats."

So I did change at that time, but I didn't make a big announcement. And so I told Vard that.

And he said, "I will take care of that." So when he announced his retirement, he endorsed me on the capitol steps. So the Republicans in Cassia County they didn't like it because they called me "the anointed one." But it all worked out. And he was always a great advisor.

But that's what he was concerned about, was the water rights, you know, and the economic welfare of the whole valley. And that's why he saw some kind of vision in me. I don't know. But at the time I was really – I was a reluctant suitor.

It was kind of just the launching pad, actually, for me. Because that's all I came to the legislature for was to see this through, you know.

BRUCE NEWCOMB I came to the legislature in 1987. I was elected in the election of '86. And then I spent two years as a grenade thrower and 18 years as a grenade catcher. I mean, in other words, my second term I was elected caucus chair. And then I was assistant majority leader. And then I was majority leader for six years when Simpson was speaker, and then I was speaker for eight years.

And there the joke was always, well, we can't go home because Newcomb's got a water bill we got to pass before we go.

The department develops methods for adjudication

KEN DUNN The responsibility for the Snake River Basin Adjudication is the Adjudication Bureau's, and they do have people assigned directly to the regions and, in fact, they have a mobile unit that is in addition to these units. Again, to the extent that a regional manager manages on a day to day basis the resources that he has in the region, both his that are assigned directly to him and those in the adjudication assigned to his region, he has the flexibility to assign the people to the job that needs to be done.

The adjudication and the Swan Falls agreement required data collection and resource study programs. The funding of that whole program, it was recognized that there was going to have to be start-up money, that there was going to have to be general account moneys put in. And so because the fees could not be collected until such time as the adjudication could be - petition could be filed with the court and fees could be collected, that start-up money was initially spent on these studies, then became available to the legislature to continue that specific data collection program associated with the adjudication.

CLIVE STRONG A lot of credit for the success of the adjudication has to go to Dave Shaw, who was the original adjudication bureau chief. Dave had a really good mind for how to put together complex issues. He did a good job of integrating technology resources and staff. Dave and I spent a lot of years together working on adjudication issues. He participated actively in the steering committee.

We had a lead attorney for the Department, Lynne Krogh-Hampe. Between Lynne, Dave and myself, we did a lot of the planning efforts for the adjudication.

DAVID SHAW I started working for the department's predecessor agencies in 1973. One of the first things I did was help work on the Payette adjudication. So I had gained a little bit of background right along.

And then in 1977, I moved to the western region office of the department. And that's where the people that we call the adjudication unit were located. And they were finishing up the Payette adjudication. During my time there we did an adjudication on Reynolds Creek. There were some other little adjudications around the state that we spent a little time on, but it was primarily those two.

So prior to the SRBA, I did have some experience with Idaho law, at least, and the adjudication process here in Idaho. I was raised on a farm, still have the farm over in Emmett, so I understand a little bit about water use that some other people don't. My background is an engineer, ag engineer from the University of Idaho, so I have some background that's applicable as well.

KEN DUNN We'd had experience as a department in two other reasonably large adjudications in recent years, recent at that time. The Lemhi adjudication, Lemhi River basin, and the Payette River basin. And we took the number of water rights that were in our records before the adjudication and then looked at how many water rights were claimed in each of those adjudications and said, all right, the number that actually come in was about, if I remember the factor, 1.74 times the number we knew about to start with, and I think you'll find that a constant factor all the way through.

NORM YOUNG The idea that the water right was more than a diversion rate was pretty difficult to sell. I stood in many, many public meetings where people just couldn't buy the idea that two acres of alfalfa consumed twice as much water as one acre and that that made any difference.

But the face of the water right has always included basically the same elements, right? You've got the point of diversion, the rate, the number of acres, purpose of use, those types of things. Or was there a time when that wasn't the case?

You're baiting me, aren't you?

You've read enough of those old decrees. Some of them say a certain person owns the entire stream.

And that's all it says. When the department was doing the Lemhi Adjudication back in the '70s, the idea of putting a diversion volume as part of the elements of a water right become very contentious. And as a compromise, as I recall, the volume of consumptive use was agreed to but not the diversion volume.

So, no. Water rights don't always have it. And if you look at the decrees coming out of the Snake River Basin Adjudication, they don't all have exactly the same elements.

You know, early on in the adjudication, the idea of decreeing the consumptive use got taken out of the mix. And for the most part, you don't see a diversion volume on a surface water right. You usually see that on a groundwater right. So, no, they don't.

DANIEL HURLBUTT The one challenge that was raised was by parties who had been involved in previous adjudications, and they felt they should be excluded from having to file claims and go through this process. It was primarily based upon the McCarran Amendment that I ruled, and the Idaho Supreme Court affirmed, that they would have to be included.

Some of them were relatively contemporary. There were a couple of adjudications that were underway at the time the Snake River Basin Adjudication was commenced. They were folded into the SRBA.

There was the Bancroft-Lund Adjudication near Soda Springs, is the one that comes to mind. There may have been one or two other smaller ones that I'm just not thinking of. But the Bancroft one was a larger one that was rolled into it.

DAVID SHAW I sought it out. The department opened for a position to be the manager of the adjudication. They were called bureau chiefs at the time. And I applied for and was selected for that job. So officially I started working on the SRBA on July 1, 1985.

My role was more to develop a plan. And it was probably unique that we had pretty much free rein to rewrite the adjudication statute. And I think that's probably a linchpin piece of making this process be successful, because we knew our own history was not stellar.

We looked at the states around us, found the same thing. So I worked with David Barber. I don't know if he's somebody that might be interviewed or not. But the two of us basically went from beginning to end of the adjudication statutes in Idaho and rewrote them.

And we made sure we had a process that would give adequate notice so it would be legally sufficient; we had a process that allowed the use of new technology – and I'll talk more about that in a minute – a way to give notice that was, we thought, more efficient than what had been done in the past, because the past notice was basically personal service, and it was awfully cumbersome; and check-ins along the way where the department could ask the court to approve various steps.

So we tried to be sure we didn't leave anything undone along the way. And like I say, probably the opportunity to rewrite the adjudication statute was a linchpin piece of making this whole thing finally come to a successful end.

. . . But the first rewrite was passed by the legislature in 1986. So we basically spent the year planning and writing so we had a plan to take to the legislature that they adopted, governor approved, and we had our road map, so to speak.

CLIVE STRONG When we started planning for the adjudication, the one thing we wanted to avoid was the history of other state adjudications. Typically these large general stream adjudications go on for decades and don't get resolved. They just keep going on.

At the time we were beginning this adjudication, there were several western adjudications going on. One was the Big Horn adjudication in Wyoming. It was of particular interest to us because the state of Wyoming was quantifying the reserved water rights for the Wind River Reservation. The Wind River Reservation was created by the same treaty that created the Fort Hall Indian Reservation, the Fort Bridger Treaty.

Adjudications around the West

That adjudication started, I believe, in 1977. It was highly contentious. The state of Wyoming, the tribes, and the United States were fighting each other, and litigating each element of the claims.

And we looked at the Big Horn and said, we don't want that to be the outcome. We also looked at the Aquavella adjudication in Washington that started back in the early 1900s and was still unresolved.

We looked at the Montana adjudication that started in 1977 and hadn't decreed any water rights. We also looked at the Gila River adjudication in Arizona, and what was going on in New Mexico. I visited a number of those states and just tried to find out what worked, what didn't work. We came to the conclusion that we needed to rewrite our adjudication statutes.

So we did that in 1986 to make sure we met the terms of the McCarran Amendment. We also had provisions for incorporating negotiations.

DANIEL HURLBUTT We looked at, and had lengthy discussions with the people and presiding judge in the Yakima adjudication in Washington. We spent a lot of time speaking with John Thorson, who was a special master in the Gila River adjudication in Arizona, which was a very significant adjudication there. Those were the two primary major adjudications ongoing in the United States that we looked at. And actually traveled on to Phoenix to meet with court personnel, and the presiding judge in that case, as well as John Thorson.

Looking at those different scenarios, we tried to figure out what would be the most economical, efficient, and timely manner to try to design our response to proceeding with the SRBA.

DUANE MECHAM Most of the work for Interior was done through the regional attorneys and the justice attorneys at Denver. Because there were a lot of adjudications that were becoming really active in the late 80s and early 90s, I was asked to follow the issues on the Yakima adjudication and the SRBA, primarily on the Bureau of Reclamation side.

By the mid 80s there was a big push to negotiate Indian water rights and not litigate them. Idaho saw that handwriting on the wall as did Montana but in a different way, and integrated into their adjudication process the ability to have stays et cetera that would allow negotiation to proceed rather than just full bore litigation on Indian water rights.

From my perspective what that did, the Indian negotiations were popping up all over the place, they needed to have staff and I was happy to volunteer. I ended up pretty early on in my career at Interior working on Indian water right settlements, in Arizona and also in the SRBA, first with the Fort Hall settlement. I was brought in primarily because I had background in the [Bureau of] Reclamation side of things, and the parties were starting to look to reclamation to some degree either as a resource for additional water supplies to accomplish the settlements, or for technical support or other support generally for the negotiations. That was kind of my entre into the Interior side of Interior water work.

I in no way was the lead but working with Peter [Monson] and others, Lyn Collins, worked kind of in the middle of the Fort Hall negotiations – I'd say toward the latter half of this, primarily in a support role with those negotiating on the federal side. I was impressed that the state had tried, in that instance, and took the initiative themselves to start a negotiation and weren't even waiting around for the feds. Which was fine: It needed to be done.

The tribes have to live with these settlements. The tribes whether they're litigated or negotiated, the tribal water right claims have to cover their current water use and future water use. This would be the one time you get a chance to do it. In a negotiation context, we're going to want to make sure on the federal side that there is adequate water secured as part of the settlement, that it's an enforceable settlement, that it's not left open in big ways.

Another key principle would be that the tribes have the opportunity to bring forward their priorities for the settlement, for the types of water uses that are important to them. Another key one is administration of the water rights once you have a settlement.

DANIEL HURLBUTT The statute set up a process first that required the Department of Water Resources to investigate all the water rights in the 38 counties that comprise the Snake River system. And it was known that that would be approximately a two-year process, for them to begin the significant work of both investigating, and it also placed the responsibility of notice with the Department of Water Resources, so the department had to both identify all the known rights in the system and to notify the owners of those rights of the pendency of the action and the fact that they would be investigated.

Investigating the claims

That was a very extensive, extensive process, and I thought was extremely well done by the Department, because the Department not only looked at the permits and licenses that resided with them, but they went and searched county records, tax rolls, property records, and used satellite imagery to identify parcels of land that they knew water was being used on, and then to cross-reference that with all of the other documentation they had, so that they could get notice, as best as possible, to everybody that would be a potential claimant.

I think that in hindsight it was extremely well done by the Department, because there were relatively few situations where there were water users or people with water rights that did not receive notice, and had to ultimately file late claims. Some of the late claims were because people just weren't paying attention, didn't do their job and get filed, but had received notice. But there were a very few people that didn't receive notice. I continue to commend the department. It was a mammoth effort and they did a terrific job.

ROGER BURDICK You know, one of the problems is the enormity of the issue and the conflicting interests and overlapping interests of everyone when it comes to water. One of the concepts in the SRBA is you can object to a drop of water coming in at Driggs, even though you may live in Lewiston. Well, you combine all of those business interests, all of those political interests, all of those economic interests, all of those personal interests, and then try to sift them out into a court system where everybody gets heard but you don't get bogged down like every other adjudication has in the nation.

DANIEL HURLBUTT Initially the state had a statutory duty, but then in developing how we were going to handle the litigation phase of the case, once claims were filed and director's reports were filed, we had to work together with the water users and the Department to determine how court notice would be effectuated when you had, you know, what appeared to be initially 185,000 water rights. Now, that represented probably 120,000 claimants that we knew of at the time.

So while the statutory notice was being taken care of by the department, we, the courts, the Attorney General's Office, and other major claimants in the adjudication, were meeting and discussing how to administer the court case, and that's where court notice came up. That's where, with the administrative office of the courts, I started working on constructing a mini court system to handle the entire adjudication matter.

I was working with the then administrative director of the courts, Carl Bianchi, who was and is one of the most distinguished court administrators in the United States. We spent a lot of time going over the adjudication legislation, trying to determine how we could accomplish what was set forth in that statute in a way that was consistent with how courts were run, how due process was met by court action, and also looking at, from a functionality standpoint, how could we get this case done within anybody's lifetime.

At the time the adjudication was filed, the average district judge disposed of perhaps as many as, well, 250 to 450 cases a year. How do you then look at a case with 185,000 claims? Clearly not all of those claims would be litigated, but a significant number would be litigated. How do you match those kinds of judicial dispositions with the amount of work that the adjudication presented? That's when we started designing a court system that could accomplish that goal.

DAVID SHAW One of the essentials – and this, I think, was included in the original authorizing legislation in 1985 – was to be sure we had an adjudication that satisfied the McCarran Amendment. The McCarran Amendment is the authority that allows the federal government to be joined in state water law adjudications. So of course in rewriting the statute we had that in mind to be sure that all of our steps would comply, we felt, with McCarran.

Then the next step was to apply that on the ground. And one of the things that McCarran says is you have to do a water system. Well, what's a water system? And there was different opinions in Idaho.

We were sure we had to do everything above Swan Falls because that was the reason for doing the adjudication. The people on the Boise said, "We're real happy. You just leave us alone."

But to get jurisdiction on the tribes – you know, we had the Fort Hall sitting on the Snake River, near Idaho Falls, Pocatello; the Nez Perce reservation sits on the Snake River at Lewiston, so the question that we had to ask ourselves was, was it necessary to do the whole Snake River Basin Adjudication so we were sure we got the Nez Perce tribe included?

What we finally filed in our petition was a request for the court to determine. We know we have to do this much down to Swan Falls. "We think we may have to do the rest of it to comply with McCarran. Judge, you decide."

The judge decided to do the whole basin. And this was after there had been notices going out, of course, and everything of the hearing, the initial commencement hearing.

That decision was appealed to the Supreme Court. The United States Supreme Court was asked to look at it, and they declined. So we were set then. We had to do the entire Snake River Basin from border to border.

CLIVE STRONG As we were moving forward with the adjudication, the Shoshone-Bannock Tribes became concerned about it.

Tribes are reluctant to participate in the state court adjudications. They feel it doesn't afford them the same protections as in federal court. So the Shoshone-Bannock tribes, through Howard Funke, their attorney at the time, approached the legislature and said that the tribe would like to engage in negotiations to see if the tribal claims could be resolved through negotiations.

At the time of the approval of the adjudication, the legislature passed – I believe it was House Concurrent Resolution 16 that directed the attorney general and the governor to embark upon negotiations with the Shoshone-Bannock Tribes to see if their federal reserve water right claims could be resolved through settlement negotiations.

And that ultimately led to a delay in the commencement of the adjudication, because the tribe didn't want to be litigating at the same time we were negotiating. So we started negotiations with the tribe in August of `85. We held off on beginning the adjudication to see where those negotiations would go.

DUANE MECHAM I would say in large measure it is a supportive role, but underlying that foundation we have the trust responsibility, so that's why we from the federal side tend to have the tribes take the lead on developing proposals, on developing their priorities for the settlement.

We'll be there in at least two roles, one, to ensure their proposals are going to be adequate to meet our trust responsibility, that this settlement will provide adequate water for future needs. The other key aspect of the trust responsibility is that if we litigate these claims, the Untied States is on point as trustee to develop those claims, to have the experts with supporting information and testimony, how we've qualified the appropriateness of those claims. And likewise the federal lawyers will be assuring that we've developed the right legal theories, adequate legal theories, to support those claims and support any legal challenge. So in a pure litigation context the role is narrow but very important.

We're rarely out front but we're there when we need to be.

Finally, the adjudication commences with a simple family road trip.

The adjudication is formally filed

CLIVE STRONG I drove to Twin Falls on June 17, 1987, and filed the complaint with the Fifth Judicial District Court. I can remember driving down with my wife and kids to file the complaint and then going out to dinner.

It probably warrants talking a little bit about what an adjudication is. An adjudication is a determination of the elements of each water right within a water system. And in the prior appropriation system, priority is very important because it determines who gets water in times of shortages. So you have to have the interrelationship of all water rights determined.

That's why you have this large lawsuit that brings all water users into the adjudication so they all have an opportunity to assert their claims and their defenses to other water rights.

The sheer magnitude of an adjudication really makes these a very complex lawsuit. When we complete this process, we will have adjudicated about 159,000 water rights. And that represents the water rights within 87 percent of the State of Idaho. Basically from all of the Clearwater drainage basin south, with the exclusion of the Bear River Basin in the far southeast corner of Idaho.

PETER MONSON The federal reserved rights claims in particular were controversial and complex and the evidence needed to present them in court was quite voluminous.

I was asked to do it but I did actually volunteer for it. I heard rumblings from my boss that this case was coming on. It was a general stream adjudication in the northwest – it sounded like interesting work.

As I alluded earlier, in 1992-93, the workload got to the point that we needed more than one attorney on the case.

BARRY WOOD It wasn't just a flip on the light switch. It was a transition. And where do they have the court? We used the SRBA chambers and courtroom to hear regular district court trials early on.

CLIVE STRONG Typically in adjudications there's a lot of planning that has to go in. In fact, the claims-taking didn't get intensive until about 1992. So we had about five years in which we were doing service of process, so there was an opportunity for us to use that period to kind of design procedures. We developed first and second round service of process. Got agreement with the United States and the stakeholders on the adequacy of that process.

We developed a docket sheet. If you can imagine in a case this size, we expect the decree, the final decree in this case, to be somewhere on the order of 250,000 pages. And, the pleadings obviously exponentially larger than that. So if you're trying to serve everybody, that would become cost prohibitive.

The docket sheet procedure provided a way to give notice of actions in subcases. Each water right became a sub-case. If you wanted to participate in that sub-case, you filed a notice of an objection or response to get into that sub-case. Those that had a specific interest in the sub-case got personal notice. But other claimants got notice by the docket sheet. Every month the docket sheet identified what pleadings had been filed, and parties were obligated to review the docket sheet.

DANIEL HURLBUTT Administrative Order 1 was an important piece of it, but given the size, scope, complexity and time that could be involved in this case, really the first determination was to set up a system, which was adopted, approved by the Supreme Court, and funded by the legislature, to have a multiple master system, so that initial disputes in the case would go to special masters, who would be full-time court employees. They would really be functioning like lower court judges. They would hear initial cases, and then make recommendations to the district court, and the appeal from the district court would then go to the Idaho Supreme Court.

Administrative Order 1

Now, in determining how that structure would work, integral was Administrative Order 1, and Administrative Order 1 was our attempt, and it was my absolute goal to try to dovetail the structure that the legislature had created in the SRBA statute with the Idaho Rules of Civil Procedure and how courts normally operate. They were – they did not look identical when you put one side-to-side, and the statutory components presented some quandaries about how you could dovetail the two together and have this case look like as ordinary an Idaho district court case as possible.

And the reason that that was important to me was, there weren't enough water lawyers in Idaho to represent all the claimants, so I thought it was important that the practicing bar look at this case, and even with its procedural complexity, have it look as much like an ordinary district court case as possible, so that they could participate and understand what was going on. It was important to honor the structure that the legislature set up, but at the same time, there were both Idaho court rules that we had to honor, as well as constitutional requirements like due process.

Clearly one of the big hurdles was, where you have a case with as many claimants as there were, how does everybody that's a party to the case, that is, all of the claimants, 120,000-plus folks, how do they receive notice of each and every aspect of what's going on in the case? The answer is it's not feasible. If I'm a farmer by Arco, Idaho, and I file a document in the case, do I have to file that document or copy that document to a hundred-plus-thousand other people? That's not feasible. It's not workable. So one of the things we accomplished in Administrative Order 1, and I think the Attorney General provided some wonderful ideas on this, as did the personnel in the Yakima adjudication, who came up with what was called the docket sheet procedure. That was an important first hurdle to get over.

What that initially was constructed to do, it was a monthly report put out by the Department of Water Resources. That report would be placed in the county seat of the 38 counties where the adjudication took place, and any party could subscribe with a minor fee, I think of $7.50, to receive a copy of the docket sheet. And the docket sheet would reflect all of the actions that were filed in the preceding month in the adjudication. It would serve as notice of any claims that were filed, objections to the directors' reports that are filed, and any other motions or aspects of any of those proceedings.

CARTER FRITSCHLE The sub-case process established for the SRBA has worked well, and represents a sound and logical approach for managing thousands of water right records. The weakest link in the process occurs when a claim is split after the director's report is filed. While IDWR creates a parent record, the court decrees the "parent" right as disallowed. I do have some concerns that this could lead to confusion down the road if IDWR ever has a problem maintaining a water right pedigree.

BARRY WOOD The AO1 process was absolutely genius. There is just no other way to express it.

A number of things have made the SRBA successful. One is the AO1 process. Two was the docket sheet notice, that you could not complete the job without the docket sheet process – it would just be an impossibility. Three was the cooperation of the water bar, the water bar for the most part has been extraordinarily helpful. And a great staff. Those things all came together to make an extraordinarily difficult and important process happen in record time and at not at all that much cost in the scope of things.

DANIEL HURLBUTT In addition to that, what we had to do was figure out how we could break the case down into distinct, segregated components, where you had an actual controversy. That is, the statute required the director to file reports in different reporting areas, outlining the results of the director's investigation of claims that were filed in those areas. And that report would basically be a – the department's rendering of how they thought those claims ought to be approved by the court, and what those decrees for those specific claims should look like. We called those, you know, separate and distinct – well, they would result in separate and distinct decrees for each water right.

When the department filed their report, of course actual notice would go to anybody whose water right was included in that report. Those claimants had the opportunity, if they agreed with the director's report, to simply allow the recommendation made by the department to go forward, and result in, it's called a partial decree, because the unified decree would be every water right in the system.

But each distinct water user filing a claim would receive a partial decree as a decree about their specific water right. If, on the other hand, the claimant disagreed with the manner in which their claim was reported by the department, that would trigger the opening of what we called a sub-case. That is, we had a dispute between a water user and the recommendation made by the director. That of course would be noticed in the docket sheet monthly.

Anyone else who was affected by either the director's recommendation or the claimant's objection could also file an objection, so you might have contiguous water users who had a dispute either between themselves or with what the department was recommending, so you could have multiple parties in a distinct, separate sub case.

After the period of time went by that any objections that were required to be filed were, the matter was then referred to the special master, and the special master essentially handled that as a separate, distinct case, and just as with any other Idaho piece of litigation, a scheduling conference would be set. The parties would be notified, brought in, and they would discuss possibilities of settlement. They would discuss how the matter would be scheduled so that it could be litigated before the special master.

The Special Master then would ultimately either work with the parties to achieve a settlement, or after litigation would issue a recommendation, essentially a decision. The recommendation would go to the district court, the parties to that sub case could file objections with the district court to the master's findings, and then the district court has – as really the final arbiter, would either hear the case – or would hear the case, and the parties could present argument, additional testimony, and then it would be up to the presiding judge to either confirm the decision made by the Special Master in whole or in part, and issue a final decision.

In some cases, the presiding judge could refer it back down to the Special Master for additional hearings and resolution of issues, and then once the presiding judge issued a partial decree, that could then be appealed to the Idaho Supreme Court.

Essentially the Administrative Order 1 was designed to construct this mini court system using the three special masters, to provide notice to parties and to dovetail the adjudication statutes with the Idaho Rules of Civil Procedure. In other words, to provide the framework for proceeding in the case.

THEODORE BOOTH You can't adjudicate all 150,000 claims at once, right?

So I believe it was mostly the department decided which claim, how to group the claims for the reporting. First of all, they were split up by basin, which typically is a surface water hydrology basin. Sometimes those basins were split into multiple parts like Basin 63, Part One, Part Two, Part Three. You had other times when some groundwater was peeled out of a basin and put on a track, for instance, in the Eastern Snake Plain Aquifer, the state was anxious to get that done, to get that in a water district and start administering those groundwater rights. I think Basin 37 has some groundwater in it, so a portion of 37 was peeled out and those groundwater claims came through.

One of the other ways that subcases were categorized was based on the size of the claim, the reporting of the de minimis and stockwater rights being reported out on a different schedule than the larger rights. I think that's what your question goes to. It's not necessarily that those claims could be deferred, in other words, they don't have to be claimed. I think the question goes to the reporting of the claims, correct me if I'm wrong. So you have to take this thing in chunks, and a chunk based on the size of the claim versus geographical location seems to make as much sense as any.

I think there maybe was some difficulties encountered, particularly on the stockwater rights on the federal land. Some issues arose out of that with the way those were claimed both by the federal government and then by the ranchers claiming sort of the same water use, but in a different way, so that the federal government's claims showed up in those de minimis and stockwater director's reports, and the ranchers' claims showing up in the irrigation in other director's reports. Obviously, there were some issues that arose around that. No matter how you do it, no matter how you divide up the chunks, it seems like there's potentially going to be some issues that arise.

DANIEL HURLBUTT There was mostly work with the administrative office of the courts, but it was pretty much left to me to try to figure out how to do this.

There was collaboration with the administrative office, but there was not a lot of discussion with the justices themselves, because ultimately it was going to be their discussion, and we wanted to let them approach it from a fresh perspective, and not be so involved with the creation of AO1 that the justices would feel wedded to it in the event that someone objected to portions of that, and they could look at it independently and from a rather fresh and fair perspective for all involved.

Sending notices, reviewing claims

DAVID SHAW So from '86 to '87, we were doing the planning, getting the initial notice out. And the notice was specified by statute what we had to do for the initial hearing. In the meantime we started putting together plans for how are we actually going to do this once we got the commencement order.

And technology then – this was mid-'80s. We didn't have e-mail. People think e-mail's a nuisance now. We didn't have it. I probably have more computing power in my cell phone today than we had in the department at that time. So state-of-the-art at the time is almost prehistoric today.

We found the USGS was producing something called orthophoto quads that would take a black and white photo and register it and lay it over a quad sheet. We thought that was wonderful. That was new technology for us to look at fields to see how big they were.

DAVID SHAW A quad sheet is a USGS quadrangle map. They come in two varieties: 7 1/2 minute, 15 minute. And it's got the public land survey on it. Most of them have topographic lines to show elevation. They have roads, streams, cities, the usual landmarks on them, on the basic quad sheet. And then the GS had laid this photo over the top of it so you could see outlines of fields and those sorts of things.

About the same time the USGS again, I believe, flew some high-altitude color infrared photography. Infrared is useful because it shows growing crops as bright red. So they had scheduled a flight of Idaho. I think it took two years, 1986 and 1987.

This wasn't digital stuff. We got 8-by-8 color transparencies that you'd lay down on a light table and look at. This was state of the art. This was new stuff, because prior we had the black and white, 8-inch-to-the-mile maps that would more than fill this room for the maps that would be required to do one basin, let alone all of them.

There was no ArcView. ArcInfo was the state of the art GIS mapping. The learning curve on ArcInfo, I recall asking, was about three years. So you didn't hire somebody today and have them be productive in a short time. It was archaic.

There was satellite imagery. And we used satellite imagery with all of its infirmities. It does not have the precision to necessarily identify fields. Didn't then, still doesn't.

So the things we take for granted today, like looking at something on Google map, didn't exist. It was a different era.

The department's water right database at the time was functional, but didn't have the capability that we needed to do what we were going to have to do. So we started out fresh to design a new database. It had to be interactive so people in Idaho Falls, Twin Falls, here, could all see the same information.

About that same time our friends at the Department of Health and Welfare were implementing probably a new payment system for something, and it failed. People weren't getting paid. There was an uproar. And we were trying to implement our own system at the time. So we were under a microscope. The governor's office was here once a week, it seemed like, making sure he wasn't going to be in the headlines again.

But we designed and implemented a successful data capture system. We had a mobile office that we would send out to the various county seats. A cloud at that time was what we expected rain from. It was nothing to do with data processing.

So my staff would order phone lines, be installed. We'd go in and wire in our modems and set up our PCs and start taking claims. And it worked, remarkably.

So from 1988 – I don't think we started taking claims immediately after the commencement order. It took a little while to get fired up. But we figured we had a two-year window to get the claims taken so we had enough revenue coming in to keep the ship afloat. So in that two-year window we took – I don't know – a hundred thousand claims or something like that.

DANIEL HURLBUTT The statute provided that the department was to investigate, the department was to file their recommendations with the court, and then the court was to determine ultimately what the partial decree would be for that water right. But the mechanics of how the court was to handle that, the mechanics of how parties would be notified in a way that's consistent with due process, were things that we had to put together. And by we, I mean the court.

We had meetings with the parties, had a steering committee for a short period of time that looked at and discussed a lot of these issues. Ultimately it was my responsibility, with my staff, to draft an initial set of rules, you know, the precursor to AO1, and we met with the parties, talked about it, tweaked it. Ultimately the court announced it would adopt these rules, but set the matter for hearing so that I could hear objections or concerns about it.

And once that was completed, it was submitted to the Supreme Court. And it was up to the Supreme Court to finally adopt Administrative Order 1, or approve it, because it did require some different procedures than the strict interpretation of the Civil Rules of Procedure. It had some nuances dealing with due process notice rights that were clearly different than Rules of Civil Procedure, but under the circumstances I think provided a good blend of the rules, the statute and due process concerns, that would allow the case to go forward in a manner that was consistent with the statute, the rules and the constitution.

The Steering Committee

CLIVE STRONG One of the things I learned in visiting other states was that some of them had used steering committees. What the steering committee was, if you've got issues that you see coming up, you get a group of stakeholders that sit around the table and you try to talk through those issues and see if you can resolve them through settlement discussions as opposed to litigating every issue.

We approached Judge Hurlbutt, who was the original judge on this case, and suggested the idea of the steering committee. Judge Hurlbutt had a good mind for how to organize the case. And he saw the benefit of trying to get parties to work together before we got into the contentious issues.

DANIEL HURLBUTT Initially there was just an informal series of conferences that I conducted with representatives from the Department of Water Resources, the Attorney General's Office, the United States, and other significant parties, that wanted to participate, and there were attorneys from Idaho Power, some of the larger irrigation districts, canal companies.

And that – they participated really for a couple years – yeah, for a couple years on an informal basis, until, looking at what had been done by steering committees, primarily Yakima set up a steering committee, which is a more formal structure of designated representatives of different groups. For example, still, the steering committee are representatives from the Idaho Attorney General's Office, from the United States, and from certain other water users in different categories of water use; hydropower, agriculture, municipal. The intent was that that smaller representative group could work more quickly and expeditiously on certain issues.

But very quickly, once we got to the adoption of AO1, the need for a steering committee pretty much dissipated, and it then became sufficiently a stand-alone court case that it wasn't helpful, it wasn't necessary, and in fact probably, given notions of due process and fairness, it was more appropriate that everything then be done in more formalized court sessions.

BRIGETTE BILYEU I think it was a way for attorneys to be involved in the process in a different way than they would be if they were just bringing the matter up before the court.

I think there was some thought in the initial years before we had a formal steering committee that people misunderstood that process and they felt like they could come up with a process, present it to the court, and it was a fait accompli and the court was supposed to be, in Judge Hurlbutt's infamous words, "a rubber stamp." That was not the way the court ever thought that process would work. Certainly, I don't think any of the presiding judges has been a rubber stamp to the process.

But, that being said, I think that the steering committee process in those beginning days, and that was talking about, you know, the role of the director and how we were going to get back on track and how all of that was going to work, I thought it was a really useful process because people weren't in front of the judge trying to argue vociferously about their position. It was a way everybody could try to come up with something that would work.

DAVID SHAW Early on in the process the court set monthly status conferences to keep up to date with the Court on what was happening and what the department was doing. And we would always give a report.

But he also established a steering committee that was an informal process where the department, the court, any of the attorneys or water users that were involved could get together and talk about process. You know, what can make it better, what were people missing out on over the misunderstandings that needed to be addressed, what were the recommendations for the Department.

And I think that was probably another linchpin piece of making this whole thing flow smoothly, because there was good dialogue in those meetings, at least initially.

What the court saw as challenges, how they could best be addressed, what we saw our challenges were, and from the water users' standpoint particularly it was a forum where they could say their piece, so to speak, on what they thought needed to be improved or changed or how it could be done better. I don't know if that still continues today or not. I don't think so.

. . . And depending on the issue of the day, we may have gone in prepared to give a report, we may have provided material, we may have listened. It was just a good, open discussion for us to be involved and everybody else to be involved.

DANIEL HURLBUTT Now, we did have set up a monthly status conference that anybody could attend, where essentially the department would spend time reviewing what it had done, what the progress was, the court could report on progress of what was going on, and discuss ideas for maybe different procedures or tweaks to the process that needed to be made in an informal context before it went into a more formal court proceeding where people could file objections and be heard.

. . . Given all the difficulties many of these parties had already gone through with the Swan Falls dispute, their participation in the Swan Falls agreement, which led to the SRBA legislation, which was adopted by the legislature, there was a certain spirit of cooperativeness.

Certainly there were battles about specific issues, but everybody, I think, was on board to try to see that this thing got going, and that it worked. And by everybody, I mean really most all the water users, and the United States and the State of Idaho, as well as the courts. And so I think, you know, everybody wanted to make this process work and go forward. It was, I think, felt by the water users that this was necessary.

DANIEL HURLBUTT One thing we did, I guess, that I didn't address, again, to open the process up to folks, we did develop, along with AO1, forms that parties could use to file objections and responses, so that it both was – there was a standard mechanism available to anybody and everybody, and really most everybody had to use, so that we could understand what a pleading looked like in this case.

It wasn't a traditional pleading that one might see under the Idaho Rules of Civil Procedure. And I think that AO1 accommodated pro se [participants] extremely well, and standardized things in a way that, even for attorneys, it was easy to see who was who and what was what and what was being filed and objected to in separate subcases.

. . . it may have been used in other adjudications, but it was something that we pretty much designed for this case. And it was designed, again, to help dovetail or integrate our mission as set forth in the statutes, but also to provide consistency with the Civil Rules of Procedure in Idaho, and consistent with the constitution.

But also, we were very attuned to trying to make this accessible to either lawyers who had not been involved in water law, to pro se claimants, and even to the lawyers that had been involved in water law, but try to get a format that everybody understood and were consistent with what had to be done in the adjudication.

. . . as I indicated before, there was a question originally over domestic and stockwater uses, de minimis uses had to be included, and I decided they had to be included.

To try to deal with that and to streamline it, essentially the department would recommend any and every domestic and stockwater right that was claimed in the adjudication without separate investigations, and they were pretty much just decreed, and I think there were very few situations of domestic and stockwater claims that were ever litigated or of any real concern, but they were included in the decree.

The first round notices arrive

DAVID SHAW The initial notice that we sent out notifying people that they needed to take their claims, we basically gathered up every mailing address we could find. We got them from the counties, I think we got them from the power company, from our own records. We knew they were poor and out of date. But we gathered up everything we could find, tried to sort the duplicates out, and mailed out these notices. I think I still got some. I was going to bring them in today and I forgot. So that's what produced this first round of claims taking.

The statute said once you have the claims you need to compare those claims to your own records, to any other information that you can access to be sure you have them all. And it's what we called second round service.

So as we started going through these claims, if we discovered here's a field that doesn't have a claim on it, then we need to find out who owns that field and send them a notice. That's where we got crossways with the realty lobby, because we knew the title companies had the best information for finding out who owned this piece of ground here.

But the title companies and the realtors didn't want any responsibility to do anything with water rights. We finally found a couple of young men who had a title company or worked for a title company who were willing to do the research for us to help us find out who owned this piece of ground.

But, you know, we tried to put literature in realtors' offices. They wouldn't allow it. It was as if it was another world that they didn't want any part of. And later on I'll talk some more about that.

So after we had the claims taken, we started this process of reviewing them. One of my concerns from the very beginning is we had a pretty good plan how we were going to first round notice take claims, second round notice, so on and so forth, except for the domestic and stock rights.

If we had to record all the irrigation, that's identifiable with photography, with other means. If we have to get all of the domestic wells, there's no way to know for sure if this house is on city water, has its own well, where it gets its water.

So I don't think people outside of our little group recognized how important it was that we got the domestic and stock deferral, because the gap in the plan was how were we going to give second round notice to domestic and stock users.

NORM YOUNG People would receive the notice, and in some of the areas, they would get a rumor started around that first in line is first in priority. Our claims-takers would get to the courthouse and find a line around the street, around the block.

And Lynn Krogh, she was a master at writing the processing procedures memos. And so a great deal of how the processing was going to be – going to proceed – was set forth as she drafted the memos probably during the claims-taking period.

DAVID SHAW Let's back up a little bit to the claim filing process. There had been a big effort to sell the adjudication starting in 1985, of course, when the enacting legislation was passed. But then when it came time for claims taking, there was another public education effort to tell people about this process, why we were doing it, what the result was going to be, and their obligation to file a claim for any water use that they had.

So we did television spots, radio spots, met with county commissioners, did public information meetings in one end of the basin to the other. We, Gerald Grimmet at the time was our public information officer, and the two of us did this traveling dog-and-pony show to try to inform people about what their requirements were.

Well, somehow in Idaho County – and that public information meeting was an experience all to its own, but word got out that priority for water use was important, that the senior right got the best right.

Well, they didn't understand that priority was when you started using the water. They thought it was when you filed your claim. So we opened an office at the Grangeville courthouse, like we did in virtually every county, and our people showed up Monday morning, or whenever they were going to open, and there was a line around the courthouse of people ready to file their claims because they wanted to be the first to file because they thought that would give them the best water right. So it was an interesting process from beginning to end. But I think the public information part was critical to get people out to file their claims. The first round was pretty successful.

When the domestic and stock deferral came along, we had already taken a lot of those claims. So we had to go back and give people the opportunity to withdraw. And some did, some didn't. But, you know, there were all these little side shows going on at the same time that we were trying to produce the result that we wanted, which was the adjudication.

DEAN STEVENSON The biggest thing I heard from people about problems with the adjudication was that there were errors in the place of use from the original licensing.

VERN CASE As an irrigation district we hold the water rights along with the Bureau of Reclamation, for the whole district. But everyone was notified, even for their well rights, to file for their domestic well. Everybody got a notice to file on their domestic use rights, and cattle rights, and other rights. And it was handled very well.

VINCE ALBERDI The water filings for the two companies I worked for, we hired folks who were in attorneys office to do that kind of work for us. There were reports back to us at our monthly board meetings, but the actually filings were done by our attorneys office. Thats the only way it could be. It was an added burden where we were managing the day to day operations for the company, and then all this added filing had to be done.

JEFF RAYBOULD In the beginning you filed a claim, and for canal companies and irrigation districts that was an onerous task. To put acres and volumes against those acres, for 100 or more water users, it was a huge amount of work. If you're an individual and you've got 160 acres and there's a water right attached to that 160 acres, it is pretty easy to describe that area and your use of the water and file it.

CARTER FRITSCHLE Claims taking in the SRBA started in February of 1988 with the mailing of the commencement notices to property owners in the Salmon River drainage within Adams County, and all of Idaho County.

While a few claimants came to Boise in February through April of 1988 to file their claims for water rights, most of the claims taking activity did not begin until May of 1988 when Forrest Luthy and I set up the first mobile claims taking office in New Meadows. Forrest and I were unprepared for the turnout, as lines of claimants were already in place when we arrived at the rented office space. The people were generally patient with us, and once we had a signup sheet in place with phone numbers to schedule appointments, order returned and we were able to assist the public in filing their claims without making them wait in a long line. As each subsequent commencement notice was mailed over the next two years, the mobile office would move from county to county assisting the public in filing thousands of SRBA claims. The only county that did not have a mobile office was Ada. This was because both the state office and Western Regional Office were easily accessible to residents of Ada County. However, while the commencement notice stated there would not be a mobile office in Ada County, at least one claimant interpreted that statement as saying they could not file a claim for water used in mobile homes in Ada County.

There are hundreds of examples of claimants going from fearing us and the process to embracing both in the end. My background in agriculture allowed me to relate to the claimants with irrigation rights, and understand their frustrations with the process. One of my fondest memories is when Forrest and I were working in the mobile office in New Meadows. We would work late into the evening, and all of the local restaurants would be closed by the time we finished with the last appointments of the day. On one occasion, a claimant that we had assisted earlier in the day brought us "boxed" dinners when she saw that we had not had a chance to leave the office that day. And I still get phone calls from people asking if I remember assisting them file their claims nearly 25 years ago. Idaho has a lot of wonderful people who have been extremely grateful for the help IDWR has been able to provide throughout the SRBA process.

PETER MONSON Initially I think our biggest concern was the vast potential extent of federal claims we would have to deal with and how the state would process them and adjudicate them ... There were lots of different specific claims to be investigated and asserted. Some of these were not very controversial, such as water for campgrounds and national forest buildings. But others were very controversial. It was the tribal claims that were the real driver of why the state would want to adjudicate ... They needed to know what the extent of those Indian tribal claims were.

NORM YOUNG I think that we had the department represented at the bureau chief adjudication, bureau chief level at the SRBA court very rarely with Director Higginson being there. And you can count on one hand the number of times that I was ever there. So I think that there was not the kind of cooperation early on that ultimately came out. And there was some misunderstandings and some concerns. There was the concern about the department having shadow files or files that were not directly reported to the court, and I think that caused some concerns.

So ultimately, the role of the department changed. It took some of the burden, I think, off the department. Probably streamlined it where the department and the court were able to function much better.

PETER MONSON We set up an office in Boise called the Boise adjudication team, just to manage the paperwork for the SRBA. ... I think they've started to wind that down. But in that office we had attorneys, hydrologists, engineers, people to keep on top of it. They worked with the field solicitors in Portland. ... There was a large ramping up of federal staff in the adjudication. Early on in the case that was one of the things we foresaw.

What processes allowed the SRBA to move faster than other western adjudications?

DANIEL HURLBUTT There are several things.

One is setting up the multiple masters, spreading the workload in a way that allowed the matter to proceed. I didn't do this, but the – again, the work of the department to notify water users and make sure everybody was included was a very key aspect to it.

The other thing was that this differed from prior Idaho adjudications, and adjudications in other states, in the sense that previously many adjudications were more administrative than court driven. And even though they were court proceedings, it was a situation where the water agency and respective state would file the case, and then the water agency would handle everything until it finally had to be written up in a final decree, and the court was not intimately involved in many of the stages of the adjudications.

Here, though, there were a couple things driving the case that made it different. One was its comprehensive nature. It involved every water user. It didn't matter whether you were a surface user, a groundwater user, it didn't matter whether you were an individual or a corporation, a municipality, and it included both the State of Idaho and the federal government and their rights. And once you involve the federal government, then you're talking about what's known as the McCarran Amendment Adjudication. And as you well know, the federal government cannot be sued in a state court unless it consents to be sued in a state court.

The split: Two kinds of water claims

Different types of claims were handled differently. A procedure was worked out for rapidly managing the vast number of stockwater and de minimis claims, which were relatively small in water amounts, and usually relatively uncomplicated.

DANIEL HURLBUTT The federal government filed ultimately, I think nearly 70,000 claims for water rights. These claims were filed on behalf of, I think seven federal departments or agencies. BLM, the Forest Service. They were filed on behalf of Native American Indian tribes, which added a different scope and complexity, because while they were represented in some measure by the U.S. Attorney General, they still are separate, sovereign entities, and that their rights were based on treaties between the sovereign entities and the United States dating back into the 1800s.

And there was some controversy about what all this meant, but one of the decisions I had to make to ensure that I honored what the legislature of the State of Idaho crafted in their statute, and that was that this be a McCarran Amendment adjudication. There's a question about, what do you do with domestic and stockwater rights, which are very small? They're referred to as de minimis rights. And initially the state did not include those in the commencement. And I ultimately required that they being included so that there be no question, but that this qualified as a McCarran Amendment adjudication and the United States was required to participate, and to be bound, ultimately, by the decrees that were entered in the case.

CLIVE STRONG There was an agreement that we reached with the United States to defer de minimis domestic and stockwater rights. De minimis refers to small water rights like a domestic water right of .02 CFS or less. And stockwater rights that divert less than 13,000 gallons. They're so small that the effort to adjudicate them would be large, without much benefit.

I can't give you an exact number, but the number of de minimis domestic stockwater rights was well in excess of 100,000, I suspect, within the Snake River Basin. So if you can imagine, we would essentially double the number of water rights to be adjudicated if these had been included.

So the agreement we reached with the United States with court approval was to not require these water rights to be adjudicated, but the holder of rights would be bound by the decree. In other words, everyone is served, and everyone is a party to the adjudication. If a person elects to defer adjudication of a de minimis water right, he is still bound by the determinations in the case. If in the future he wants have to administration of the right, he must come into the court and have it adjudicated.

I think this was one of the more important decisions we made both because, it reduced the size of the adjudication to a manageable level, but also because, as we go forward with the administration, we have this class of water rights that will have to get resolved.

DAVID SHAW Well, [think about] just the mass of claims we would have to deal with if we had to take all of those claims and process them. The filing fee was $25. I didn't believe there was any way we could process them for $25, nor could we be sure we had them all. And that was really my biggest concern and what motivated me to try to get some kind of deferral.

The concern for a deferral was to maintain McCarran jurisdiction, because McCarran basically says you have to include all water users. So how could we not do domestic and stock and maintain jurisdiction?

So Clive and I worked with the federal attorneys and the tribal attorney for Fort Hall at the time to devise a plan that basically said all these people are joined to the adjudication that have domestic or stockwater rights, but they don't have to file their claims right now. And if they ever do decide to file a claim, they have to go through this process, as Judge Wildman has adopted the process now for doing deferred domestic and stockwater rights.

So I was motivated to get that done because I saw that as a huge hurdle for the department that we really didn't have an answer for. And finally we were successful and got the deferral order.

CARTER FRITSCHLE The ability to defer the de minimis claims certainly helped defuse some anger towards IDWR during the claims taking phase. When it was implemented in January of 1989, the IDWR agent no longer had to tell the claimant they would lose the right if they did not claim it. And while IDWR always encouraged the filing of de minimis claims, giving the potential claimant the option to defer the filing had a calming effect. Also, the procedure established for recommending the de minimis claims that were filed allowed for IDWR to commit more resources to the more complex water rights. However, I do have concerns that the deferred de minimis rights that are diverted from surface water, and are not based on a decree or license, will eventually be a challenge to deal with as fewer people are left that have personal knowledge of what occurred prior to May of 1971.

KARL DREHER Had I been the holder of a *de minimis* right, I would have filed a claim. ... I think you're better off having the decree than not having it.

DANIEL HURLBUTT A second aspect of ensuring that this be a McCarran Amendment adjudication: What does one do with prior adjudications that have been conducted in the state of Idaho, some of which included the federal government? And there was a contest [over that], and it went up to the Idaho Supreme Court. I had decided that, even though there was a prior adjudication in a separate, distinct area of the state, that involved the federal government, and seemingly all of the water users in that separate, distinct area, that

that still had to be included in the Snake River Adjudication because, not to do so, I think would violate – potentially violate – the McCarran Amendment.

Not everybody in those previous adjudications had been, obviously, parties to all of the other matters that would be included in the adjudication. Nor had all of the new parties in the Snake River Adjudication been parties to what went on in the prior adjudication. And there were situations where they needed to be included in those previously adjudicated claims in some measure in the SRBA, in order for this to be truly a McCarran Amendment adjudication.

One of the key things was to ensure that this was a McCarran Amendment adjudication, but then I think what was important in this case was that it became ultimately a court-driven case, and I was bound and determined that this case would be managed and moved along consistent with the workload that was required, but also consistent with what I feel is important, and the Supreme Court of Idaho felt was important, and it has to have good careful, timely case administration.

So while we were very much attuned to make sure that all claimants were involved, make sure that all parties were heard and had an opportunity to be heard, we were also insistent on the time frames that were set out in Administrative Order 1, and we were going to hold parties' feet to the fire, when we had some cases, and we were going to move those along and get them done. And it wasn't, you know, we had seen situations in -- I'll just say the western United States, where the typical adjudication was more a situation where the Department, you know, or parties, would initiate and adjudication. The court would sign the commencement order, and the court didn't want to deal with it. Would hide.

The respective water agencies and major water users would work to try to resolve differences, get matters in shape to get back to the court. Frequently there would be a lot of browbeating, intimidation, all kinds of things going on, to try to work out these larger adjudications, and then they'd trundle into court, present it to the presiding judge, who just wanted to see it go away, and that's what would happen.

With the United States in this case, that couldn't happen. You know, I think some people expected the old model to maybe prevail, but the United States wasn't going to let that happen. Nor was I, as the presiding judge. So the court, the statute allowed, took control of the case, and tried, and was bound and determined to move it along.

The special masters and the various presiding judges, I think, have done a wonderful job to see that that happened.

DAVID SHAW Another provision that was added when we did the 1986 amendments was the opportunity for interim administration. We knew this was going to be a long, drawn-out process. And it didn't make sense to have brand-new, fresh information from a Director's report or what turned out to be partial decrees that we couldn't implement on the ground and use for administration.

So we added the provision that if a Director's report was filed, we could ask the court. If the court approved for interim administration, we could use that new information for water distribution.

Well, we did that in the Lost River. And that just elevated acrimony between the court and the director because the court wanted nothing to do with water administration. The court believed that was a ministerial process, the court should not be involved, so the court was not interested in interim administration. And I remember a lengthy hearing on interim administration in Basin 34.

When we finally did get it approved, as I recall, it was approved without some of the instructions that we thought were important to carry out water administration, but we did get it approved. Of course, subsequently lots of basins were approved for interim administration.

Over time, the federal government involvement in the adjudication increased along with the number of federal-related claims.

DANIEL HURLBUTT They were very involved. Their primary attorney, Peter Monson, with the Department of Justice out of Denver, Colorado, was at virtually every meeting, status conference, court proceeding, those first couple of years. The United States participated and very responsibly, and had many good ideas. I think the United States, in western water adjudications, historically has been hesitant and somewhat untrusting of the state courts, and I think in this case we developed a process and a relationship where the United States felt very comfortable and felt they were in a fair, independent court, and would be heard and could prosecute their claims in a fair forum.

Large numbers of individual claims came in too, and in many cases the claimants represented themselves. In legal lingo, they were called "pro se" participants in the case.

CARTER FRITSCHLE I have a lot of respect for the pro se litigants I have worked with. While working with some did prove challenging, the majority were genuinely interested in coming to an accurate and reasonable description of their water rights.

DAVID TUTHILL I will say that one of the entertaining fellows was Harvey Walker.

He's a water user and a local person. He developed an interest through the SRBA in water rights and still today is working in the water right field in eastern Idaho. He added a lot of color to the process – in a nice way. Harvey told me a joke every time I talked with him, and I was finally able to use one of them. So that was a lot of fun.

PETER MONSON Fairly cooperatively, I think, on the technical side of things. We filed all our claims electronically. ... We exchange databases. I know we filed paper claims. But behind those paper claims we shared databases with details of each claims.

DAVID SHAW One of the things that was included in 1985 was a resolution to negotiate the water rights of the Fort Hall Indian Reservation. And the governor then issued an executive order that said the Water Resource Board would be the lead agency in negotiations, which is provided for statutorily.

The Fort Hall negotiations

HOWARD FUNKE It was a complete surprise to us, so we went into the legislature. . . . Pretty much on the spot we put together House Concurrent Resolution 16 and went before a joint session of the House and Senate natural resources committee, and discuss the Swan Falls negotiations and the potential for adjudication. I was arguing that if they wanted to adjudicate the tribes' water rights and come after the Shoshone-Bannock, we were in fact ready for them because I had been preparing their water rights for several years. I believe at that point they were asking about $20 million for the adjudication, and I suggested that $20 million was not near enough, if they were going to get into a fight with the tribe, it would be more like $60 million, because it would take a lot more time and cost a lot more money and become a very contentious process. . . . They approved the negotiation process.

The primary reason for suggesting negotiation as opposed to litigation was, I laid out several cases that had taken 40 or 50 or more years to complete an adjudication, also the fact that the cost factor involved, as well as the nature of the adjudication of water rights in a complex system like that, courts are bound by precedent, and their hands are kind of tied in how they go about interpreting water rights and priority dates and quantities. It seemed to make more sense to be able to sit down with the people who were being affected by it to try to fashion and agreement based on the regional needs.

Tribes don't like being in state courts. Never have, and history is full of reasons why. We don't trust the state court system. It would be like the tribe telling the state of Idaho and all of its water users they've got to come into tribal court to claim their water rights when they're located in or affect the reservation. You can imagine what kind of reaction you'd get from non-Indians or the state.

DAVID SHAW So prior to the commencement order, those negotiations began, discussions between the attorney general's office and the Water Resources Board and the tribe and the United States. And it started like most negotiations, you know, the shape of the table and all of that stuff.

By the fall of '86, I think it was, I got involved personally to provide the technical support for the state in those negotiations. One of the provisions of the Memorandum of Understanding that got the negotiations started was we wouldn't start claims taking until the tribe or the United States said it was okay to do so. So it didn't delay the process too much, but it delayed it a little bit.

HOWARD FUNKE We began meeting, over months in the attorney general's conference room, myself and the attorney general, Clive Strong, the attorneys representing the middle and upper snake river. And over that period of time we revamped the code to federal reserved rights negotiated settlements, put that in a bill, and the legislature approved it, and the code was amended to allow for negotiated settlements. And the negotiations commenced.

We determined that a four-party table would probably be the ideal. The tribe was one of those four parties, the United States, the state of Idaho and the water users, and the water users deciding among themselves who they wanted to represent them at the table. . . . The four-part table became the process for negotiations, and each had their own exports as well as their own lawyers. We scheduled meetings as needed on a pretty regular basis.

. . . The United States came in late in the game in this process, so the tribe basically represented itself and the United States definitely participated – they were at all the meetings, there were there I think primarily to protect federal interests, and they were significant in the adjudication and in the negotiation.

PETER MONSON I can't recall if they actually intervened as a party ... I understood the Sho-Bans were involved in the early and mid 80s, and we were made aware of that the around 1985, and we knew the Sho-Bans were going to be involved.

I was the attorney for the United States, the lead Justice attorney. There were Interior department attorneys, and we had policymakers from Interior. There was a fellow named John Bushman who was chair of the federal negotiating team.

DAVID SHAW But the negotiations had to build a track record to have some confidence – I guess on both sides, or all sides of the table. There were four sides – so that we could actually start sending out notice and getting claims from all the water users, but particularly the non-federal water users.

As part of that process, the executive order or the resolution – I don't recall which – called for water user input. And since this was on the Upper Snake, the Committee of Nine was selected or appointed as the water user representatives at the table during those negotiations.

The Committee of Nine is technically the advisory committee for Water District 1. Every water district in the statute can have an advisory committee. And it varies from district to district. Typically, it's the officers.

The Committee of Nine originated – I won't get the date right, but there was a conflicted water delivery in the Upper Snake. The governor actually called out the National Guard to regulate headgates or keep peace at the headgates, whichever. And after that incident the water users, basically above Milner Dam, agreed to form this nine-member advisory committee that since has been called the Committee of Nine. They're politically potent because they represent a large area of the state and quite influential.

So they were selected to represent the water users. And they had their own counsel. They had their own technical advisor. And the technical advisor is now my partner. That's how I met him and how I got associated with ERO. I was a technical advisor for the state.

And the attorney general's office had also hired Boyle Engineering out of California. They had some experience with federal reserve water right negotiations, so they were our backup, so to speak.

But the tribes had Tom Stetson at the time. You'll love this. Waldesion Mesghiana was the person on the ground for Stetson. Wald eventually formed his own firm and still works for the tribes today on their water issues. And we're still trying to tie up loose ends on the Fort Hall negotiations.

So that process was kind of laid over the top of everything else that we were doing to get it off the ground and build a comfort level, really the personal relationships among the negotiators to build some confidence so the tribe and the United States would be willing to let us go do our job in collecting claims and start this whole adjudication.

Those negotiations were ultimately successful. The 1990 Fort Hall Indian water right agreement was the result of those negotiations. It was decreed in 1995 as a partial decree. We're still tying up some loose ends, not from lack of cooperation, but lack of information. We just didn't have the information to do a good job of completing some of the pieces of what needed to be done.

HOWARD FUNKE The tribe was looking to fulfill the purpose of the reservation, a mix of irrigation needs as well as preserving water quality and habitat and fisheries. The Fort Hall Indian Reservation is an absolutely unique, beautiful ecosystem thanks to the Shoshone-Bannocks. They were very concerned about preserving that system and natural order. They were also looking for basic fairness, being treated fairly, making sure that things that occurred to them in that adjudication did not impair the future generations of the tribe and their ability to use water supply.

DANIEL HURLBUTT The Shoshone-Bannock tribe had significant claims in the adjudication, and actually had been, I think, talking to the Department of Water Resources and Clive Strong in the Attorney General's Office even before the adjudication was commenced.

There were discussions about their rights and how they could be resolved. Their rights variously related to treaty rights as well as rights acquired under Idaho law. And really the court's only involvement was to both monitor the negotiations, make sure they were ongoing, to assist with questions the parties might have, but ultimately, it was a Titanic effort on the part of Clive Strong in the Attorney General's Office, the Department of Water Resources and a group of water users that were negotiating with the tribe, and they were able to reach an agreement early in the case and submit it to the court, and my review of their agreement was consistent with the rights as we knew them, and so it was approved by the court, and a partial decree entered.

It was very interesting. As we learned really even before the Shoshone-Bannock settlement or the Nez Perce settlement, Native-American tribal rights can be the claims that – the tail that wags the adjudication dog, in the Gila River Adjudication in Arizona the – it was ruled that the Native-American claims down there were not only significant under treaty rights, but the tribes down there, it could be demonstrated, had actually set up canal systems, and used irrigated agriculture, and were given substantial rights.

So it was understood by everybody the impact of Native-American tribal rights on the adjudication could be very significant, because both treaties and even prior use that could be established. Now, we didn't have the irrigation aspects of the Native American rights that they had in Arizona, but what was significant, and was I think consistent in many of the treaties the United States entered into with western tribes, were the abilities of the tribes to maintain their fishing rights at customary locations and times, whatever that might mean, but what that implicated was, where they were fishing, as they frequently did, for both sustenance and religious reasons, fishing for anadromous fish that would spawn in tributaries through the Snake River system, and the smolts would travel downstream to the ocean and return to spawn, it meant that minimum in-stream flow requirements were – could be very much impacted by Native American claims under their treaty rights to fishing.

And that was something that was very important in both the Shoshone-Bannock tribes' negotiations and decrees, as well as the Nez Perce claims.

RAY RIGBY Before the adjudication, there was an organization called the Committee of Nine, and the purpose of that organization, which by the way was established several years ago, was to work together in the distribution of the water that came from all of these sources, natural sources from Fremont County and up above Ririe. In other words, the North Fork of the Snake and the South Fork of the Snake that joined down here near Menan, all of those rivers that were so connected, you know, you go to Buffalo, the Warm River, the Fall River, and the Blackfoot River, all of those rivers had been organized. And they were distributing their own waters, but it involved then eventually the people in the American Falls, Twin Falls, Rupert and Burley area.

And arguments would arise because those people down there said we were using more than our share of the water. And so they eventually organized the Committee of Nine which put those people together. And they worked pretty well over all of the years in that Committee of Nine relationship.

But then when the adjudication came along, the first thing that we did was to try to settle the dispute of the Indian rights and the people that belonged to the Committee of Nine.

RAY RIGBY [Among the Shoshone-Bannock Tribes] the big dispute was a priority date, and the Indians saying, "Hey, we were here before the settlers were. Why don't we have the first priority?" That's the first arguments we heard.

HOWARD FUNKE Within the reservation internally there was a lot of dissension or disagreement over whether or not the tribe should be negotiating or litigating. Some thought it ought to be litigated, and some thought it should be negotiated. There was a lot of discussion and heart-felt concern over what was the right approach.

That was coming on the heels of the Colorado Conservation District and San Carlos Apache confirming that the tribe really – at least some of the people in the tribe did not like face the fact that the state courts had potentially jurisdiction over their water rights and the adjudication of those rights. That created a problem. In fact they never did submit to the jurisdiction of the state court throughout the entire negotiation. Basically reserving a decision a decision as to whether to enter that case. Since the adjudication had been put on hold in light of CHR 16, we went through the negotiation and were successful, and came to an agreement five years later and then the adjudication petition was filed and formally got underway at that point. But we never did formally appear before the court in the Snake River Basin Adjudication.

JOHN ROSHOLT The adjudication was in '87. So we probably had some early meetings in '85. ... It was pretty contentious.

The Upper Valley people . . . had never asserted the Winter's Doctrine priority. So – and, mean, that was pretty basic. There's no sense going to fight about the Winter's Doctrine.

So then it was how are we going to get through this. And they seemed to be more concerned about the other features, fisheries and aesthetics and the environment water quality on the reservation than they did about their irrigation projects. And, in fact, other than the Fort Hall project, which included both the tribe and the farmers, individual farmers, non-tribal members, they didn't care much for irrigation, didn't seem to.

Early on, there were – in the early '60s, maybe late '50s, groups of farmers got to the tribe and at least substantial blocks of land, you see it as you drive from Pocatello to Idaho Falls, all that was just desert, and the deal was the guys would put in – make all the improvements in exchange for a 15-year lease so they could spud the ground. And then they gave it back to the tribe with the improvements. And then the tribe, when they got the land back, and, of course, it had been spudded for 15 years, or how many years it was in potato potential at that point, they had trouble getting people to actually take the lands and farm them for them. And I don't know who's doing it now. I've kind of lost track.

But the tribe was pretty systematic. They had – you know, once they asserted the claims for the reservation, then you bring in the justice department, you bring in the Department of Indian Affairs, or the Bureau of Indian Affairs, and then you had the local Bureau of Reclamation lawyer, the local – we must have had six or seven federal lawyers attending all of the negotiation sessions on behalf of the tribe. And then the tribe had their own counsel. And they had some colorful people over the years. And they were good hearted. They were trying to get the best they could for their people.

This may surprise you, that this would be my opinion, but we kind of just blew by the tribes in previous years. We didn't pay much attention to them. Except that I was also concerned about the Winner's Doctrine. And I came on some correspondence in one of my old files where we had actually hired hydrologists, experts on behalf of Twin Falls Canal Company in the late '60s, early '70s to consult with us if the tribes put together a Winter's Doctrine claim.

DANIEL HURLBUTT Well, first there was initially a question whether there were four or five denominated Native American tribes that existed and could claim water rights in Idaho. The United States Bureau of Indian Affairs only recognized four tribes, and I did have to hear whether a claimed distinct band of the Shoshone-Bannock nation existed and was recognized and could file claims, and I ruled that they could not. So the claims were all filed ostensibly through the Bureau of Indian Affairs, the Department of Justice, although working with tribal counsel.

Again, early on, none of the tribes were in the three test basins, and early on it was a process of getting the two major tribes, that being the Shoshone-Bannock and the Nez Perce, into discussions and negotiations to avoid litigation. And you know, the Attorney General's Office had already initiated that with the Shoshone-Bannock tribe, and everybody agreed it needed to be initiated with the Nez Perce tribe.

In other adjudications, Native American rights had been a real linchpin, sticking point, hotly litigated to extraordinary expense and consumption of resources that I think everybody recognized it was really a losing proposition to try to get involved in major litigation, and that the better way of dealing with Native American rights was through negotiation to see if it couldn't be resolved with a negotiated settlement.

They did appear through separate counsel, and their attempt to file claims and participate as a separate, distinct tribe was opposed by, primarily the Bureau of Indian Affairs and the Department of Justice, and the Department of Justice prevailed in that.

CLIVE STRONG The 1994 Fort Hall Water Rights Agreement is quite remarkable for how it started and how it finished. If you survey western states, historically most of the tribal reserved water rights settlements start with litigation. Only after the parties fought for a period of time did they actually come to settlement.

I have to give a credit to the Shoshone-Bannock Tribes for their foresight in approaching the state. And, also to the legislature for saying, let's sit down and see if we can find a solution without the need for litigation.

We had the benefit of looking to the Wind River adjudication and the conflict that had developed there. Recognizing that ultimately there would be a reserved water right, the important thing was to figure out how to resolve the tribal claims in a way that didn't impact existing users.

HCR 16 directed the attorney general and the governor to begin negotiations with the Shoshone-Bannock Tribes. We did that in August of 1985.

Governor Evans issued an executive order appointing the Idaho Water Resource Board as the lead negotiator. I thought that was a great move on his part. The board has the responsibility for dealing with federal water issues.

We had the leadership of Gene Gray, who was the chairman at the time, and Dave Rydalch. Gene was from Payette, and Dave from eastern Idaho. So we had good representation from across the state. They approached negotiations with the idea of, let's be candid and up front with the tribe about our expectations and constraints. The board made it clear the state could not enter into a settlement that would affect existing water right holders. The board insisted on protection of all existing water rights. The board further stated that the state would not recognize the Tribal in-stream flow claims.

The board also informed the Tribes and the United States the state wasn't willing to contribute financially to the settlement. Historically, the United States has insisted upon a significant state contribution as part of reserved water right settlements. Generally, the federal government seeks a 25 percent contribution from the state.

We told the tribe these conditions up front. Likewise, the tribes were equally adamant about the importance of having federally reserved water rights.

The Fort Hall project was originally developed in 1907, and many of the water rights for the project were created under state law. In fact, some of the water rights were acquired from Barzilla Clark who later become governor of the state of Idaho. And that was particularly the water rights for Grays Lake. That's a story for another day.

Early on in the negotiations water users expressed concern about the state and the tribe negotiating without private water user representation at the table. Water users approached the board; and the board responded by holding hearings in eastern Idaho for the purpose of designating private water user representation in the negotiation process. Ultimately the water users selected the Committee of Nine – or recommended, I should say, that the board appoint the Committee of Nine to represent water users in the negotiations. The Committee of Nine represents the surface water users that divert water from above Milner. It was created in 1920 as an advisory board to the Director of Water Resources.

That was a good move in the sense that we had actual water rights holders at the table helping in the negotiation process. They were represented by Ray Rigby, the original father of the Swan Falls trust concept. He represented what is oftentimes referred to as "the Committee of Six". Those were six members of Committee of Nine in the upper basin. And, John Rosholt represented the Twin Falls and North Side Canal Companies. Roger Ling was involved on behalf of A & B and Burley. Kent Foster was also involved in this process. Those four individuals were very helpful in the negotiation of the Fort Hall Water Rights Agreement.

We had a number of meetings, as you might expect. Early on there was a belief by the water users that the tribes had no reserved water rights. There was equally a belief by the United States and the tribes that they had the earliest rights on the river.

I had the benefit of having a very good attorney working for me, David Barber. He was a very well respected water attorney, and also a very good historian.

We did a lot of historical research. David, through his work in the national archives, uncovered a proposed lawsuit that the United States had intended to file for reserved water rights in the Blackfoot River. It laid out their theory for the reserved water right claims. We also found a number of prior decisions, *Hibner* being one I can think of, that talked about the tribes reserved water rights.

We looked to the Wind River adjudication. It was apparent to us that the tribes were going to be successful in getting reserved water rights.

We had large and raucous meetings early on. We weren't making a lot of progress, and frustration was building. So in September, actually September 1st of 1989, we had a meeting in Boise, and decided we needed to get a framework that we could use for the negotiations.

We developed a one-page term sheet that laid out where the water supplies were going to come from. And, just like the Swan Falls Agreement, we started with the proposition that the Snake River was largely fully appropriated during the irrigation season, so we set the water supply from the Snake River at 115,000 acre-feet of water, the amount available under the existing state water rights for the project. And, we agreed upon 580,000 as the total water supply for the Shoshone-Bannock Tribes. We then identified water supplies from the other water supplies to bridge the gap.

We changed the priority date on the Snake River from the late 1800s-early 1900s to 1867, but agreed that water would be made available to mitigate for any impacts of that change. And that was the Ririe and Palisades storage space.

One of the things the tribe wanted to do was to market water off the reservation. That was a place that we would not go because if you marketed water off the reservation, you'd impact other existing users.

A compromise was reached that allowed the tribes to rent their storage water under a state-created water bank. Federal reserved water rights, however, had to be used exclusively on the reservation.

There was also an understanding that the tribes would be able to manage their water rights on the reservation, but the state would manage delivery of water to the reservation. That was how we dealt with the distribution.

The Fort Hall Indian Irrigation Project serves both Indian and non-Indian water users. So we needed to carve out a portion of the state water rights for the Fort Hall Project sufficient to satisfy the Fort Hall project non-Indian water users needs.

That's the real nubbin of the agreement, and it was all on one page, which I thought was remarkable. From that date in `89, we then, within a year, negotiated the entirety of the agreement. We took it to Congress and got congressional approval of the agreement, and then got legislative approval of the agreement.

The agreement has withstood the test of time. One of the things we included in the agreement was a provision for an intergovernmental board. The intergovernmental board meets on a yearly basis so we can talk to one another about issues that arise out of the agreement.

We had an opportunity to test this process. When we put together the agreement, we didn't know the full extent of the non-Indian use in the Blackfoot River Basin. So we included in an equitable adjustment provision in the Tribes' Blackfoot River water right. We estimated the amount of non-Indian use of Blackfoot natural flow to be 45,000 acre-feet. And we said, to the extent the non-Indian use is ultimately determined to divert more than 45,000 acre-feet, the parties would negotiate an equitable adjustment to the Blackfoot water right.

Around 2004 or 2005, as we were decreeing the Blackfoot water rights, it became apparent that we need an equitable adjustment to the Blackfoot water right. We spent several years negotiating the equitable adjustment to the tribal water right.

It was somewhat contentious. Nonetheless, because of the relationships we developed, we were able to negotiate an equitable adjustment. I think we finally got that approved by the SRBA district court in 2013.

It's a testament to the parties and the strength of the agreement. Because at the same time we were negotiating this issue, we were in the middle of trying to resolve the conjunctive management issues between the surface and groundwater users. The water supplies in that area are very tight, yet we were able to find a solution that satisfied everyone's needs.

The Shoshone-Bannock negotiations were interesting in the sense that the state and the tribe initially started out as adversaries; but, toward the end of the negotiations we were aligned against the United States on some issues.

Particularly when it came to the tribal trust fund. We made it clear early on the state would not contribute to a tribal trust fund. Yet, the federal guidelines for settlement required a state contribution. With the collective effort of the tribe, the state, and the water user representatives, we were successful in obtaining federal funding for the Tribes. The state contribution to the settlement was $250,000 of in-kind services and payment of adjudication filing fees for the tribal water rights.

I don't think the agreement would have been possible but for some of the creative efforts of the parties. One area we had a problem was Sand Creek. Sand Creek is a stream that is connected to the Snake River and empties into the Blackfoot River. Historically, there was a storage reservoir that captured excess flows for use by the Fort Hall Project. But, the reservoir had silted in and it would have cost millions of dollars to dredge the reservoir. What ended up happening was the Northside Canal Company agreed to step forward and do a water exchange, which eliminated the need to rehabilitate the reservoir. John Rosholt thought of this creative solution.

We had some really interesting people that worked on this negotiation. Dave Shaw and I have been involved in the settlement from the beginning. Dave has been very helpful in crafting creative solutions to ongoing issues.

The tribes had a consultant – his name was Woldezion Mesghinna; he was critical to the settlement process in terms of bringing creative solutions to the table. We've been very fortunate to have that kind of collective effort throughout the history of the agreement.

The Fort Hall Agreement became the template for our future negotiations. A couple of things that we learned is that you need ta framework to guide the development of a final agreement. If you don't, parties tend to focus on their issue of concern as opposed to the broader agreement.

Oftentimes in these settlements the way you get to the settlement is you make the problem bigger. It sounds counter intuitive, but you have to find a place – like a Venn diagram – where the parties' interests overlap sufficiently to achieve an acceptable resolution.

The important thing for water users is to have certainty that the integration of the tribal rights will not impact their water rights. From the tribe's perspective, the certainty they seek is the ability to have wet water as opposed to paper water.

From the state's standpoint, we are concerned about how to administer the water rights and impact that the quantification of the tribal rights will have on existing and future uses.

When we put together the one-page term sheet, then everyone could see feel certain their interests were protected and could see the benefits of the settlement. From my perspective, that's the most important lesson we learned. You'll see this as a recurring theme as we go forward. Typically as we get into very complex issues, it's the development of the term sheet that becomes critical to providing essentially a template for settlement.

PETER MONSON The federal government contributed water and money to the settlement, and helped to sweeten the pot, made it easier for non-Indians to agree to a settlement ...

HOWARD FUNKE All sides were committed to making it happen. There was nobody playing games, there was no conspiracy going on. No one came in with a hidden agenda. It was straight up trying to resolve matters in a way that worked, make it a mutually beneficial process while protecting your interests.

I think the settlement is good. It provided a good water right for the tribe. It took in consideration the other water users in the basin, including the federal storage system and the water uses in the Magic Valley. While preserving them as federally reserved water rights we were able to integrate them into the overall Snake water system.

If we had litigated? I don't know how long that might have taken.

DUANE MECHAM The Shoshone-Bannock on reservation water right claims were resolved very well. I've had the opportunity especially since I moved to this Portland regional solicitors office in 1996 to be involved in implementing that settlement, so even though I came in on the tail end of the negotiations I became quite familiar with it in the implementation of that settlement.

I think the state was fair in that settlement. They recognized that the tribes did have some Indian reserved water rights for irrigation. Other states sometimes really aren't willing to go in that direction, they want all the tribe's water rights to be state law based. I think the quantities were in the right arena for what the tribe's needs were. And the state was willing to, post settlement, have the tribe administer those rights, and I think that's gone forward pretty well. And there were some issues that just had to be left open after completing the settlement because we just didn't have all the information to finalize some of the pieces of the settlement – groundwater, the Blackfoot River adjudication of the non-Indian water rights, what we called an equitable adjustment. My personal sense there was that the state again was pretty fair and forthright in recognizing the need to deal with this equitable adjustment and ensured all the parties worked together to complete that adjustment, which we needed to do about two years ago.

DAVID TUTHILL The involvement of the Tribes and the major impact of the Tribes was recognized early on, and that resulted in a major effort being put forth toward coming up with a negotiated agreement with the Shoshone Bannock Tribe, first of all. A lot of department assets and state assets were directed toward that.

The resulting agreement was quite successful. It was ultimately approved by the state, and by the federal government, and by the tribes.

It had some provisions that have just recently been reviewed -- and just the fact of coming to an agreement doesn't mean the whole process is resolved or certain aspects that were yet to be resolved. One of the things that Idaho I think can be proud of is the way that it has handled the tribal issues – as compared with other states.

I personally was not directly involved with the negotiations; that was before my time. Dave Shaw, and Clive Strong and others did a very good job, from the state's behalf, of negotiating those agreements which have been successful.

DAVID SHAW After the Fort Hall Agreement was done, the Fort Hall Project Water Users – they're the non-Indian project users – were not happy with it, still not happy with it, as far as I know. So there was a public meeting. There's an old school building on the reservation that's used for meetings.

And the United States was there with their attorneys. I think the tribal attorneys were there. Clive and I were there.

Well, by that time I had done public information meetings from one end of the basin to the other, and I could tell this was not going to be a good situation. And all of us were up on the stage. So I found a chair in the back behind everybody and went and sat down.

Well, Clive is up on the front edge of the stage shaking his finger at the crowd. And the media is there. And they got it on tape. And that played on the local news for I don't know how many days. So I continually remind Clive of that.

The storming

1990-95

Much of the early work in the adjudication, done on an almost experimental basis – though legally it was very much a part of the case – occurred in three "test basins," in the Lost River area (Basin 34), in the Hagerman area (Basin 36) and in north-central Owyhee County (Basin 57).

The three test basins

DAVID SHAW We came up with this idea of doing test basins because we wanted to go through the process. We knew we couldn't do all the basins at one time. And there were reasons to do the Lost River, for example. There was lots of contention up there, still is, but worse at the time, so that was a test basin for eastern Idaho that we selected.

Basin 36, the Hagerman Valley and the groundwater users on the North Side of the Snake River down by Twin Falls, one of the issues was the interface between the groundwater users and the spring users and surface water users. So we selected that as a test basin because we thought how we'd do conjunctive management is going to be a critical part of this overall adjudication.

We selected Basin 57 out in Owyhee County, it was not spectacular, but it had some unique characteristics about it. And there's a couple of Supreme Court decisions out of that test basin, so it was not for not. We got some law out of it.

DANIEL HURLBUTT That was up to the Department of Water Resources, and I think they selected it because there were ongoing water disputes there that needed to be addressed, and it just seemed to be ripe for addressing early. Same situation with the Hagerman area, which was one of the test basins, and because of the vagaries down there of having surface water rights that were very old, but the source of that water was really the Snake Plain Aquifer, because that water was coming out of springs in the canyon walls.

You know, there was always this notion that ultimately surface and groundwater would have to be administered together, "conjunctively" is the term that is now used, and that that was an area where there had been a lot of disputes, and it was an area that, because of the interface between surface and groundwater, the department felt it was important to early address some of those water rights and get them resolved.

There was some bitterness down there. I think historically there were water users who felt they had not been heard and treated fairly by the Department of Water Resources, and I don't know what the genesis of those feelings were. Nonetheless, that was one of the initial basins addressed, and I think it was dealt with in a very fair, responsible manner, and I think while there were some disputes, I think, again, by investigating each water right and dealing with each water right as it was presented, worked out very well. Those disputes were resolved.

BARRY WOOD I would have selected the basins where water is leaving the state of Idaho, so if you screwed something up, and you're getting the kinks worked out of the process – I think they could have chosen some better basins to make the initial law of the case. I understand why they did it. They accomplished their mission – they wanted difficult basins and they sure as hell did that.

DAVID SHAW The test basins themselves, like I say, were selected because they had specific issues that we, the Department, felt needed to be addressed in the adjudication. But there were also the opportunity to refine our processes for reviewing and recommending claims.

We had separate staffs, separate offices with claims that were different yet similar. So my staff from the state office and I made I don't know how many trips to the different offices where we would sit down and go through the claims that they had set out as being problems. "This is something new. How do we deal with it?"

So we would work through that with the Idaho Falls office, for example. Come back to Boise, and as we needed to develop our process, do whatever research we needed to do, and how we were going to deal with that. And then we go to Twin Falls and do the same thing, and here to our western region, and produced I don't know how many memos describing different situations and how they should be recommended in the director's report. And that was an evolving process, because as soon as we thought we had one particular situation addressed with appropriate procedures, somebody would find a claim that was a little bit different, that it didn't fit, so we'd go through the process again.

We were probably gone more than we were in Boise for that first one. I don't know how long as we started and went through the review process, up to completing the first set of director's reports.

And this was the time when we had the conflict with the Court over what should be included, even the season of use became an issue. We had historically in the department set out a season of use based on climate conditions because we don't think most people irrigate in January.

The court wasn't willing to do that. So if you look back at some of the first partial decrees that were entered, the initial decree simply said "irrigation season," no definition. That ultimately got changed, but it was that kind of contention that was going on between the department and the court. And it's unfortunate, because that took a lot of energy.

And as we were doing the claim review, of course we were identifying the unclaimed rights. And we needed to refine our second round notice process, our refined owners of these old rights that hadn't been claimed or this field that looks like it's irrigated and doesn't have a claim for it.

Then as the Director's report started coming together, the theme of the adjudication was to try to resolve problems rather than litigate problems. So one of the things that was in our grand plan was to have a process where our recommendation could go out to people, they could look at it, if they didn't agree with it, we'd have an opportunity to sit down with them and try to work out the differences.

Well, as we were developing the initial recommendations, the situation occurred where somebody was working on a claim, and at the end of the day it wasn't finished, it was lots of loose ends, but it was in the computer.

Well, the claimant, the next day came in and asked for a copy and got a printout, and of course it was so jumbled because it wasn't the finished product, and we had all kinds of problems. Here was somebody who believed what was not a finished product was what was going to be recommended for their water right. And, you know, it was terrible, we were taking their water, and all that sort of stuff.

So no good intention goes unpunished. We decided, let's keep our work product private until we finish the review, we've gone through our process, checked everything off, reviewed by somebody else if necessary, and then we'll make it public.

Bad choice. We put those working products in red files. I don't know if you've heard the tales of the red files. But anyway, we created a separate electronic record and a separate paper record to give staff an opportunity to work on their product and not worry about at the end of the day leaving something half done that ultimately gets out on the street and creates a problem.

And this was during the time of the Court when things were not going smoothly, a particular attorney took advantage of that and said, “Here's the Department, a public agency, keeping secrets. They can't do this.” And I don't know how many court appearances there was over the red files because, like I say, no good intention goes unpunished. It was a good idea that didn't work out.

But it takes time and energy and resources to go through that process. No harm intended, but it didn't work out that way.

DANIEL HURLBUTT After the initial claims taking and investigation process, notice, claims taking and investigation by the department, they designated three test basins, where they would report the rights. They filed those reports, and we began taking objections, and the masters began doing hearings.

Now, to try to make this workable, the one thing the court did, after the claims-taking process was accomplished and the report was filed in those three test basins, we went out and had meetings in

Arco and in the Hagerman area, to meet with water users and explain the court process, and how it would work. And I think that helped, one, dissipate concerns that water users had, helped them to understand what the process would be, and help them understand how they could participate and have their rights protected, and have their disagreements with the department heard.

And then each of the special masters was assigned to one of those sub-basins and they proceeded with hearings. I'm trying to think. There was another aspect to this that was problematic. Oh, the issue that arose, what do you do with issues that might arise in a sub case that not only affected the sub case, but could potentially affect all of the claimants in the Snake River Adjudication? And that was provided in AO1, and it was called a basin-wide issue.

And for example, one of the first basin-wide issues was the issue of whether domestic and stockwater claims would be included. Another was the issue of whether the previously adjudicated water rights necessarily needed to be included. Why this was important was it then gave us a mechanism in the test basins, when these issues came up, that potentially affected everybody, to provide notice to everybody that these issues had been identified.

They would be then designated as basin-wide issues, they would be heard by the presiding judge, and then we could expedite appeal of those issues to the Supreme Court. You know, normally you can only appeal cases when the final judgment's been entered. Well, the final judgment, final decree of this case wouldn't be entered for a decade or two. So this gave us a way to identify those issues that would encompass everybody, potentially, to get them litigated before the presiding judge, and then referred by the presiding judge on, essentially an interlocutory appeal, that is an appeal before the final judgment was entered, so the Supreme Court could decide the matter, and we could then proceed with that issue resolved.

KARL DREHER Idaho through the SRBA became the first state to use GIS shape files in the definition of irrigation rights. Nobody else had done it. We developed the technology, and then we proposed changes to our laws which the legislature adopted, to recognize GIS shape files as a legitimate definition of a place of use for rights.

Why did that make a difference?

For whatever reason, individual right holders and some attorneys believed or claimed or asserted that the reason the state had initiated the adjudication was to take their rights away. To some that might sound unbelievable, but it actually happened. Without naming names, I had to confront one of the attorneys that was sending out notices to right holders claiming the state was seeking to take the holders' rights, and his firm was willing to represent them. That actually happened. How widespread it was, I don't know. But I do know I had to confront this one attorney. And, I also know that early in my tenure I attended a public hearing in Hagerman where the audience was angry, and they repeatedly made this assertion, you're just trying to take our rights away.

New tech:
GIS shape files

The GIS shape files were critical to defusing these assertions. In many cases the claimants claimed an irrigation place of use that was say 640 acres, fence line to fence line. They didn't subtract out the footprint of their house, the footprint of their feeding lots, footprint of the ditches, and the footprint of roads. With us subtracting that in our recommendations, that became proof to them we were trying to reduce their right. But, when we laid down a series of pictures at different points in time showing the extent and quantifying the extent of irrigation, the acrimony dissipated. We would go out in subbasins and meet with individual claimants that had these irrigation claims, and they would say we have a right to irrigate 640 acres or whatever, and you're just trying to refuse us that right. We would say, actually we're not trying to reduce your right, but rather just trying to give you a right to irrigate the area that you have historically irrigated, and here it is. And, you know, a picture is worth a thousand words.

This idea that we were simply out to reduce their right, just dissipated. It also created a perception that maybe the department wasn't trying to take things away from people, that we really were recommending a right to irrigate the extent of their historic place of use. We weren't willing to recommend more than that, but we weren't willing to recommend less than that either.

VINCE ALBERDI Anytime somebody's messing around with your water rights, there are suspicions: What in the world is going on? Why are these people so involved? Are these chances I might be losing what I have here?

Hagerman valley, they were worried abut … in my project we were worried about when this is said and done … Theres always the concern abut the restriction on the amount of water were going to have in the future …

Basin-wide issues, partial decrees

CARTER FRITSCHLE I believe the process of establishing basin-wide issues was extremely helpful from the perspective of the claim reviewer. Because once the basin-wide issues were decided, certain parameters for reviewing particular types of claims were established. For example, Basin-wide Issue 12 was particularly useful for reviewing in-stream stockwater rights. Being able to recommend a 0.02 cfs cap on the diversion rate for de minimis in-stream stockwater claims was extremely helpful in attempting to achieve consistency among the numerous recommendations for that type of water use.

JOHN MELANSON A partial decree, I always thought, was maybe not the best terminology for it, but it's what we've used, and it sort of fits. The reason we called it that is this, that decree was final as to that water right. But we knew that we were going to be issuing at the end, a final decree that would say, okay, all – how to put this in understandable terms – all the water rights that have been decreed with all these partial decrees are now a part of this final unified decree. And so we called them "partial decrees." I think people, when they received them, sometimes had concerns about that. Well, what does this mean? Does this mean that it's only part of what I should have? But, you know, our staff would always explain to them, why we called it that, and that's how that worked.

DANIEL HURLBUTT There were a lot of concerns. One of them, of course, was the Big Lost River. There had been historically water battles up there for many, many decades, and ongoing water battles because of scarcity issues, and there were some, I think very hard feelings between certain surface users and pumpers in that basin.

We did have, you know, a very significant series of informational meetings in Mackay and Arco, meetings with water users who, because of their interest, participated in both the steering committee and many of these other informal meetings, and were frequently present at monthly status conferences.

And Brigette Bilyeu was assigned to that basin, and she just did a wonderful job of working with those folks, and we were able to avoid, you know, some of the bloodletting kind of disputes that had gone on for a long time up there. That's not to say there weren't heated disputes. There were. But we were able to get those water rights decreed in partial decrees without too much difficulty.

DAVID SHAW But then I was still working on this process for the opportunity to have the face-to-face with somebody that didn't agree with what was the initial recommendation. And it was one of those things we talked about in our little staff meetings and I had been thinking about for several years now, because it was going to be fairly complicated and expensive because we needed to contact people, we needed to mail the information out to them, give them the opportunity to sit down with us. That takes staff time. And I thought I had devised this scheme that was going to work. And I was supposed to talk at the annual meeting for the Committee of Nine over in Idaho Falls.

So the night before I started writing out the process that I had sort of built in my mind and, oh, my gosh, it was a page long. This will never work.

So I flipped the page over and rewrote what ultimately became the error correction process that night. And that's what I presented to the Committee of Nine the next day.

But it was an effective process because we gave people the opportunity to look at what had been recommended, simple checkoff card, they agreed, they didn't agree. If they didn't agree, there was a process they could go through where we would sit down face-to-face and try to work out the differences.

And I think ultimately the report got to the court, and the Court had the mandatory settlement conferences and all those sorts of things. But we probably headed off twice as many, three times as many conflicts in our error correction process – and that's what we call it, the error correction process – than were resolved in the settlement conferences.

Some we simply disagreed, and those had to be resolved by the court. That's what the court's for. And I think that was another big step in getting through the process fairly quickly, and nobody thinks it was economical, but less expensively than if every conflict had gone to the court.

And I don't know if they're still doing error correction. I know they're still submitting in a few Director's reports, or have, but that was a process that I think carried through until the last Director's report was filed.

Will the feds pay? goes to court

One of the first areas of dispute between the state of Idaho and the federal participants concerned the question of filing fees: Simply, the federal position was that while it was obliged to participate in the case, it did not owe any filing fees. The dispute was fought in court intensively, with decisions coming in favor of the state in SRBA Court and the Idaho Supreme Court, and in favor of the federal government at the U.S. Supreme Court. It was the first big legal battle in the adjudication, and in some opinions, one of the most significant it generated.

CLIVE STRONG When we started the adjudication, the expectation was that the United States would pay filing fees. We expected the number of claims from the United States to be of significant magnitude, and our expectations were fully satisfied. I think ultimately the United States filed nearly 50,000 water right claims in the adjudication.

But it took the position that, under the McCarran Amendment, the United States had only waived its sovereign immunity to participate in the adjudication, but not to pay filing fees.

Recognizing early on that this issue was going to have a long term implication on the financing of the adjudication, Judge Hurlbutt scheduled the issue up for early resolution. It was a hard fought trial in which we argued the difference between a fee and a tax. Ultimately, Judge Hurlbutt determined that it was a filing fee. A fee is something that relates to the services being provided. So we were saying that the service that the United States was getting was equivalent to the benefit that it would get out of the adjudication. Whereas a tax is way of spreading costs across a group of people. So that was the real issue, was this a fee or a tax? And was it within the scope of the McCarran Amendment?

PETER MONSON So when Clive Strong first approached the department of justice and with preliminary issues, the variable nature of the fee was what really caught our attention, our claims were not only numerous and but variable in terms of quantity. we were getting hit harder than anyone else in the adjudication ... We felt like we were being unfairly asked to pay for it, not only out costs, which were quite a lot, hiring experts to quantify the claims, litigation support staff, attorney time, travel time, add all that up – I know we spent several million dollars inn exports alone.

We felt that was not only unfair but also contrary to the provision of the McCarran amendment. ... I was very much involved in that. We filed a writ of mandamus a way of asking the court to require the state to take our claims without payment.

I certainly think the financial litigation was important law. From the standpoint of precedent, it was probably from our perspective one of the most important decisions that came out of it. It will affect all adjudications throughout the country.

DAVID SHAW About midway in that time the United States came in with their claims. I remember them sitting in an office over in our old building, filled an office, and then refused to pay filing fees because McCarran says the United States won't be assessed for costs.

Idaho said, "These are filing fees. They're not costs."

United States said, "They look like costs to us."

And Director Higginson said, "You can't touch the claims. Until they pay the filing fees, as provided by law, you can't touch them."

And I thought they initially would be inventoried, but they sat there.

Well, the United States filed a writ of mandamus to force the Director to do his job.

DANIEL HURLBUTT What happened was in the adjudication statutes the legislature set up a formula for filing fees for claimants in the Snake River Adjudication. More or less the filing fees were tied to the kind of water use you had and the amount of water you were using. The United States looked at that and objected, and indicated that they were being taxed unfairly and inconsistent with the nature of their agreement to be sued in a state court under the McCarran Amendment.

So they challenged the filing fees as they related to the United States. I determined that they had to pay the filing fees. Between the time I decided the case and it went to the United States Supreme Court, the Supreme Court had entered a decision that related to filing fees. Notwithstanding that, the Idaho Supreme Court affirmed my decision, and the U.S. appealed to the United States Supreme Court, and the United States Supreme Court, citing that decision that they had made after I had made my initial ruling said no, the U.S. did not have to pay the filing fees as constructed in the Idaho statute. They did say that the U.S. could be required to pay what would be considered normal court filing fees, based on how courts set up the requirement to pay filing fees, but that was different than the statutory formula relating to water type and usage and quantity that was constructed in the statutes.

So they reversed the Idaho Supreme Court, and the state legislature, I feel, could have changed the adjudication statute to conform to the ruling of the U.S. Supreme Court and require the United States to pay some court filing fee, but the state legislature chose not to do that, so they were essentially exempted from paying filing fees in the case.

[It was] pretty much federal government versus the state. I don't know that – well, before me there were other parties who joined with the state in arguing against the U.S. claim for exemption. I don't know if, once the matter got before the Idaho Supreme Court, the U.S. Supreme Court, whether the parties were actually involved. I'm sure they were in spirit, and they might have counseled with the Idaho Attorney General. I don't know if they filed separate briefs or anything. They could have.

There were many changes made, and the matter just, for whatever reason, the legislature determined not to go forward and at least charge them a court fee. But it would have been so little, I suspect the legislature didn't feel it was even worth getting involved.

PETER MONSON At the time we estimated them to be in the tens of millions of dollars ...

CLIVE STRONG We argued the case in the U.S. Supreme Court. In 1993, the United States Supreme Court issued a decision reversing the Idaho Supreme Court's decision, holding that the filing fee was not within the scope of the McCarran Amendment waiver.

So we were confronted with the situation that the United States would not pay filing fees. One aspect of that decision, though, that later became important, was the rejection of the United States argument that it was immune to the procedural laws of the state of Idaho for purposes of the determination of those water rights. The decision made clear that the United States had to follow the procedural laws of the SRBA District Court.

It was interesting arguing before the United States Supreme Court. It's a very intimate setting with nine justices surrounding you.

DANIEL HURLBUTT I think they [the federal agencies] were focused more on the nature and extent of their waiver of sovereign immunity under the McCarran Amendment, that is the consent to be sued, and I think the ground of their argument was this went beyond the waiver that was granted by the U.S. Congress in McCarran, and I'm sure that they argued due process, equal protection kinds of claims as well.

And I think there was also a question of whether this -- the filing fees as applied to the U.S. constituted a tax against the United States, which was – is not allowed, and certainly was not a part of McCarran.

CHARLES McDEVITT I think the first significant case after I got on the Court was the *United States of America vs. State of Idaho*. The United States said they weren't subject to the jurisdiction of the State of Idaho and they didn't have to submit their claims.

And I wrote that opinion for the Court. We decided that they were subject; and I went a step further and I said, "Not only that but we get filing fees." The United States Supreme Court affirmed us on everything except the filing fees. They weren't prepared to go that far.

CLIVE STRONG Without the United States filing fees, obviously we weren't going to have sufficient funds to complete the adjudication.

This was a time when the executive, legislative and judicial branches came together and really determined that the adjudication was important and warranted the expenditure of resources to quantify all water rights. The legislature began using general funds to support the adjudication. Basically the filing fees and general funds were the way we got through the adjudication.

Appointing special masters

As the recommendations on claims and rights poured through the Department of Water Resources and headed to the SRBA Court, more help was needed to handle those where some issues remained. That led to the hiring of three special masters, who worked for and reported to the SRBA judge much as lower court judges are reviewed by appellate courts.

Judge Hurlbutt decided to appoint three masters, though some people wondered, why not two, or five, or some other number?

ERIC WILDMAN I think it was just based on looking down the road and what the caseload was going to be and looked at the number of basins and the department's tentative reporting schedule, three was probably the minimum at the time.

I know in setting up with the special masters there was the issue as to whether they should be set up as special masters or, in fact, magistrates. They opted to, the decision was made to have them be special masters and have their jurisdiction and authority be derived from the presiding judge. I know when you look at Montana now, they have 13 special masters now and two presiding judges. They're looking at trying to – they're looking at the end, too, trying to get it done by 2028. They're looking and saying, well, we need this much staff. I think three special masters was probably the maximum amount you could get by with, given the size of the water bar here. Idaho has a relatively small water bar and the department has limited resources. I mean, if you're staggering trials and hearings and that type of thing and trying to process cases, I think if we had more, we would run into conflicts where counsel just wouldn't be available.

I think when Judge Hurlbutt started, though, they started out with two special masters and then realized he needed a third. But it's worked out well. I mean, the way we've assigned the cases has been by basin to a special master.

BARRY WOOD The SRBA was going for a while, Hurlbutt was assigned, but in '93 the Idaho State Bar helped the courts get a third district judge position in Twin Falls, because Hurlbutt was moving over to the SRBA full time. That really increased our awareness of it. There was a lot of discussion at the time about who's going to fill the role of the fact-finders [special masters]. Were they going to use existing magistrates? One of the proposals was to use informal – discussion about, let's use magistrates around the state in the role of special masters. ...

DANIEL HURLBUTT The process was that we, that is the courts, advertised the positions, essentially nationally, and took applications. And then I interviewed all of the applicants who looked qualified, and initially there were three Special Masters hired.

Terry Dolan, who is still a special master. Terry had significant work and was working as a special master in Wyoming, the Wind River Adjudication. Hired Brigette Bilyeu, who was in private practice with Elam & Burke in Boise, but was – is an extremely bright and talented person. And she's still a special master. And initially Richard Sims, who had been involved in the water area all over the western United States.

Richard's participation was objected to at one point by the United States because he had litigated against the United States in a number of matters, and I ruled that there was no conflict, and that he could continue as a special master. He did for a while work as a special master, and then he determined that he wanted to leave and pursue other matters.

And again we advertised for a special master. The Supreme Court set up a process to assist me. They appointed two other district judges to join me in the interview process, and decide on who to hire. That's when Fritz Haemmerle was brought in, initially to work as a special master. That was – Fritz Haemmerle and Brigette Bilyeu and Terry Dolan were the three Special Masters who were working when ultimately I left the bench.

BRIGETTE BILYEU My husband got a job here in Twin Falls. We commuted for about two years. So when the job came up here, one of my friends from law school was Fritz Haemmerle who had been Judge Hurlbutt's, the presiding judge, the first presiding judge, had been his law clerk. So he called me and said, "Hey, you should really apply for this job since you're thinking about getting closer to Twin Falls." So that's kind of how it evolved and how I came to apply for the job.

TERRENCE DOLAN I met Judge Hurlbutt at a water conference, I think it was a water users meeting down at the Red Lion Inn in Boise. That was back in '92, late '92, maybe early '93. He asked me if I wanted to come over and work as a special master, and I said yes.

About the same time another administrative tool started to be used: Designation of basin-wide issues.

CLIVE STRONG One of the things we recognized early on was the need to divide the adjudication into subcases. We recognized, however, that there would be some issues decided in subcases that could have impacts across the entire basin.

And so we set up a process for designating issues that would have that kind of impact. We set up a process for notifying claimants so they could come in and participate because we wanted to be able to get a binding decision that would control in all the other subcases.

When we saw issues that had overarching effect on more than one water right, or multiple water rights, we would ask the court to designate the issue, a legal issue, that could then be noticed up as a basin-wide issue. All parties that had any interest in the resolution of the issue would then have an opportunity to intervene and participate in the sub-case.

DANIEL HURLBUTT I think it existed in some measure in other places, but I think it came out of just many discussions with the Attorney General's Office. I know Clive Strong participated to a very large extent with some wonderful ideas. And I think it just sort of was a seed that germinated as a result of all of these discussions, and finally blossomed into the basin-wide issue designation that was placed in AO1.

It helped prevent a situation where a significant issue that affected potentially multiple users all over the 38 counties from being decided separately, discreetly in a sub-case, and then all of a sudden having to be readdressed when it came up in another basin, when the director issued his report. So it did allow for us to confront certain issues early, and get them resolved once and for all so they didn't have to be readdressed, and everybody knew what the landscape was on some of those issues very early in the process.

DANIEL HURLBUTT On the basin-wide issues, I thought the quality of lawyering, representation, was excellent. I think that you had people like Clive Strong from the state, and Peter Monson from the United States. You had Jim Tucker from Idaho Power, who was just titanic, I think, in the work he did, and the quality of the work he did. You know, those people stand out, with a bunch of others, I mean, who just did a terrific job, – whether they prevailed on their arguments or not. They gave the court, always gave the court the best information and the most solid arguments to assist in trying to get matter resolved.

There were gradually rising tensions between the court and the Department of Water Resources.

The court and the department

DANIEL HURLBUTT I had concerns, we had many discussions about what we would do with partial decrees and how would they be handled between the time they were entered and the time the final decree was entered, given transfers and sales and splits and all of that kind of stuff. The long and short of it was, the court, while I was there, just left to the department to take care of those. They said they wanted to take care of them.

My concern was that, and still is, in fact, that with all that can happen with water rights between the time a partial decree is entered and a final decree is entered, who's keeping track of that, and how do we know when the final decree is entered, we're really entering an accurate final decree?

I thought that it would be most appropriate if, as part of the SRBA, the department basically kept all of the partial decrees, and every claimant would be required to notify the department and properly take care of any transfers, splits, what have you, in the interim, and almost like the Torrens Title System, in the sense that that partial decree would be to the Department, that would be the water right, unless and until someone came in and changed it with the Department, and that any changes that were made that had not been both approved by the department and made on the partial decree, would not be recognized. Like with your car title.

Well, they chose not to do that. And that meant two names and addresses of the owners. They didn't want to do that. That means the final decree will be entered, and if you were then to try to notify everybody in the basin of some action that was going to be taken, you wouldn't have an accurate list of who the water right owners were or even necessarily an accurate rendering of what the water rights were. But that's not something that has happened.

DAVID SHAW At about the same time there was a conflict over water rights on Niagara Springs. The State Department of Fish and Game had water rights, Idaho Power had water rights, and Rim View Trout Company had water rights. And Rim View Trout Company complained they were not receiving their entitlement.

So Bill Ringert, their attorney at the time, filed a motion with the SRBA Court to have their right be delivered.

Well, the department had taken claims, I think, and done some work, so the department showed up at the hearing with our attorney, Judge Krogh now. Fish and Game was there with their attorney, Idaho Power was sitting in the bleachers. And Bill Ringert was there for Rim View. Judge Hurlbutt had a fit because here was the state with two heads and he didn't want to deal with it or didn't know how to deal with it. I won't say. So that cascaded into a struggle with the Court over what the role of the Director was.

In the initial statute the director was a party. He was under the Court's jurisdiction. So as being a party, the judge felt the state, entire state, was a party, and he was not going to decide any conflicts between what the department might say or what Fish and Game might say. The state had to speak with one voice.

That was about, as I recall, the same time we were trying to do the test basins. The judge didn't understand or didn't like the way the basins were laid out and didn't like the concept of doing test basins. He wanted things done, as I recall, he said "in an orderly fashion," whatever that meant. And that started a really difficult time in the adjudication because of the contention between the court and the department. Going back, if there was a way to avoid that, I think we would have had a much more productive adjudication because we burned I don't know how many years just trying to resolve how the department was going to function in the adjudication, culminating in the 1994 amendments to the adjudication statute that removed the department as a party, or the director as a party, became a technical advisor to the court.

But we did ultimately go on with the test basins. And in the test basins we started reviewing claims. We polished our second round service procedure so we could go out and get those claims that hadn't been filed. We started writing director's reports that recommended the water rights, and also those matters necessary to administer the water rights. We, the Department, thought that was – I do personally still believe that's an essential part of the water right decree.

CLIVE STRONG Once the claims were filed, we then had to begin preparing what were called director's reports. A director's report is where the department investigates the claims that were filed and then makes a determination of what it believes is the appropriate elements for each of the water rights.

We recognized that in the director's reports there would be a number of issues that could become important. So we set up what are called test basins. We had three test basins. One was in Hagerman Valley, one was in the Big Lost. And I'm forgetting for the moment where the third one was.

Lo and behold, the issues started coming forward. The department took positions that some of the water rights were overclaimed and should be cut back, which resulted in some very contentious litigation down in the Hagerman Valley and up in the Big Lost. And we ended up in a lot of litigation with an organization called the Hagerman Water Rights Owners Association. And questions began to be raised about what the department's role in the adjudication should be.

Historically, the department had been a named party. So we had the State of Idaho as a named party and the department as a named party.

From the state's perspective, we viewed them as separate parties. set up representation for both the state and the department.

The District Court took the position that the department was subject to all of the traditional discovery rules, which created a real crisis for the Department.

Tension built between the District Court and the state about how this process should be set up and whether the state should speak with one voice.

When we talk about speaking with one voice, the question was, could an agency like Fish and Game with a water right come into the adjudication as a party and then have the Department of Water Resources report on that water right?

This issue played out in a case involving Rim View Trout Company just south of Wendell. The court ordered the state to speak with one voice. In other words, the director had to speak through the attorney general. I had to file an emergency motion with the Idaho Supreme Court to obtain relief from the District Court's order. It became obvious we needed to do something different. Given the orders that were coming from the District Court, the decision was made to go to the legislature and amend the adjudication statute. That was done in 1994.

As an interesting aside, the tension had gotten so high that it was determined that amendments would be pursued even though it was near the end of the legislative session.

So Speaker Newcomb directed us to prepare amendments to the adjudication statute. We did so in a week. It was the week of spring break. I sent my kids off with my wife to Arizona, and I stayed here rewriting the adjudication statute.

The amendments removed the director as a party so that the director would no longer be in contention with the district court or with the other parties, but more of an advisor. In fact, we called him an expert, a court expert. The amendment recognized that the state could appear as a party.

Needless to say, the amendments were not greeted uniformly by all participants of the adjudication. The Hagerman Water Right Owners filed a challenge to the constitutionality of the 1994 amendments. There challenges were designated as basin-wide issue two and three.

Basin-wide issue two dealt with the role of the director in the adjudication. Basin-wide three dealt with the constitutionality of the amendments to Chapter 14, the adjudication statute. Judge Hurlbutt issued a decision striking down all of the amendments as unconstitutional.

When we appealed to the Idaho Supreme Court, the legislature took the unusual step of intervening in the case and hiring outside counsel, Tim Hopkins, to represent their point of view. They viewed the court's decision as impinging upon legislative authority.

DAVID SHAW I wish I knew. I can speculate. I have speculated. I don't know. I speculated it was a personality conflict between the director and the judge. I don't know what caused the conflict.

And I've talked with Clive about this. And I don't know what the root cause was. But I know the working relationship with the court I thought was excellent while we were taking claims. You know, if we had questions, the court was always very open to discuss them and make recommendations, make rulings if he had to. Steering committee dialogue was very open.

Once we got down to about the point of filing Director's reports, the Niagara Springs thing, the red files, it may have been a combination of things. I don't know. But it finally got to the point that I think in Basinwide 3 the Court's decision called out Clive and I by name in his decision.

LAIRD NOH There was a lot of concern among legislators about just the amount of knowledge and understanding the court had in some of the proceedings. Bruce Newcomb and I have always been very good friends, we go back a long ways, and this water issue was one of the main reasons Bruce got into the Idaho House. He and I were almost always on the same side, we teamed up.

We wanted to meet with the Supreme Court, not to discuss any legal issues but just to discuss some of the procedures and see what could be done to improve the flow of knowledge between the adjudication court and the history of various things. Chuck McDevitt was the chief justice then, and Chuck was very concerned about ex parte communications. He didn't want this to happen at all. Of course Bruce had a little more clout than I did, and so we finally got him to agree to sit down with us. It was a very formal proceeding. Bruce and I were in front of the chief justice in the court room, and he insisted the court reporter was there and transcribed everything, I don't know if those things are ever available or not for historical purposes. It was very formal. Bruce and I had our discussion and he dismissed us and that was it.

Much of the legislative concern focused on Judge Hurlbutt. It got to the point where the interim water committee really pushed to have a meeting with Dan Hurlbutt, an open meeting. He's in control of the meeting, so we're very aware of that, we want to do this right. So it was set up. It was agreed to. So at considerable expense the legislators, some from north Idaho, gathered in Twin Falls to have a meeting with Judge Hurlbutt. And we sat down and waited, and he didn't appear, and waited, and he didn't appear. Finally we got a call from court saying, Dan's not going to be able to be there after all, there's a big bar association gathering at Sun Valley coming up and he had kind of an emergency and went up there, to get that straightened out. We adjourned. Everyone went home. But Stan Hawkins, a very bright, somewhat cantankerous legislator from Eastern Idaho, who was usually on the opposite side from me of most issues. Anyway, Stan stopped at a fast food place in Twin Falls to get something to eat on the way home, and there was Dan Hurlbutt. He wasn't in Sun Valley; it had been a put up deal.

At any rate things moved on and got settled down. But there were some repercussions from all this, and some effort in the House and the Senate went along, to put a little financial pressure on the court.

The legislature adjusts the adjudication

DANIEL HURLBUTT Well, there certainly was the issue of the legislation that was adopted to modify the initial adjudication statute, that was challenged, and the principal issues in that, as I recall, were, one, to what extent could the legislature statutorily adopt changes in the adjudication that would modify or materially impact the Rules of Civil Procedure. They did change the role and function of the Department of Water Resources technically, and that was challenged and had to be addressed.

When I decided the case, I pretty much declared all of that legislation unconstitutional. The Supreme Court agreed in the sense that the legislature can't get involved in modifying court procedure. That was a violation of separation of powers. The court did rule that the role of the department could be modified by the legislature. The consternation was, you had a state agency in the Department of Water Resources that could both recommend water rights that were filed by other state agencies, and the question became the degree of weight you could put on the department's recommendations. The department was ultimately determined to be an expert witness, and not a party to the suit, and the Supreme Court affirmed that that would be an appropriate way to proceed in the case, and could be allowed. One of the problems that that presented, at least initially, was you had the Attorney General's Office representing the Department of Water Resources, representing private state claimants, opposing other claimants, and the question was, how many States of Idaho could participate in a McCarran adjudication case. And that finally got sorted out through that process.

They were the driver of it because I had been pretty insistent that we be antiseptic in how we proceeded with the State of Idaho in the McCarran adjudication, trying to give proper deference to the waiver of sovereign immunity to the federal government had acceded to in that statute. And through this process it got sorted out.

CLIVE STRONG It wasn't so much that the district court didn't want to remove the director as a party, the district court viewed the adjudication as being a judicial proceeding and that was under the control of the judiciary, not the legislature. So we had a direct confrontation between the legislative and judicial branches about their respective authority.

You throw into that conflict the tension between the department and the court, you get the kind of intergovernmental conflict, that rises to the highest level. So there was a very difficult period in which the adjudication was essentially on hold while we went forward with litigation over the amendments.

We appealed the district court's decision to the Idaho Supreme Court. It was the first Idaho Supreme Court argument ever videotaped.

The Idaho Supreme Court reversed the SRBA District Court and held that the legislature had authority to remove the director as a party to the adjudication and upheld most of the statutory provisions. It recognized that the adjudication was kind of sui generis – different from all other cases – and that the legislature had the authority to establish procedures for the adjudication.

My recollection was the Supreme Court held that the Legislature did not have authority to designate the director as an expert. The Court said that, while the director's report would be given prima facie weight, it would become just evidence if challenged.

As you might suspect, these kind of battles are difficult ones to overcome. But I think, to the credit of the state officials, , the parties ultimately came back together and found a pathway forward.

The 1994 amendments were another turning point in the adjudication. It probably was one of the biggest factors in the completion of the adjudication.

Over time a strong relationship developed between the court and the department.

DAVID SHAW And everything basically came to a halt while the role of the director got sorted out and what should be included in the water rights as they were decreed got sorted out.

CLIVE STRONG I wished we had the `94 amendments in 1985. Maybe some of that conflict could have been avoided. It's inevitable in something this big and this number of players involved that there's going to be some conflict.

The legislature decided to step in and restructure part of the SRBA, changing the role of the Department of Water Resources.

DAVID SHAW I remember going to Twin Falls, the co-chair of the joint finance appropriation committee is Maxine Bell. Was then, I think she still is. And this interim committee had set up a meeting with the Court to talk about procedures and what have you. And the judge stood the committee up.

So it was contention not only between the department and the court, but between the legislature and the judiciary. And it went on up. Somewhere in this same time the Supreme Court issued a decision referred to as the Musser decision that was contentious. The legislature was concerned about what was going on. There was push-back from that decision by the legislature.

As I recall, there was a request for reconsideration. And the court refused, I think. But this expanded from just the department and the court to include the legislature and the Supreme Court. It was a very contentious time.

. . . But under different conditions I think we would have made much better progress during that – oh, it must have been three to four years where we probably spent as much time being not productive in what we were really trying to do in the end, as we did actually doing our job.

BRUCE NEWCOMB I think I have to say if Clive Strong hadn't been in the attorney general's office none of this would have been as successful as it has been, because I think people would have rolled over.

And when I was majority leader, Randy Smith was the chairman of the Republican party and Blake Hall was a national committee man of the Republican party. And they called me out. And Al Lance was running for attorney general.

And so I told him, I said, "Al, I'll tell you what also, I'm going to support you," but I said, "there's going to be a lot of people wanting you to get rid of Clive Strong." And I said, "If you do that, I won't support you. I'll come out against you."

So Randy and Blake Hall called me out, and they started ranting on me about doing that because, you know, Batt was upset with me. So I said, you know, "I don't really care about you guys, or even Governor Batt or, you know, potentially Governor Batt at this point because I care more about the state of the water rights than I do any of you." And I said, "You're both lawyers, and neither one of you could carry his water." So I said, "That's why I came here. That's why I'm here."

And subsequently Governor Batt was elected. And he gave his gubernatorial address in Kellogg in the high school gymnasium, and he made a beeline for me and really, really took it to me. And Dean Cameron was standing so close. He said, "I was so close to you there I thought I was getting my butt chewed too."

But anyway, Batt eventually said, you know, in one of the joint leadership meetings he looked at me and he said, you know, "I've come to the point where I wouldn't talk water or to the tribes unless I had Clive Strong on my side."

And in his book he said, "The best thing I did was keep Clive Strong. One of the best things I did." I mean Clive was the linchpin of getting this all done because if he had gone somewhere else where he made a lot of money, you know, he could have. Might have been out of state because he would have been conflicted on everything here.

But that being said, he chose to be a consummate public servant. And so I think that was one of the linchpins of this whole thing being successful, you know, at this point.

DANIEL HURLBUTT I think that one of the concerns expressed, and that I ruled on, was the extent to which the state of Idaho, who was a party in the case, could then in the middle of the game change the rules, and by some people's arguments, change the rules in their favor. I know the U.S. was concerned, as were a number of private litigants in the case. That was hotly contested.

That, and you know, other changes that would impact essentially the Rules of Civil Procedure or court procedure, and whether or not the legislature could move in and fill that role, and one of my concerns with that particularly was maintaining the adjudication as a McCarran adjudication. The United States had consented to be sued in a state court, not a state administrative agency. And in a state court there are stern rules to be followed, and to the extent the legislature could come in in the middle of the case and modify those rules, I think implicated the integrity of the adjudication as a McCarran adjudication.

Basin wide

1996-1999

Changes in the court-department dynamic

KARL DREHER Governor Batt was elected in 1994, and my predecessor Keith Higginson had decided to retire. So Idaho, through the governor's office, formed a search team largely made up of water attorneys to do a nationwide search to find someone to, I'll say, re-start the SRBA. The relationship between the presiding judge and the department was not good. From my perspective, there was reason for the problems and the failure on both sides.

Normally it would be very unusual for a state to recruit from outside the state for this kind of position. But, in this case, most every candidate – at least the likely candidates for the position within the Department of Water Resources – had the baggage from what had previously occurred in the SRBA. I won't say it would have been impossible, but it would have been very difficult for someone in an existing leadership role within the department to restore a working relationship with the court.

I mentioned how well known and respected Greg Hobbs* is in the west. So the search committee contacted Greg to see if he had any recommendations. And his response was, I know just the guy.

DAVID SHAW I left in 1996.

* A highly respected attorney and currently a member of the Colorado Supreme Court, who was a colleague of Karl Dreher in Colorado.

My work for the attorney general office has continued. There's probably – well, I don't see a difference in what I do for them today than what I was doing when I was with the department. Clive may have different ideas, but I see it as being the same.

But some of the work for private water users, you really see a different perspective of water use, the concerns of the private water users, their view of the department. It's been an opportunity to really get a much broader understanding of water use and water users than what you see from inside the department. Now, I thought I understood. I had been a farmer, an irrigator all my life, and did have some background about water use, but from working for private water users since I've been a consultant has certainly broadened that perspective.

DAVID TUTHILL I went to school as a water engineer. I came to the department as a water engineer in 1976, and my first assignment was as the supervisor of the adjudication section for the department. It was a very small section back in '76. We had a few adjudications across the state; the largest was the Payette River adjudication. I served in the state office for about a year in that role. An opening became available at the western regional office for the manager of the Payette River adjudication, which I did not apply for, but which I was assigned to.

Because I liked my job in the state office, I really wasn't looking for a change, but it was my good fortune to have the assignment of the Payette River adjudication, and I learned about the judicial process through that role. I served in that role for about three years.

In the Western Regional role as the supervisor of the hands-on adjudication, I learned about serving potential claimants, about claims-taking, about taking the claims that were made, and developing recommendations for the department to the court – because in Idaho we're fortunate to have a process where the claim is considered to be just a claim to the department, and it doesn't become prima facie evidence until it has been evaluated by the department of Water Resources and sent to the court.

So the department accepts the claim and a variety of other information – hydrologic survey, the records of the department – all information that's available and develops a report to the court called a "Proposed Finding," and a "Finding" to the court.

The court then takes over the process and allows opportunity for claimants to come in and either agree with or object to the findings of the department.

In some other states the process attributes more weight to the claim; for example, in Montana the claim is considered to be prima facie evidence, and it's much more difficult to correct the information that's on the claim.

With Idaho, our claim is considered to be part of the evidence and becomes part of an overall assessment that goes to the court.

So in my role with the Payette River adjudication, I became familiar with the preparation of claims, the reporting of those claims to the court, working with the court, and evolving that process to a final decree by the court.

In 1996 when Dave Shaw retired, I was asked by then Director Karl Dreher to serve as the chief of the Adjudication Bureau because I had the previous experience with the Payette adjudication. I turned him down. I was happy with my job at Western Region.

Then Karl assigned me for a month to be in that position. During that month, I had the good fortune of going down to the court and seeing court operations.

I drove down with Nick Spencer and was very surprised at some of the things I saw with the adjudication. Some of the contentiousness that I saw was surprising to me in the hearing – the first hearing I was at.

Coming back, I wasn't too sure I was interested in this whole process, but Nick and I had a nice talk, and Nick told me that his vision was to be part of something that would be major for the state of Idaho. He wanted to be involved in an adjudication that would really leave its mark on this state – and by the end of that drive, I was in.

DANIEL HURLBUTT The initial hearings and basin-wide issues were at the court, but we were committed that when it came to hearings on individual water rights in the test basins, that the Masters would go out into the field, and for example, Brigette Bilyeu held many, many hearings in Arco and Mackay. We were going to the water users, and with the – at least with the test basins that was a feasible, doable proposition. And we did go out and hold hearings in the field.

I think as things progressed, and certainly after my time on the bench, we had basins that were more distant, and there was, with the advent of video technology there was much more opportunity to take advantage of that, and to hold hearings remotely.

But initially we wanted to be where the water users were. And the Supreme Court was very supportive and sought the funding, and agreed with my philosophy that we needed to go to the water users, rather than -- they already felt put upon, I think, by having to do this, and rather than drag them to one location, we tried to go out to them wherever possible.

One thing we were able to do to advance – two things we did to advance technology in the court system. Early on, the Idaho courts had had a computer system to monitor and administer cases throughout the state, and that had been developed by the Supreme Court internally. The Supreme Court provided us with an old IBM machine, and with their programmers, who had devised the system for the Supreme Court, to develop iWaters, the separate, segregated court – computer system that we could use to try to administer the Snake River Basin Adjudication. That was developed. I think there was a lot of skepticism on the part of many about this. I think there were many who were nervous about what kind of control the court might exert over an adjudication. But this, in my opinion, was standard operating procedure for the courts, to monitor cases, and to do as much as we could to get them on a computer system so that we could monitor progress and keep things moving and be very active in the administration of the case.

An offshoot of this was that once the system was developed, we could do two things. One, it meant – and I think this caused a lot of consternation to a lot of people. We allowed any water user, virtually anybody could get on the iWaters system remotely through the Internet and look at everything that was on the system.

Some people are fearful of having too much information out there. I was not. I insisted on it. So we had farmers, ranchers in Mackay, Idaho, that were on the system and able to monitor what was going on, remotely from their own computer.

This also allowed us to do another thing, which caused some consternation initially. When we were devising iWaters, I pointed out we could probably print out the docket sheet very quickly and easily and get it to water users. Heretofore the department had done it. Eventually the department came to me and they had a problem. It was taking, I think it was 80 or a hundred hours a month for their personnel to put together the docket sheet and mail it out to everybody. So we ran a test at the SRBA court, and using the administrative staff that had been set up there, I asked them, you know, to run a docket sheet off iWaters, and we talked about the steps that would be necessary, the information that would be necessary, and I had them time what it took for them to go through those steps to produce a docket sheet.

Well, our very first one, it took them only about six hours. I mean, we could save thousands of dollars a month just to produce it ourselves. So while – when I first broached that topic, and there was a lot of resistance, now the department really wanted to take advantage of it and have us do it, and we could do it a lot cheaper. So we began, then, publishing the docket sheet and sending it out. And the docket sheet was then available on the computer, online, it was consistent with AO1, available at the various county courthouses, and anybody that wanted to subscribe and get a hard copy could get it.

CLIVE STRONG If you look at the period `95 to `99, what really strikes you is that 14 major cases were processed through the SRBA District Court and the Idaho Supreme Court. It's virtually unheard of, to have that amount of litigation in one case go to the Supreme Court in such a short period of time. We were hitting most of the large basin-wide issues and establishing, really, the foundation for a lot of the later decision. For instance, in that `95 to `99 period, the court dealt with the issue of whether the public trust doctrine was a limitation on water rights. The Supreme Court also rejected a challenge of the conjunctive management rules and upheld the enlargement and accomplished transfer statutes. It addressed how general provisions would be incorporated into the decree.

And we began dealing with the federal reserved water right issues, too, which was a huge component of the adjudication. So if you look at this period of time, it was quite remarkable, the efficiency with which the court processed all of those cases and laid the foundation for a lot of the subsequent decisions.

DAVID SHAW I've worked on the Klamath adjudication in Oregon. And now after however many years since the '60s, I don't know how many millions of dollars in litigation, finally they're sitting there at the table and trying to find a resolution.

And in the case of federal reserve water rights, in my experience, litigation doesn't produce a good result. The court seldom answers the questions you want answered. And if you can sit down and find a solution that you can look at yourself in the mirror the next day, it's likely much better than what you'll get out of litigation. And I think if you look around the West, that runs pretty true.

My partner on the Gila River and the Little Colorado had the same experience where he and his client have negotiated for years and finally got settlements with the tribes that everybody could live with.

The central Utah project was supposed to be resolved a number of years ago, and the court entered the order. And now it's come apart. And I don't know if they're in the process of litigation yet, but it has not worked and so they're back trying to fix it.

So far that's not been the case in Idaho. Once the negotiation was done, people have been able to move ahead, both the tribes and the non-Indians, and work with what was included in the agreement without needing to litigate any further.

DAVID TUTHILL Typically, the finding of the department will result in about 80 to 90 percent acceptance by the claimants. Those that don't accept the findings of the department can make their objections, and that's typically between 10 and 20 percent.

The pro se claimants

People often appeared in court without legal representation.

DANIEL HURLBUTT We knew it would be the case because, again, if you had 120,000 claimants, you knew there weren't enough lawyers in Idaho to represent them, and it was also clear that not everyone could afford counsel, and that there were a lot of matters that could be addressed without counsel. And so it was known that there would be a lot of pro se claimants in the case, people appearing on their behalf.

The masters were trained and very attuned to dealing with pro se claimants. Pro se claimants, I think, were assisted by meetings we had in the field to address, you know, their concerns, and to familiarize them with the process. Pro ses were allowed to contact court staff who clearly could not represent them but could inform them of the procedures, timing, various requirements that they would have to meet.

Ultimately the process of having status conferences in sub cases evolved into a process where before there was even a status conference or scheduling conference on those subcases, the department worked extremely well in meeting with claimants, represented or unrepresented, to try to see if they couldn't resolve some of the issues. Some of the department's work, I'm sure, was to help educate claimants on what the recommendations really meant. And a claimant could point out to the department where there were clearly errors made. And some matters were resolved immediately before they went in before the special masters on a scheduling or status conference.

And in that way a pro se's – I think the system evolved to allow pro ses to participate freely and fully and be dealt with very fairly.

I'm not aware of it being a big problem with pro ses. Again, because the department worked very well, and we were able to – they were able to, you know, be sure that all water users were given notice and opportunity to file claims. And there was a process for taking late claims, where people had legitimate reasons that they hadn't filed. Either for some reason it had fallen through the cracks and they had not been notified by the department, or other factors attended. I think there was more tension with actually attorneys seeking to file, not so much late claims, but late objections to claims that had been filed, and that would be – more often that was a situation where it was not attorneys representing the claimant who wanted to enter in late and file objections, but where a claimant may have had an objection, may have filed an objection, and there was an ongoing sub-case, and some other water user felt that they might be affected, so they wanted to file, and they could, and were allowed to under the rules, file an objection, but were very late to the party.

We in the court held the line and said, No, you have had adequate opportunity, through the docket sheet, through getting on to iWaters remotely, to follow and understand the progress, or the initiation and progress of any separate sub-case, and we didn't allow a lot of the Johnny-come-latelies to come in when they thought maybe they needed to get involved.

DAVID TUTHILL One of the principles of water is the smaller amount of water, the more contentious the fight. People are very interested in their little bit of water – and we see that in many situations.

There was a re-definition of the statutes early on in the adjudication describing the definition of "domestic." That's Section 42-111, and the statute helped to clarify what "domestic" is. "Domestic" is generally enough water for a single household – generally – the exempted domestic. It's 13,000 gallons per day as a limit in the amount. Another limit is up to a half-acre of irrigation for an exempted domestic – or stockwater of up to 13,000 gallons per day, which is about enough water for 1,000 head of stock. So that's the exempted domestic where people had the option to file.

People think, "Gee with my 13,000 gallons a day, I can provide water for five homes." That's really not allowed. The exempted use can't provide for multiple ownership subdivisions. It's single ownership, and it's basically for a home – for an individual's home.

People were very inventive as far as adding additional domestics and "glumping" them together and so on, and the department has some memorandums describing how to handle those. Also, the special master [Fritz] Haemmerle wrote a good decision on domestics at one point that was key in our understanding -- mutual understanding -- of how to handle domestic water rights. I would say that is an area of nice cooperation between the department and the court on how to consider domestic water rights.

One of the biggest initial challenges was in managing the sheer immense volume of paperwork – until much of that data could be located in computer systems.

DAVID TUTHILL When we began to issue Director's Reports or our findings on the water rights, we were required to provide those to all the counties that were involved so people could come into the county and look at everybody's water rights – not just theirs.

We have kind of a famous picture where Danni Smith, who was the person in charge of report distribution, is standing by a stack of reports that she would have had to give to the county -- and a CD – which she offered as an alternative.

At first, maybe a couple of the courthouses wanted the paper. That didn't last long.

The director transitions to an expert

DAVID TUTHILL My predecessor, Dave Shaw, I thought did a wonderful job of bringing the adjudication from the commencement in 1987 until the end of claims-taking in about 1991. This was a very challenging and demanding time for the agency.

They developed a computer system that had worked very well for the initial processes. They had worked through some very difficult situations where the department was considered to be a party. Then in 1994, in the midst of that process, the agency and the state had a major reset in direction when the 1994 laws – led, I believe, by Clive – were changed to more match what the state of Arizona had where the department was not a party, but rather was a technical expert to the court.

That transition from party to technical expert was the key to the success of the adjudication, in my view.

When the department was a party, it was treated as a party by the court and was not allowed to provide information to the court in the way that a technical expert would have been allowed to do.

For example, some days when department staff would go down to the court, they didn't know if they would be held in contempt of court for not providing information demanded by the court. As a party, they had a different status and developed what I would call a "contentious relationship" with the court and with the federal government and other parties.

In that party status, things were not moving forward very rapidly. There was a lot of contention. That was my observation – not being directly involved – because this all happened before I became directly associated with the adjudication. That was my observation and that was, in part, the reason why I didn't want to be a part of it.

But in '94 this major change happened, and when I was asked to be a part of this in '96 I was able to see that there was another potential way to move forward. With the department as a technical expert, we had the chance to work with the court and provide the court information in a way that would lead to better solutions and not be held to the same standard as a party.

So one of the things that I felt from the onset was the power of Idaho's adjudication in that the legislature provided steady funding for many years which enabled the hiring of long-term staff, with some certainty in the expectation that the adjudication would be completed.

The legislature provided good laws, as exemplified by the 1994 laws. So I felt that the legislature did a wonderful job -- as compared with other western states – because we benchmarked with other western states, and Idaho's position was much better than other states. So the legislature did a wonderful job.

The courts have done a wonderful job in that the five judges and the special masters that the state has had in the SRBA have all been exceptionally talented and dedicated.

CARTER FRITSCHLE The removal of IDWR as a party to the SRBA was welcomed.

Prior to the legislative change, IDWR was required to file responses to all of the objections filed to the Director's Report. This was especially challenging for Basin 36 (one of the test basins) in that technical and legal staff at the state office had to work all night on the eve of the response deadline in preparing those responses. Also, the change resulted in a better working relationship between the court and IDWR. I definitely believe the change was a good idea, and I doubt that we would be this close to the completion of the SRBA if the change had not occurred.

KARL DREHER I didn't exactly know what I was getting myself into. I couldn't have. I didn't fully understand how significant the conflicts had been, and the importance of the 1994 amendments to the adjudication statutes to resolving the conflicts. The reason they turned out to be so significant is they removed the department as a party and reestablished the department's role as technical advisor to the court. I could not have done what I did in terms of establishing a working relationship with Judge Hurlbutt had I not been able to talk to him. And, I couldn't have talked to him unless the statutes had been changed, because it would have been ex parte communication. By changing those statutes and removing the department as a party, they opened the door for communication between the department and the court in a way it had never occurred before.

DAVID TUTHILL Early on, the special masters and the judge did not seem to be comfortable with the department's role as technical expert because they had several years of history with the department being a party.

So early on Karl Dreher, as the director, and I as the bureau chief met with Judge Hurlbutt to go over some of the difficulties in this relationship. It was just a divide sometimes between the court and the department that we had to work on.

So we established a monthly briefing for the court where we presented the administrative status and received input from the court. This presentation was supported by efforts from supervisors Don Shaff, Carter Fritschle, Jan Shurte, Doug Jones, Ernie Carlsen and Michael Ciscell, and by many others throughout the department.

That became very much a mainstay. We had almost 100 of those meetings while I was at the department, and those became very important for information exchange and to be on the same track.

I would say that all of the judges that we had were very supportive of that kind of liaison and effort.

KARL DREHER I came in from outside, I wasn't labeled, I had a good reputation, and I was able to start clean. There was a capable internal candidate, but he wouldn't have been able to start clean. So what I began to do was drive to Twin Falls, numerous times every month, to sit down and to communicate with Judge Hurlbutt about the process. In the beginning – and this is a lesson all of us should remember – I listened, I didn't do much talking. I just listened. And I began to assimilate where Judge Hurlbutt was coming from, what his perspectives were, and I began to develop a very healthy respect for him. I found him to be extremely intelligent and academically well prepared for what he was doing. He's smarter than I am, hands down – this guy was very sharp.
So it behooved me to listen.

Speeding up the claims through division

I think this process went on for at least six months, maybe nine months, before we began to jointly explore possibilities. Through that nine months which started with listening to each other, we developed trust in one another, which allowed us to explore ways to begin to make the adjudication successful.

We jointly decided the SRBA should be bifurcated between the simple rights and the complex rights. One of the things that was happening is, you had all these claims, and every time there was any kind of a notice or anything, all the claimants had to be notified and given an opportunity to attend if not participate. And, from an administrative stand point, that was overly burdensome. So what Judge Hurlbutt and I realized is that if we separated out the complex rights – the federal reserved rights, the Indian rights, the complex irrigation rights, the Bureau of Reclamation storage rights, the forest rights, all of that – they probably could care less about somebody's right for an individual domestic well. That's not something they're going to want to participate in. So we decided to set aside the irrigation rights and the reserved rights and all of the other complex water rights and focus on the simple small rights that could be decreed and removed from the adjudication, which is what we did.

. . . When you're involved in a process that's been plagued with failure, small steps of success are critically important to achieving larger steps of success. And, that's what happened. Even though these rights were small we demonstrated the process could be successful. Those smaller steps of success led to eventually larger steps of success, and eventually settlement of the Nez Perce claims and the completion of the SRBA. It all progressed from the relationship Judge Hurlbutt and I developed and those early small steps of success we achieved.

ERIC WILDMAN A lot of the cases are the single-party subcases. I think before '94 when the department was a party, it made it a little more difficult processing those cases. Now the department just comes in and gets on the stand and puts on the record the basis for their recommendation, and then they're subject to cross-examination by the claimant. Then the claimant has to put on their case.

A multiple party sub-case isn't just when the claimant objects, but it's when you have the neighbor or third party objecting. Those can range from, you know, one or two litigants to hundreds of parties. Same thing, though, the recommendation gets the prima facie weight, and the party opposing it has to come in and burst the bubble. The claimant always has the burden of persuasion on the water right claim. For handling multi-party subcases – well, before I get to that, then we have the general provisions. A general provision is a provision that affects a significant amount of water rights within the basin, either in the sub-basin or the entire Snake River Basin.

Sometimes the department would make a recommendation as to a general provision. Other times parties would object because they felt like there should be a general provision and there wasn't one. But the implication is, because it affects a lot of water rights, you're going to have a large number of parties.

The same is true with basin-wide issues. It doesn't pertain to, necessarily pertain to a general provision, but it's just one issue that has basin-wide significance. Administrative Order 1 has a process for getting an issue designated as basin-wide and the process for handling it. But again, that is a process that lends itself to having a large number of parties.

I have some processes that I use for managing a case with a large number of parties. It's real important in that situation to get everybody on board right at the outset who is going to participate. Typically, in those type of situations I want to get it on a dual track: a settlement track and a litigation track. You don't want somebody coming in, after you've started the process, you don't want somebody coming in at the eleventh hour and undoing everything, all the progress that's been made to date. So we really try to bend over backwards on giving notice and getting everybody on board up front. And then a lot of times you'll have people involved that may have filed an objection, but it doesn't really affect their water right or they did it to preserve their status and now they don't want to be in the sub-case any more. So it uses a series of processes, incremental processes to winnow those parties out. Then the parties that have the same issues, they can be aligned and designate a leader to represent their interests.

The other issue that I guess I'll bring up with respect to case management and handling a large number of claims within a basin that may or may not be interrelated, and a process that wasn't always used, was the department goes through and files with the court a case management report that attempts to identify overlapping claims.

Groupings of issues. You know, that was a lesson we learned in a couple of the cases when we didn't have that.

There's the old legal principle that the claimant should rely on the strength of their water right, not the weakness of their neighbor's water right. Well, that isn't necessarily true when you have a limited source, either on a ditch, or you have a limited amount of water that everybody is claiming by the same decree. If everybody is not brought into that case from the outset and you have the potential of decreeing more water than is available, not everybody is going to object to everybody else's water right that is claimed by that same decree. They're just going to focus on their own claim.

But because the subcases have the potential to go through the process at different times, and if nobody objects, the claims that go through the process earlier are going to end up with all the water. We had that experience a couple of different times .

DAVID TUTHILL The federal government had been a very contentious party in the early years, and there was more to it than just that – and other speakers will talk to that who were directly involved – but by the time I became involved, we were able to establish a nice relationship with the federal government and other claimants while being able to provide technical information for the court.

In 1996 the court was just transitioning from the department being a party to the department being a technical expert, so there were a couple of difficult years where the special masters really weren't sure how to treat us. However, over time the special masters began to rely on the staff of the department in a mutually beneficial way. In recent years there has been a very nice relationship where the court could count on the department to provide objective information.

DAVID TUTHILL That was one of the biggest evolutions in the SRBA because early on there was great contention between the federal government and the state when we were a party.

Some of the participants federally had come from other states where there was great contention between state and the federal government – that's part of the culture in the west in many cases.

By the time I became involved in 1996, much of that rancor had been resolved, and I enjoyed a very nice relationship with the federal government. We had a mutually supportive perspective. We didn't see eye to eye on all cases – we had differences of opinion – but I would say much of the rancor had left by 1996.

One of the more complicated issues to hit the adjudication abut that time was the question of what should happen in the case of changes of water use, if use was expanded beyond the original limits or if other changes had been made by water users.

Expanded water use

CLIVE STRONG There had been a number of what we call private adjudications where some water rights were determined but not all. And as with most water rights over time, ownership changes, the way you use the water changes. And while the state law requires that those changes be reflected through a transfer process, in many instances that hadn't occurred.

We recognized that if we had to force everybody to go through the transfer process that would not be a very efficient way to move forward. So we developed a process in the adjudication for doing what are called accomplished transfers. If somebody had made a change in the use of water right, they could come in and claim that in the adjudication, and the department would review and report that as part of the director's report rather than going through the administrative process of doing that change.

There had also been what we call enlargements of water rights, or expansions of water rights, where through irrigation efficiency, maybe you switched from gravity to sprinkler irrigation, you were able to irrigate additional acres.

In 1986, there were statutes enacted that provided for a recognition of enlargements and expansions. Those were struck down as unconstitutional by the SRBA District Court. So when we amended the adjudication statute in 1994, we rewrote those particular statutory provisions and addressed the constitutional issues.

Those 1984 amendments were upheld as constitutional and were another important factor. Rather than having a separate administrative process, we were able to incorporate them into the decree at the time we were doing the review process.

In February 1997 Charles McDevitt stepped down as chief justice of the Idaho Supreme Court, and Linda Copple Trout was chosen by the other justices to replace him. Some personal dynamics changed at the court as a result.

LAIRD NOH After Chuck McDevitt was gone, Linda Trout became the chief justice, she wanted to get this all settled down, so she invited Bruce and I to come over and sit down with her, and maybe two other legislators came along also. We sat down and shot the breeze in her office. It was all very friendly and we had an open discussion and healed things up on an appropriate basis. That was kind of the end of the friction between the legislature and the court system.

DANIEL HURLBUTT I think there were four [main appeals from my time at SRBA Court]. Filing fees, inclusion of prior adjudications, and the case – I don't know whether the domestic stockwater issue was appealed. Perhaps one other that I'm not thinking of.

I think I was affirmed completely two or three times, and one time on the legislation it was partly an affirmance and partly a reversal.

I was advised by a Supreme Court justice when I first went on the bench, don't worry about what happens on appeal. Just call them and decide them the best way you can and as honestly as you can, and don't worry about that stuff.

BARRY WOOD That's why frankly I liked decisions to be appealed. What's on the table is so important. To me the district judge's decisions are more like the first cut by a law clerk. Then get it on up to the appellate level where you have five good minds and lots of law clerks. Because the whole idea is to get this right. What happens here is going to be here for a long time.

DANIEL HURLBUTT There was a decision I'd made dealing with wilderness water rights that was appealed to the Idaho Supreme Court. Initially it was affirmed, and later on it was reheard, after an election, and was reversed, and I was disappointed that the United States didn't appeal it. But under the Bush administration, the George W. Bush administration, the determination was made not to appeal it.

It was essentially about the nature and extent of the rights the U.S. could claim, and whether they could claim water for wilderness purposes under the Wilderness Act, where supposedly the land is supposed to be retained in a primitive and pristine fashion, and I ruled that they could, and that would preclude further appropriations by any non U.S. claimants in the area, and it was fought vigorously, and I was initially affirmed by the Idaho Supreme Court, and then overturned by the Idaho Supreme Court.

Actually, that generated some law review articles about the independence of the judiciary and elections, because that was a time frame when Justice Silak was defeated by Justice Eismann, and one of the issues was water, and U.S. claims to the rights to use water, and it was then the new court with Justice Eismann that reversed course and overruled me on that issue.

Hurlbutt departs the bench

After 11 years presiding over the adjudication, Daniel Hurlbutt resigned from the case and from the bench in December 1998.

DANIEL HURLBUTT I was at a point in my career that I'd been on the bench a total of about 20 years, and determined that it was time to move into a new direction.

I thought my goal in setting up the court administration of the case was to set it up in a plan that would work, would move through, and that if I dropped dead the next day, any other district judge in the state of Idaho could move in and pick up the case and move it through. It wasn't my case. It was an Idaho court case, and I think it's proved that it has moved through. There have been some very capable judges, and I think the essence of what was set up by the court, and with the assistance and cooperation of the parties has worked out extremely well.

. . . I watched, and, you know, read Supreme Court decisions that came down on water law issues. You know, I think everybody's worked hard to make it work. I think the process has evolved into -- once you get beyond the test basins and all those initial issues and fears and concerns, I think there's a sense that there's a much more cooperative process with the Department of Water Resources and claimants, and it's limited both the tension and the litigation in the matter.

It was nice to participate in a process that dealt with one of our more precious natural resources, and that needed to be dealt with, both in terms of protecting the resource, and in terms of its impact on the environment, although environmental issues were not directly impacted or addressed in adjudication. And it encompassed every type of use and user, and so, you know, there were a lot of meetings where you felt like you were at the UN, because you had the federal government, state government, private users, municipal users, and four Native American Indian tribes who were separate, sovereign nations.

That was both unusual, and it was gratifying to work with all those people, and I felt a real responsibility to the people who were water users to try to get a handle on this case and put it in a position where it would be accomplished and finalized, as many western, if not most western adjudications, never have been able to do.

. . . I'm very gratified to see it's going to be finalized. I always felt, and people laughed at me and said, Oh, you've got a job for life. And I said, No, I felt it was my job to get out of a job and get this case done.

DAVID TUTHILL In my experience, Judge Hurlbutt was tough in many ways – and sometimes tough to deal with – but one capability he brought to the SRBA was use of technology, including the Court's own website . . .

It's very much cutting-edge. He brought the whole organization of the court, the courthouse. The rules that he developed were excellent. So, in overall analysis, I think he was a very important part of this whole adjudication.

The special masters

This chapter is from a joint interview of the three special masters about managing the nuts and bolts of processing subcases – the actual water right claims – over the last 20 years.

THEODORE BOOTH Certainly learning how to deal with pro se litigants – I don't mean this in any demeaning way – is a little bit challenging because you're sort of walking a little bit of a fine line between helping them, but maybe you don't want to – I mean, there's a little bit of hand holding that goes along with a pro se litigant, but you certainly don't want to have an appearance that you're treating anybody unfairly or giving them a leg up because you might be explaining how something works.

I certainly do like to take the time to explain how things work in a particular case with respect to a pro se litigant, of course, on the record so there are no surprises. That's one thing pro se litigants will try to do is contact you ex parte and you'll have to explain to them, no, if we're going to have this conversation, we need to have it on the record.

BRIGETTE BILYEU I do remember when I first came here that it seemed overwhelming to me the number of cases that we had. We were very early in the process of figuring out how to function, how to manage, how to finish or begin even the subcases in the test basins.

I had Basin 34 and I remember that just looking at the number, the sheer number of litigants, the sheer number of objections and the sheer number of subcases, which I couldn't even tell you how many subcases we had in Basin 34 now, but it was hundreds, hundreds and hundreds, maybe thousands. I don't know. I would have to go back and look.

But I remember talking to Judge Hurlbutt about it and being very, I guess, stressed out about how were we going to do all of this. His words of advice I've always tried to operate by. He said to think of it like football. You can't think of the whole football game at once. You just have to block and tackle one thing at a time. You know how to litigate. You know how to go through the cases and do what Special Master Booth was talking about, you know, go through the process, go through the litigation, get things set. The ones that don't settle go to trial one case at a time, one piece at a time, and you'll get them done. That was great advice. To me that was, at the time anyway, the biggest challenge. When I look at it at the other end, you know, we're almost ready to do the final unified decree. I think truly that was the biggest challenge was just the sheer number of cases.

TERRENCE DOLAN It became clear to me, at least from the very early stages, that a case like this does not work like a normal civil case. We had a lot of people who wanted to represent themselves. All along we got the impression IDWR and legislators were encouraging us to work better with pro se litigants, to encourage them to represent themselves. We didn't want everybody to have to hire a lawyer, and there aren't enough lawyers in the state to handle a case like this.

So trying to meld a civil case with a case that's actually going to get the work done, to hear the people, what their claims are and not force them to hire a lawyer and trying to meld that together was tough. Another problem early on, it was a mighty struggle between contacting IDWR and the position that the court first took that we cannot contact IDWR; they are a party to the lawsuit, end of story. When we could finally work together with IDWR, they were taken out as a party, the light bulb went on and all of a sudden the case got much, much easier. It works, and it still works today.

THEODORE BOOTH I think that sort of three special masters, you know, having access to each other for purposes of settlement moderators was really a good benefit to the parties, too, because we're all on the state's payroll. So when you show up to a settlement conference and sit there all day, it's not costing the parties. They're not paying for a high dollar lawyer to sit there; not that they couldn't have done it equally or a better job, but it certainly saves a lot of expense. So I think that's something that's worked out real well.

BRIGETTE BILYEU At the beginning in the SRBA, we did not have a formal settlement conference type of process. The thought at that point was these are all, you know, big boy, big girl lawyers that know how to settle a case if they want to. They're litigators and that certainly was true. But you find in the beginning, well, for one thing you have additional governmental parties, including the state and the federal government in its different capacities.

We found after a while that the parties really wanted a way to have a settlement procedure without seeming to be weak. Gee, Your honor – we really think you need to order us to come in to court. So it really, I believe, came as a suggestion from the parties and the attorneys that were involved in the early days of the SRBA that we began to have the formal settlement conferences.

In fact, for a while I believe they were mandatory in every sub-case that didn't settle at what became the initial hearings. We didn't even call them that in the beginning days. So it was really something that evolved.

Just like we did in the sub-case process and everything else, we learned along the way, the department learned along the way, and we tried new things. We kicked the tires. If they weren't quite inflated right, we tried to fix that. That was one of the things I was going to say that I have felt like has been one of the most important parts of having successful settlement conferences is the involvement of the department.

In fact, the first thing I ever do, I'll come into the room and say, okay, department, explain to me why and what you recommended. Just start us out. Explain what you recommended for the director's report. I did that because, number one, probably half the time even though I might have had some idea of why or what, I really probably didn't know what the department really had in the back of its mind as to why it recommended it. So that was the first reason.

The second reason was to get the parties focused on what was going to be the thing that got prima facie weight. It was really important for them to understand we always start with the director's report. So the fact that they would explain that, and Carter Fritschle and whoever the agents were would draw something up on the board and explain visually where we started. Then the parties would come and talk about that and about what they saw as the necessary changes from that. So that was really important to start out the tone of the settlement conferences. In addition, the department, especially once it became a non-party, was kind of an additional facilitator in the settlement conferences as a neutral individual. Even though they came up with the director's report, it wasn't their land and it wasn't their dispute and they weren't mad at anybody, so I have felt like the neutral arbitrator that the special masters have provided and that the department has provided have been the things that have been key to the success.

TERRENCE DOLAN Early on IDWR, as an independent expert to the court, was involved in the subcases for settlement purposes in some cases before we even saw the case or before we got a director's report. We learned that IDWR massaged the issues with the claimants explaining to them what the issues were and trying to get them focused on what we're talking about. By the time the cases got to us, most of the work had already been done.

One particular basin I'm thinking about. Nicholas Spencer, a former attorney with IDWR, and Steve Clelland, a senior water right specialist with ISWR, did a wonderful job mediating water right disputes in the town of Rockland. They spent hours down there talking with nearly the whole town. I don't know what the county population is, but I think they talked with everybody in the county trying to work out the water rights because they had been swapping their water rights without talking to IDWR and without talking with some of their neighbors. For instance, a water right might be transferred from one bank of the creek to another bank, but nobody told anybody else about it.

So the mediation that Nick Spencer and Steve Clelland did just trying to get the facts straight went probably 85 percent of the way toward settling those cases. In the end we had very few contested cases come out of that basin thanks to Nick and Steve.

THEODORE BOOTH A lot of that heavy lifting, like Terry said, that heavy lifting in the settlements was by the department either before or at the initial hearing. The initial hearings are really simple for the special master because you leave the room and let the parties meet with the department and try to work something out. Then you come in, and they put on the record, you know wherever they are and what happens next. So that heavy lifting of settlement really happened by the deputy attorneys general and agents of the department.

TERRENCE DOLAN At a recent water users conference, the three special masters spoke. One of the things I said in there was about taking IDWR out as a party. In my mind, when I saw that happen, I didn't think it would happen, frankly, because it was so hotly contested. Judge Hurlbutt entered his order prohibiting contact between IDWR and the court in 1994, and the legislation you talked about was passed December 7th of '94. In the end, once we finally figured out what it really meant, I think most of us just said "amen."

Now we can work with IDWR and communicate back and forth because there's so much we have to know informally, for instance, with just a phone call. That's all we need to find out about how to contact a claimant, something simple like that. Before we couldn't do it. Now we could with that new legislation. In my mind, that was the best thing the legislature did.

BRIGETTE BILYEU I think it has been a good change. I know it was something that was thought about by Judge Hurlbutt and his staff attorney even before the SRBA process and before the first hearings began because I remember asking them during the interview process when I was interviewing for the job. They explained kind of how they saw the process working. I remember sitting there scratching my head, because I was a litigator and I didn't understand what the role of the department was, and I said, "Well, is the department a party or is the department a nonparty?" They both looked at each other, scratched their heads and laughed and said, "Well, that's the $20 million question."

So I guess I have a little bit different feel for it at this point. I think the tenor of the court was just in those days to get the thing going. If the department were a party, certain rules applied; for example, ex parte communication. If they were not a party, certain other consequences would happen; such as, they couldn't cross-examine witnesses and they couldn't file responses and they couldn't file objections.

So I think it was controversial at the time, but I think some people mistook the court's reaction to it because the court was, even before the first hearings, was really scratching its head trying to understand how that would work. Even though the court, I'm talking about Judge Hurlbutt in particular, had extensive experience in criminal law and so was very experienced with cases where you had non-parties who were critical to the process, such as the investigating officers in a criminal case, I mean, he was very used to that.

But the statute, as written in the beginning, had placed IDWR as a party. I think there were concerns when the legislature changed that process. There were concerns about how responses would be done because the department in the very beginning years filed responses in every single sub-case.

I know there was a question that came up in the initial litigation that happened right after the legislative change in 1994. What happens if you're sitting out there, you're a neighbor, and you like the way the director's report is written. The guy who has the water right has objected to the director's report in the way his water right is recommended, what do I do? Judge Hurlbutt, after this had kind of all settled down, made a rule saying here is what has to happen. If you agree with the director's report and you want to become a party to the sub-case, you must file a response.

So I guess my take on it is a little bit or my memory is a little bit different. I think the court was trying to get a process that worked all along and was just trying to figure out how that would work. But, yes, ultimately I thought it was a very good change.

THEODORE BOOTH Two things: One is I'm fairly certain that if the legislature had not removed IDWR as a party, we would not be sitting here having this sort of wrap-up interview in 2014. It would probably be pushed off a few more years. I think it tended to expedite and make the process more efficient to have that.

Then I guess the other comment I would make is if you listed the pros and cons, so to speak, there's a lot of things in the pro column of not having the department as a party, but there were some peculiarities. For example, there were some subcases that were – and I can think of one right off the top of my head. They were one-party subcases, but they involved an issue that I think the state of Idaho proper was interested in. Well, so now you had this situation where the department couldn't come in and make those arguments.

So the state came into those subcases and made those arguments, and I think that's proper and right for that to happen. But, obviously, that's not without controversy and it's not without, you know, it's subject to the argument of, well, hey, how can you remove a subdivision of the state of Idaho as a party, but the state gets to pick and choose when it's going to come in and involve itself in an issue?

The one case that I'm thinking of is the claimant was Tlucek. Scott Campbell represented the claimant and it was a one-party sub-case. There was some groundwater rights where the license did not have – it just had the cubic feet per second that you could pump out of the ground. It did not have the acre-feet per year volumetric limitation.

When the director's report came out, it took the cubic feet per second rate from the license, but then also added a volumetric limitation. I can't remember if it was 4 acre-feet per acre, whatever the number was. Of course, the claimant, through the attorney Scott Campbell, objected to that saying, hey, the license didn't have this volumetric annual limitation; therefore, the partial decree in the SRBA can't have that.

That was one of those cases where the state saw that and said, you know what – I think it was one of those cases where the state came in and said, well, wait a minute, this issue has broader implications for other water rights. So I think that's one of the ones they got involved in.

That sort of goes along with the whole rule about the summary judgment in one-party subcases because that issue seems to be a legal issue. The facts weren't in dispute, but how do you come in in a one-party sub-case? The Supreme Court made a ruling in one of those cases that talked about summary judgment in one-party subcases. So it was a little bit challenging on how to handle those.

TERRENCE DOLAN When IDWR was taken out as a party, one of the side benefits was identified by the water bar and they did a wonderful job because now that IDWR was an independent expert to the court, they could require IDWR to file 706 reports before hearings. Those reports, frankly, made all of our subcases where they filed them much easier because everybody knew the basis for IDWR's recommendation. They knew exactly why IDWR recommended what they recommended and what the resolution could be. The 706 reports were incredibly helpful to me, and I think to all of the parties.

THEODORE BOOTH Well, I'll tell you about three cases that are kind of memorable to me. There are others, but one was called the Janicek sub-case. It did not go to trial, but it did go to summary judgment. Janicek Properties was the claimant, and the Nampa-Meridian Irrigation District was an objector. It had to do with the diversion of water out of, I believe, one of the drains of the Nampa-Meridian Irrigation District. There were two things that made that case memorable. One is the quality of the lawyers in the case. Mike Creamer represented Mr. Janicek; Bryce Farris for the Nampa-Meridian Irrigation District.

I believe Dave Gehlert on behalf of the United States Bureau of Reclamation was involved. So the quality of the work that was presented was very high. And then the other thing that was interesting about it is I got to learn a lot of history about the development of the irrigation canal systems and water projects in the Boise area, which I, frankly, knew very little about. There was just a lot of historical context which, frankly, comes up in a lot of the cases, which is what makes a lot of them very interesting, just the history that's involved. So, anyway, that was the Janicek case.

Another one that was fun was the Monarch Greenback case, which was a claim by a gold mine somewhere in the headwaters of the Boise River system. That one also was resolved on summary judgment. One of the things that made that interesting was, I believe, the water right was recommended disallowed due to forfeiture because there had been this long period of time when the mine hadn't been in operation, and then the new owners were going to fire it back up. It was about right during the middle of those cases that the legislature passed a new exception to forfeiture having to do with mining operations and not mining because of the price of the mineral and whatever is too low as an exception to forfeiture.

Dana Hofstetter was representing the mine, and that new statute came out of the legislature. I remember thinking, man, I didn't know Dana Hofstetter had that much horsepower, or her client, with the legislature. We had a hearing on the thing, and she said, I had nothing to do with this.

It was coincidental in that particular sub-case, but, nevertheless, there was all of a sudden this brand new law that became relevant. So that was pretty interesting to have a change in the law right in the middle of those subcases.

Then the other case that I'll mention, again, it was a case that Dana Hofstetter was involved in, I think we referred to it as Terteling vs. Edwards.

Charlie Honsinger represented the Terteling Company. The Edwards Family LLC was represented by Dana Hofstetter. The thing that was really interesting to me about that sub-case – and that one did go to trial, or those subcases did go to trial – is that the water rights at issue were the same water rights that went up to the Idaho Supreme Court in the *Silkey vs. Tiegs* decision, which is kind of one of those seminal decisions that you hear about and everybody reads with respect to Idaho water law. I think that case was back in the '30s, and here you are in 2010 again dealing with the same subcases and same water rights, same hot water. In that case it's hot water wells that service some greenhouses and some other hot water geothermal water uses.

TERRENCE DOLAN One of my very first subcases was a claim to 31 acres irrigated land. When the facts started coming out, we found out he had land but no dirt. The state had bought all of his surface soil down to the rock to build an overpass not too far from his farm. So the question was, what are you going to do with the water? He didn't have a very good answer. I finally recommended that it be limited to just small plots around trailers that he was trying to sell sites for.

One of the things that we've had the pleasure of doing, I have at least, is going out on field trips, both to the courthouses where we hold the hearings in Salmon, Challis, Albion, Rockland, some really odd places, but also field inspections as part of the trial process where the court and sometimes the reporters will go out with us with a tape recorder. We'll actually walk the ditches and try to find out, does the ditch go left or right here?

One in Salmon was particularly interesting, but we got a chance to tour a junkyard area and basically found out this ditch didn't exist any more, but everybody knew differently from their own personal knowledge. It turns out that they were wrong.

BRIGETTE BILYEU I don't think there's a single water lawyer that I just don't have a huge amount of respect for, including the people with the department: Nick Spencer, Chris Bromley. Candice McHugh and Andrea Courtney were two that I worked with extensively and are just phenomenal lawyers and people. Lee

Leininger and Larry Brown with the Department of Justice. You know, Kent Foster, Kent Fletcher, Jerry Rigby, Chris Meyer, Rob Harris, I mean, they are all just terrific. They've got great backgrounds. They work hard. They're prepared when they come to court. I know they're all juggling a million things, but they manage to get it done and they manage to do it well and they manage to do it quickly.

TERRENCE DOLAN We haven't mentioned the judges involved in some of the old water cases and their use of plain common sense. They are so wonderful when you read how they handled them. Their concern early on, of course, was preserving the peace in a lot of cases.

But the one decision in the Lemhi River Valley out of the town of Salmon where I followed the precedent, it was just a wonderfully well written decision back in the 1970's. Then you look at some of the even older cases going back before the turn of the century when they were decided by the federal court out of Utah, they did some wonderful work. We've got to hand it to them. They got things so right back then, with few exceptions.

THEODORE BOOTH It was just a real good way to force yourself every month to sit down and, you know, fortunately the department did the heavy lifting on the preparation of it, but it was just – the way I looked at it was it was just another tool in the toolbox to make sure all of your subcases were moving. There was an event on the horizon in each one. Nothing fell between the cracks. It seems like a lot of times you would have those lingering cases that every month, you know, well, nothing to report here, still working on it. There was, for instance, those federal reserve water right claims in the old Fort Boise and there was a bunch of governmental agencies, federal governmental agencies that had federal reserve water right claims. Special Master Dolan acted as settlement moderator and the parties came to an agreement to the extent they could, but because it was federal government, they had to go up the ladder to the Pentagon and wherever else and then back down. It was just every month that was still on there. That was kind of humorous, if nothing else, but, yeah, it was just a good tool to make sure you kept everything on track.

THEODORE BOOTH As special master, I wasn't assigned any cases that were basin-wide significant. Typically, those were handled by the presiding judge. I think the one that I was the closest to, and that was as a law clerk for Judge Wood, was the Basin-Wide Issue 5 regarding the conjunctive management or conjunctive administration language that ultimately shows up as a general provision in all of these basins. That was a very interesting process. Frankly, I don't know how you would have structured that issue absent that basin-wide process and had it so everybody could get involved. So, you know, in my perspective that worked out really well.

TERRENCE DOLAN When basin-wide issues came up in the abstract, they fell flat because they didn't have facts. They didn't have specific parties. They didn't have identifiable, fundamental issues that could be addressed, you know, the meat and potatoes. Early on, because basin-wide issues were stayed in the abstract, they floated around. So when a decision came down, many said that doesn't fit my case because my facts are slightly different. Basin-wide issues work well when they come out of very specific subcases where this party is claiming this and that party is claiming that. That then gives notice to everybody, and then I think everybody benefits. The parties involved are bound by it because it was their sub-case.

TERRENCE DOLAN One of the mistakes we made early on was trying to divide subcases into class one, class two. Class one, I think, were the simple ones that were going to be wrapped up in short order. Class two were the ones that were going to be fully litigated. They'll take days and days of trial. We found, if anything, it was just the opposite. Those "simple" claims, the stockwater claims, for instance, turned out to be hugely contested. They took way more work than some of the ones we thought would be really difficult.

As Special Master Bilyeu was saying, we invented the wagon here, refined it as we were going along. If it worked, fine. If it didn't work, we went on to something else. We don't do class one, class two any more.

The de minimis exemption for filing, I don't know if it's going to be useful except for the purpose of getting us a final unified decree. Some states where they require adjudication of every stock pond or every domestic well, they've turned out to be disastrous because they can take over 60 years and they're still working on them.

How did the masters maintain consistency between their decisions?

THEODORE BOOTH We didn't even try to do that. The cases that came before you were independent subcases. I didn't go consult with – now that being said, if there was a case that went up to the presiding judge on challenge, then it's law of the case and you follow that precedent. That being said, if I have a case that one of the other special masters had worked on a similar issue and it did not go up on challenge, a lot of times the parties would point that out to you, and they would say, well, Special Master Dolan had this same situation and here is how he ruled on it.

As far as I know, I'm not bound by what Special Master Dolan ruled on a sub-case, but certainly if a party points out the opinion in a sub-case, whatever it is, I get his opinion out and read it. The more research and the more you can learn, the better, the higher quality your decision is going to be, in my opinion. So I think just the natural process did lead to consistency, but it's not something we had a particular process to get to.

BRIGETTE BILYEU I think the process was set up initially that it was envisioned that there would be three special masters. They would each come to their own conclusions of law. I think originally it was thought that we would come up with – we would have some, you know, for example, forfeiture. The three of us would maybe have a case on forfeiture, and it would go up to the presiding judge so he would get the benefit of our thinking, which in a lot of ways, I think, benefits a presiding judge if the thinking is different just to look at different lines of reasoning.

I don't think it's played out quite that way, but certainly we have never tried to copy each other, except sometimes, you know, Ted will copy the same shirt I have on. But other than that, we have tried to be pretty independent and still be mindful that the process that we come up with at least should be consistent enough that the parties are familiar with how the courtroom works. It should work the same way consistently between the three of us. We've tried to do that, but we've tried to be independent.

TERRENCE DOLAN Early on Judge Hurlbutt cautioned us that he viewed the three special masters as divisions of the court and each division is entitled to its own opinion. Then Judge Hurlbutt would make the final determination, much like a federal and state court structure.

Early on we had subcases involving fish hatcheries and facility volume. The exact same issue came in front of me and then in front of Special Master Bilyeu and then in front of Special Master Haemmerle. The same issues, the same testimony, the same people from IDWR came up and gave testimony. It turns out we all recommended the claims the same way. We came to the same conclusions. Since then I think IDWR has helped us shape our own subcases so there is more consistency in their recommendations.

THEODORE BOOTH What really comes to my mind was particularly when Dave Tuthill was director of the department and there was a big push. Director Tuthill was really pushing the agents. They had a lot of agents on staff to really get – back in I think '04, '05, I mean in that area, maybe I'm wrong on the years, but really get all the director's reports done and get them filed with the court. Frankly, at one point in time there were so many director's reports being filed that the court had to sort of modify and stagger some of the objection periods and so forth to accommodate that.

I guess in my mind the biggest challenge was really a challenge for the department which was investigating and coming up with all of these director's reports for all of these claims and that time commitment that had to happen to get those done and to the court so that they could begin being processed.

BRIGETTE BILYEU The agents are just phenomenal. From the federal government standpoint, we talk about him a lot, he's just an extroverted character, but Fred Price has found more mistakes in the SRBA and has probably done a job for the whole citizenship of Idaho in reducing at least, I mean, he's not responsible for finding all the mistakes just on his end for the federal government.

I think it was Basin 29, he went to an initial hearing. We were in a break and he said, "Brigette, I think there was a mistake in the way they calculated that man's cattle and the number of the cfs that he should have." And I'm like, "Really?" And he goes, "Yeah." He could just do those things in his head. So we went back on the record and I checked with the department, and sure enough, he needed more water based on that. He's another example of some people behind the scenes helping the public. We certainly know who they are and what a great job they've done, and Fred Price is one that I would mention.

TERRENCE DOLAN I remember one of the legislators, Mack Neibaur in Rupert, saying the SRBA could take more than ten years, but he was still committed to it. Judge Hurlbutt and several of us with the SRBA went over there and presented to him the very first SRBA partial decree and it was framed.

Unfortunately, Mr. Neibaur passed away a number of years ago so he didn't get to see completion of this. He said a number of times he couldn't believe it took as long as it has, but I think we consistently had his support.

BRIGETTE BILYEU Fritz Haemmerle was the special master in 1995. So he started here, and we had already been here, Terry and I, for a while so we had our black judges robes, and we looked very efficient and cool in our robes. That really irritated Special Master Haemmerle because he didn't have a robe yet.

He kept pestering Diana Delaney, our court administrator, and Judge Hurlbutt, "I want my robe." So they ordered it for him. He was just very insistent, "I want my robe." So they thought this was very funny. They got quite a chuckle out of it. It took a while for the robe to be made and manufactured because he's tall and they had to special order it. So when it came in, we all thought he had been making such a big deal out of it that we thought it would be fun to kind of prank him a little bit. His clerk at the time was Debbie Lash. She had a really dusty looking, old, ratty, pink robe, a bathrobe at home. So when the box came in, we asked Judge Hurlbutt, we said, "Would you play along with us?" He and Fritz Haemmerle had been close friends because, as I said earlier, Fritz had been Judge Hurlbutt's law clerk right out of law school. So he said, "Oh, I'm all in."

So when the box came in, we took out the black robe, put in Debbie's pink bathrobe, boxed it up again, and told him that we had a special robing ceremony, which we totally made up. We had never had a robing ceremony for special masters. We still don't.

So we brought everybody in. We said, "Fritz, at 2:00 is your robing ceremony." We came into the courtroom. Judge Hurlbutt sat at his chair with the microphone on, and we weren't recording it, of course, but Fritz didn't know that. He said, "Fritz, we would like to present you, this is a very honorable occasion, raise your right hand, and promise to be a good special master." "I do. I do." "You may now open your robe."

So we gave him the box. He opened the robe, and he just busted up. He stood up, this big six foot three, one of the best athletes you will ever know in your life. He's in his suit, and he put that pink bathrobe on. It went clear up to here above the elbows on him because he was so tall and Debbie was not nearly that tall. He paraded it around. He was an amazingly good sport about it.

Whenever I see a pink bathrobe in the store, I start to laugh and people wonder why.

BRIGETTE BILYEU I don't remember the name of the witness, but he was a terrific guy. He was an expert from either the BLM – I think it was the Forest Service. I think he was a Forest Service expert. So he was in that chair, not the one that the water bar bought but the predecessor chair right there in the witness box. I was sitting in the judge's chair there. My clerk at the time was Teri Hranac, and the attorney that was cross-examining the witness was John Lezamiz.

If you know John Lezamiz at all, he is extremely confident. He is extremely experienced, and he is extremely – would loud be the best word for it? Animated. He was extremely animated. So he asked for permission to go over here and ask the witness a question, and it was something very near and dear to his client's heart. He said, "Isn't it true, and isn't it true, Mr. So and So? Isn't it true?" He's pointing and stomping probably, which I should have probably controlled, but I'm very busy. I'm serious, I'm trying to take notes.

This is the lesson I learned from this.

I'm writing like mad, right, because we didn't really have a process at the time. We pretty much took notes. We didn't go back to the court reporter and have the thing printed up. We took our own notes. I'm busy taking notes. My clerk is poking me really hard. I look up and I look over at the witness. The chair, while this cross-examination has gone on – it wasn't Mr. Lezamiz's fault – but the chair has spiraled clear down so the witness is sitting like practically on the ground. So I took a time out, and we took a recess and fixed the chair.

From then on I tried to pay a little more attention to not just what they were saying, but what they were actually doing so I didn't have anybody pass out or fall on the floor again.

Norming the change 1999-2006

DAVID TUTHILL With any major project or major effort there are four phases: Forming, storming, norming, and performing.

That's what has enabled the adjudication of more than 158,000 water rights.

. . . There had to be those first three phases before we could really perform. Since 1995, the state has been focusing on really resolving the problems, issuing proper recommendations and proper partial decrees on a not very contentious basis in most cases. There have been exceptions, but that was the norm. It was remarkable to me that in most basins we had no more than two or three trials before the special masters resulting from maybe 1,000 or 2,000 recommendations.

The process for dispute resolution was so effective that the special master really didn't have to decide on many. The special masters sat in as participants in more than that, but the actual trials boiled down to very few.

. . . One reason that there wasn't more conflict is the adjudication did take into account in some cases historic practice. One example is in the Boise basin.

In the Boise basin court order – not a decree – a court order established that once the senior water rights were not all satisfied, instead of curtailing the junior right, the senior rights would back off to 75 percent of the full amount.

And once that 25 percent reduction was not sufficient, then the water rights would back off to 60 percent. So there would be a 40 percent reduction. This is the only basin, to my knowledge, in the west where this occurs. So the anticipation was that there would be a giant battle on this issue, which is – and this has been the way delivery has occurred for more than 80 years in the Boise basin for major water rights. So this is the backbone of delivery in the Boise basin.

The Agency looked at this historic practice and decided to acknowledge it and continue it even though it had not been formally decreed. The expectation was that somebody would challenge it – nobody did.

So we developed a condition – we spent a lot of time developing a condition that reflected what had been done historically. This condition of approval was put on these old decreed water rights, and it wasn't challenged. So that unusual historic practice was perpetuated.

We had a similar historic practice on rotation in the Lost River basin – and that was an area of great contention early on – but the department reflected in its recommendation the historic practice of a certain type of rotation because it had been done for many years, and that survived and wasn't challenged, either.

CARTER FRITSCHLE The most successful approach for me was to learn as much background as possible for each sub-case (water right). My preference was to conduct an on the ground field examination of the water system in order to understand how it all worked. But of course as the SRBA progressed, in office exams became much more common, and the field exam was often replaced with historical research and extensive use of aerial photography to try to establish the facts behind the development of the water use. I frequently would create a timeline for the information discovered through the research, and by establishing a chronological path for the development of the water right or rights for a particular place of use; I could usually have some understanding as well as appreciation of the history and work that went into the development of the water system.

One of the other 5th District judges, Barry Wood, was asked by the Supreme Court to step in to manage the SRBA, at first on just an interim basis.

The 2nd judge, Barry Wood

BARRY WOOD I grew up on a farm, well familiar with gravity irrigation – this was pre-sprinkler irrigation, everything was gravity. And had some legal work for some irrigation districts.

I did have some experience with irrigation districts filing objections to claims of appropriation that would arguably affect the district's water rights – the people filing claims in the Owyhee River system.

I became administrative district judge. Then Judge Hurlbutt sent his notice in 1998 that he was going to retire at the end of the year.

Linda Trout was the chief justice, and she called me up to organize a meeting. We held it in Dan Hurlbutt's old chambers in the courthouse – it was Burdick's chambers. And Bill Hart was in Hailey, got hold of him by telephone, and he wouldn't come down.

And basically she tried to get one of us to take it. Nobody would do it. Nobody wanted anything to do with it, me included.

Then it worked around, long story short, because I was the administrative district judge of the district, to go down and start filling in, to basically keep everything moving - sign the partial decrees, do whatever was necessary to keep the thing going. And then it just got bigger and bigger. In fact the original order as I recall was express on its face, intentionally so, it was an interim - you'd like to look at the exact language, but it wasn't an appointment to the SRBA, it was acting and interim while we find a replacement type deal.

And then I do remember that, it must have been February of 1999, Representative Bruce Newcomb, who was the speaker, called me and visited a little bit, and desired to get me to do it. I told Newcomb I wouldn't do it unless the legislature restored the funding for the staff attorney that had been stripped out when Carolyn Minder had that position. I said I just won't do it unless I'm provided some help. So right at the end of that session that money got appropriated and we had the ability to hire a staff attorney. I put together a team, a panel of Bill Hart, Roger Burdick and myself and we interviewed the applicants and we chose Eric Wildman. That's how Eric became the staff attorney, and he served under me and Burdick and Melanson and then Eric took my [judge] position.

Once I got in there, it's really fabulous work. It's hard work, but if you have any bent for history, any interest in history, I found it just fascinating. Plus its important work, satisfying despite all the challenges.

DAVID TUTHILL Judge Wood was exceptional in that he took a job that was not wanted by anybody else. When Judge Hurlbutt left – Judge Hurlbutt had lost a couple of decisions before the Idaho Supreme Court. The job as SRBA Court judge was seen as a tough and pretty much thankless job.

Judge Wood was willing to step up. He brought a staff attorney by the name of Eric Wildman, and between those two they did a wonderful job.

So he was courageous. I think he was a very courteous and thoughtful judge. He was the right man for the hour, and it was a real disappointment when his brother-in-law, Judge Eismann, became a supreme court justice so he had to step down. I was really saddened by that because he had done a wonderful job.

THEODORE BOOTH I had an opportunity to come up and clerk or intern with Judge Barry Wood in Gooding for the summer. I came up for a couple of months and did that. He was not, at that point, assigned to the SRBA, but he was, rather, the district judge for Gooding, Lincoln, and Jerome Counties. Judge Wildman had previously been a clerk, and I was friends with Judge Wildman from way back. He had sort of arranged that, or gave me the contact to make that internship happen. Anyway, that was a very enjoyable and educational summer with Judge Wood. At the end of it, he essentially said when you're done with law school, if you want to come back up and clerk for me, I can get you a job as a law clerk. I was like, oh, that's cool. So I took him up on that. After I graduated, I moved up to – I graduated in 1999 and moved up here in June of '99. In the meantime, the Supreme Court had assigned Judge Wood to the SRBA. So I sort of got the job before I knew it was with the SRBA. I came up and clerked for Judge Wood for about, I guess it was about a year and a half, until the Supreme Court removed him from the case, I think, in 2001.

So, anyway, then Judge Wood left. The Supreme Court then appointed Judge Burdick. I stuck around with Judge Burdick as a clerk for him for about, I think, six months or so, and then went into private practice in Gooding.

So I had that experience here as a law clerk for about two years. Then a few years later, I think in 2004 or 2005, I can't remember which, Special Master Cushman retired, a vacancy came open, and I applied for that position. I think part of why I successfully got that job was because of my experience as a law clerk here.

KARL DREHER I was never told this, but I always suspected that we [the department] were getting good reports, from the outgoing judge to the incoming judge. And, of course the other thing that played into this that I focused on was the involvement of legislators, not that they were involved in the adjudication, but they had to fund it.

During this period, the Department of Water Resources was moving more definitively on a two-track approach, splitting apart the mass of smaller and generally simpler claims from the larger and more complex – the latter often involving irrigation and other large-scale uses.

DAVID TUTHILL For the most part, the upside of recommending the small domestic and stockwater rights in one series of Director's Reports followed by reports of irrigation and other water rights is we knew how to adjudicate the smaller water rights. There were still quite a few questions on the larger ones. So we did what we knew how to do so we could tally up and make forward movement and adjudicate actually most of the water rights before we had to do the more difficult ones. So that was a major decision that I think paid off.

We had a major celebration when we got to the watershed point, the halfway point, and celebrated that achievement.

One of the aspects, from my view of adjudication, is it's a long tough process, and we had to celebrate achievements as we went with the eye on the ultimate goal, but the ultimate goal was years out, and it was a lot of tough work. So we had some satisfaction in celebrating achievements along the way – and completing all those domestics was an achievement.

Then as we went through basin by basin recommending the larger water rights, we had a more bite-sized chunk and could achieve that reasonably.

It became clear in the early years that to try to require that all of the domestic rights would be filed would be very burdensome, whereas to allow the domestic – the small domestic and stock to be optionally filed would be much more achievable and realistic.

So a change was made partway through the adjudication to move from requiring all the rights to allowing only those where people wanted to file could file.

In various basins we estimate that maybe half of the potential domestic and stockwater rights could be filed.

. . . the reason that this decision was made is that in most basins it's very unrealistic to expect delivery to individual domestic and stock; and the reason for adjudication is not so much for those small ones, but rather for delivery to the larger water rights – irrigation, and commercial, and municipal, and others – hydropower. So the benefit for requiring all those little domestic de minimis rights to be filed would be very small. The cost would be high because if it's not optional, then to require people to file those – it would take a lot of effort. So the cost benefit was very much in favor of not requiring those.

Over the years we have found that if people want to file, there are other ways where they can file, but throughout Idaho there really isn't any significant delivery of those small rights.

There might be a couple of tiny exceptions on springs, but for the most part, there's almost no delivery of the small water rights.

DAVID TUTHILL So we had a prioritized system of investigation where we spent much more time on those rights that hadn't yet been determined than we did on the smaller ones or the ones that had been determined.

I would say 10 to 20 percent of the claims required significant additional work where we spent our staff time.

BARRY WOOD The first to leave [after Hurlbutt's departure] was Fritz, and Tom Cushman took his place. And then when Tom Cushman left, Melanson was there then, and Ted Booth was hired. But I worked with Ted Booth as a law clerk. ...

They were all professional. The biggest problem in that has nothing to do with the special masters, it was the notion that some of these cases got resolved without a really truly adversarial process. I have always thought in my mind one of the two failures of the

SRBA was that there should have been - these are my words - a water prosecutor, there should have been a person hired by the state, but independent, basically an independent counsel who would serve as a prosecutor if you will, a devil's advocate on every water right, so you couldn't get friendly agreements or whatever, friendly settlements – and I'm not implying there's anything untoward. But just as a checks and balances, because water is so important, it would have been money well spent. And I think the Department of Water Resources would have been better served by having somebody who was questioning every water right outside the investigatory process. So a lot of times there have been awkward situations in the SRBA about who's the lawyer for who, and who is the attorney general really representing, are they representing the Department of Water Resources, are they representing Fish & Game – are they representing the state of Idaho generally. It's too many hats. ...

A number of legal issues percolating over the last few years were beginning to hit the court. Some of the more significant concerned federal reserved water claims.

Federal reserved water rights

CLIVE STRONG Probably one of the most significant reserved water right issues was the Deer Flat National Wildlife Refuge claims. This is another example of how water issues tend to come back around again.

When we were implementing the the Swan Falls settlement, the United States Fish and Wildlife Service opposed the settlement based upon its concern 3,900 and 5,600 CFS minimum flow at the Murphy Gage was insufficient to protect the migratory birds that used the Deer Flat National Wildlife Refuge.

The refuge consists of islands in the Snake River between Swan Falls Dam and the back waters of Brownlee Reservoir. It also includes Lake Lowell, which is part of the Boise project. But, the real focus here was on the Snake River.

A condition of the Swan Falls settlement was Federal Energy Regulatory Commission approval. I'll use FERC to refer to the agency. FERC was resistant to approving the settlement because of the Fish and Wildlife Service objection.

Ultimately we had to get Congress to pass legislation in 1988 directing FERC to approve the settlement. That became a very hot point of contention between Attorney General Jim Jones and Senator McClure.

CLIVE STRONG As the Deer Flat claims came forward, we could see that if recognized, they would undo the Swan Falls settlement. The claim sought a flow in excess of 17,000 CFS for the purpose of preventing coyotes from swimming to the islands and preying on the geese.

We vigorously opposed the claims. We retained an outside consultant, Hayden Wing, to determine whether in fact coyotes were preying on the geese.

They radio collared various predatory animals in the area, and used airplanes to track them. We discovered that it wasn't a coyote problem, but rather a raccoon problem. The way we discovered this was by placing dummy eggs in nests on the islands, and then using night cameras to photograph animals approaching the nests. We've got pictures of raccoons taking eggs from the nests. We also have pictures of the raccoons swimming the Snake River in flows in excess of 17,000 CFS.

We were really looking forward to trying the case; however, we prevailed on a motion for summary judgment on legal grounds. We argued that the migratory refuge was created as a secondary purpose over the top of the reclamation project. The district court agreed and held that a federal reserved water right can only be created for a primary purpose. And, we were successful in defending the decision before the Idaho Supreme Court.

The Deer Flat claims led ancillary litigation over the ownership of the islands. David Barber was the primary litigator on this case. And he did a marvelous job. He was with me through most of the adjudication. A very talented attorney.

We also were successful in defeating the maintenance flow claims under the Organic Act, and the Multiple Use Sustained Yield Act claims. In fact I wish I could remember the exact number, but well over 10,000 in-stream flow claims were filed.

After a decision by Wood adverse to the tribes and federal interests, federal attorneys sought to disqualify him from the SRBA, pointing out that his family has water rights which could relate to, or be affected by, determinations made on Nez Perce Tribe water rights.

BARRY WOOD When Justice Trout came down to Twin Falls to try to get one of us to take the case, the statement was made by me to her, I can't do it: I have water rights. And my family has water interests although I didn't even realize [some of them] at the time. To this day I've never been to my brother in law's place on the middle fork that became the contentious issue in the Nez Perce deal. I don't even remember the name of the creek, never seen it, didn't even know they owned it. Her comment to me in effect was, we've got water rights at our little farm at Kuna, at the time. And Justice McDevitt had hundreds of acres of water rights under the Boise Irrigation District. Everybodys got water rights; it's no big deal. So nobody ever thought about making any kind of disclosure, and it never even came up until the decision was issued. So I immediately filed this disclosure, I got hold of my brother and my sisters, what does anybody own? The filing process has been followed, as I understand it, ever since. But it never came up until after the fact.

KARL DREHER The situation with Judge Wood was unfortunate. I don't know what else could have happened, once a party made an issue of the fact that he had a claim, I don't think it affected his decisions in any way, but it created the perception that it could. I felt badly for him because I knew he very much wanted to make his contribution to the SRBA, and I think he was making a contribution. But, by then he had this perception problem. ... How far do you carry that? We all use water.

Judge Wood stayed at the SRBA after that challenge. But in May 2000 his brother-in-law, Daniel Eismann, who was then a 4th District judge, was elected to the Idaho Supreme Court – where he would be reviewing Wood's SRBA opinions. Wood relinquished the SRBA, though he stayed on the 5th District bench, and the case was handed to another 5th District judge, Roger Burdick.

DAVID TUTHILL Then we had the wonderful good fortune of having Judge Burdick, now Chief Justice Burdick, join as a judge.

Judge Burdick was quick on his feet. He had great experience. His experience wasn't so much in water rights, but it was in judicial kinds of activities.

He brought a courage to the process. He looked at the job carefully, but was willing to take – again, this thankless job that nobody really applied for, but that he was assigned to – and brought great energy to the position.

Again, he carried on with Eric Wildman as his staff attorney, and that twosome did a wonderful job.

The 3rd judge, Roger Burdick

Burdick had some previous experience in water law.

ROGER BURDICK Yeah. We had just a small ditch issue. We had a raft river – Lloyd Webb represented the canal -- Salmon Falls Dam irrigation folks. So I did some research for them. Bill Hart and I had a small irrigation dispute. So other than that – that was all of my water law experience.

ROGER BURDICK The thing that got me interested in the SRBA is I wanted to be a high school history teacher. I thought the history portion of water law in Idaho was fascinating. And every time I had a chance, irrespective of what job I was in, as a Magistrate or D.J., I went to the water law seminars, just out of interest, for the history. And I didn't realize that I would then become the SRBA Judge.

It fascinated me, number one – the SR – the water law history. I became the Water Law Judge because it was – it had been – it had hurt the careers of two other remarkable judges, Hurlbutt and Wood. They both left with some controversy, unneeded controversy, in my opinion. They were – are both excellent jurists. And I saw that as the wildest pony to ride in town. That's why I took it.

It was the hardest case that I heard of.

ROGER BURDICK I just found it fascinating. And Dan Hurlbutt was a good friend, and I saw some of the issues that he had gone through. And so I was attentive to the cases and read them because of the interest.

[Hurlbutt and Wood] They were both Fifth District judges. Barry and I hunted and fished some together, and Dan and I had been Magistrates together and then District Judges together.

Diane Delaney was head clerk, as she is now. Eric Wildman was the staff attorney.

The first thing I did was read Randy Stapilus's book on the SRBA. So I knew the political as well as the legal maturation of the court to that time.

And I bought a picture of the Light Brigade, "Those of us" -- what is the quote? "Ours is not to question why; ours is but to do and die," and I hung it over my chair.

I had kept up with the cases. I had gone to seminars. In fact, I kind of had to bust my way into the Water Users Association's seminar the first time because they'd never had a judge go to it, I guess. And was it Sheryl Chapman who ran it at that time? He said I couldn't go. I said, "I can." Then I asked him for a government – a government scholarship. He said, "We don't have them." I said, "Well, it's on the back of your brochure that you can get them." So I worked my way in and went to a couple.

You got to hear the people talk about it. You got to hear the people talk about the court, what was good and bad. They didn't know that I was a Judge and a Magistrate in Jerome or a District Judge in Twin Falls.

You know, at that time, Barry and Dan were the judge,, so that helped me understand what Water Users felt of the Court and what the Court needed. Stapilus's book, I think, gave me a really fine idea of where it had been so we didn't need to re-trod a lot of the ground.

ROGER BURDICK The first thing that happened when I got in there is everybody started pulling the same old separation of powers, the same old arguments that Dan and Barry had gone over numerous times. I think the best thing I did was I said, "We're not doing that. We're going forward. I don't even want to hear about those types of things." And we made a lot of progress after that series of discussions.

DAVID SHAW I think it was an attitude and a commitment top down from the governor, the legislature, to find resolutions rather than litigate.

The court gave the parties time. They kept the pressure on. I mean there were deadlines, reporting requirements, those sorts of things. But they gave the parties time to find agreements and solutions that would work. So I don't know that there was anything, you know, magical because of the statute or anything, but more attitude.

And I think the experience with Fort Hall – and they were the ones that reached out and said, "We want to negotiate these rights. We don't want to litigate" – was a good precedent, because even if people didn't like the agreement, they saw a process that worked. And it was successful there. So they believed there was an opportunity for success with the other claims as well.

DAVID TUTHILL We had a whole continuum of claimants being perfectly happy with what we recommended – to totally unhappy – but in most cases, by the time we met with the objector and shared with the objector what we had, in almost every case that would resolve it – but not in every case.

There was a full range of opportunity for claimants to have their day in court. The system that has been evolved I think has been a very fair system in that initially the day in court is with the special master so if the claimants were unhappy with our recommendation, they could say, "No, I want to have this heard before the special master."

The dispute resolution process included a negotiated process where there would be an informal meeting with one of the other special masters and there would be an attempt at a solution. If that was unsuccessful, there could be a trial before the special master, and that trial would then be reviewed by the district judge. In some cases, there would be more activity in front of the district judge.

In just a few cases, the issue would go to the state supreme court, and that's the final judgment in this particular adjudication.

DAVID TUTHILL We learned in the Payette River adjudication that it's best to send out the proposed findings first and then hear back and make adjustments, changes, and corrections – and that worked quite well there. In a basin where we wouldn't do that, there were just too many errors, too many misunderstandings, and so on. So we learned to do that successfully in the Payette.

That was applied in the SRBA. We would send out a proposed finding – have a public meeting allows people to come in and ask questions, and maybe make modifications before we issued our final recommendations. Then, based on that input, we would make our finding to the court – it's called a "Director's Report" – and that's basically a compilation of our findings for all the water rights in that basin. There could be objections to the Director's Report; and if there were, we would attempt to resolve those at an informal level – we as agency representatives -- so the objections could be resolved at an informal level.

If the objection was unresolved the next step as was for the court to assign a special master. A special master would have a formal meeting and, in many cases, assign it to another special master for informal resolution. If that didn't work, only then would it come before the special master for a hearing.

There was a whole variety of issues that could make it to that point. Most irrigators would accept. In most cases we could come to a resolution on lands irrigated. In some cases, we could not come up with a solution that would be satisfactory for the department and the claimant. So in those cases there was an opportunity for the claimant to have his or her day in court, and that could go all the way up.

I don't know that we lost any of those because our information was so powerful. We had imagery over time and we just had very powerful information, but that opportunity was there. In some cases, we had a series of issues relative to fish propagation and conditions of approval on the fish propagation – whether those water rights could be expanded – and the special masters had rulings on those issues.

I think every basin had its own issues, but the number of trials before the special masters in most basins was either one, two, or zero. There weren't very many trials.

The city of Pocatello case

One of the hottest cases to hit the court in that period concerned the city of Pocatello.

DAVID TUTHILL The City of Pocatello is right on the edge of the Eastern Snake River Plain Aquifer. So some of their wells are in, some are out.

The City of Pocatello also has 50,000 acre feet of storage water in Palisades as backup water, which explains some of the interest of the City of Pocatello. Some wise person invested in Palisades at a low cost – very much lower than the water is worth now.

Through the years the city of Pocatello has been very actively involved in the SRBA and old storage water, and the city has protested many of the recommendations.

In my perspective, most of the department's perspectives have prevailed, but it has been a contentious area.

The city has been actively involved and wanted certain decisions to be interpreted in favor of their views, and the department didn't always interpret in that manner, and therein lies the conflict that was settled through the special masters and beyond.

BRIGETTE BILYEU The city of Pocatello group of subcases out of Basin 29 raised some very serious issues about municipal water rights. We were all hoping that they would settle, but they didn't and we went to trial. We heard the case right here, and it was terrific because there were great experts that were really interesting to listen to. It was very interesting to me because I grew up in Pocatello, and the history of how Pocatello and how the townsite of Pocatello came about in conjunction with the reservation was really interesting to me because the farm that I grew up on is very close to the reservation.

My grandfather worked for the railroad for a short time and was a taxi driver back and forth for people going to Pocatello by rail. So it was really interesting. The historical background was fascinating to me. So that was one case.

The other sub-case or group of subcases was in Basin 27, I think, where the Shoshone-Bannock Tribes filed objections to, I believe, every irrigation right in the basin.

The reason that was so fascinating was we had a challenge in terms of trying to find a place big enough to have all of those people. The courthouse didn't come even close. So we had to put it in the Needlecraft Room at the county fairgrounds, which is the Eastern Idaho State Fairgrounds in Blackfoot. That was all well and good. What we didn't know was there was no air conditioning in these buildings. We held the hearings in, I don't remember if it was July or August, but it was without a doubt the hottest day of the year probably of the last 20 years. It was horribly hot. We put these great big fans in and had them going. Then we couldn't hear anything very well. Just calling roll took an hour. The other problem was we did not, at that time, our computers did not spit out the names of the litigants alphabetized either by first or last name either way. So when somebody would come and say, I'm John Smith, did you call my name, am I on the list, I mean, seriously, it took me forever to even be able to find the answer to that question.

It was so hot that people that were the epitome of professionalism and neck ties and everything, David Barber one of my very favorite attorneys had to ask if he could take his jacket off. By this time I have my jacket off. I'm in a short-sleeved shirt, thankfully, and I said, "Everybody is ordered to take off their neck ties and their jackets," because I knew he would rather pass out than take off his jacket. You know, he was just always very careful with his decorum. I was very grateful that he finally said something and we all took our jackets off.

Federal water rights were also among the most prominent items facing Burdick's court.

CLIVE STRONG The issue of federal reserved water rights from a state perspective was of real concern, because it meant new water rights coming on to a system that hadn't been there before that could impact existing users. A couple of them that were of particular concern were the wilderness, Hells Canyon, as well as Deer Flats.

The wilderness reserved water rights were of concern because they covered a large swath of the lands in central Idaho. The Frank Church Wilderness Area is really kind of the core part of the state of Idaho.

Our concern was if those water right claims were recognized they would impact all of the water users in the Salmon River Basin.

Wilderness reserve water right claims have been a contentious issue. The Wilderness Act was enacted in 1964, and it was really, from our perspective, it wasn't a water right statute. The intent was to protect the lands through land management, not though water rights.

It had been a point of contention in the state of Colorado and other western states where the United States asserted federal reserved water rights under the Wilderness Act.

We did a lot of legislative history research, went back to Congress, and went through the prior litigation in Colorado. And, we concluded there wasn't a reserved water right. So we filed a motion for summary judgment arguing that there was no express or implied intent on Congress' part to create a reserved water right.

The SRBA District Court, to our surprise, agreed with the United States and held that the federal reserved water right was for all unappropriated water. So essentially it would have precluded any future development in the basin.

We appealed the decision to the Idaho Supreme and the Supreme Court issued an opinion upholding the District Court, which caused a tremendous amount of consternation in the legislature. We petitioned for rehearing. The rehearing was granted. This was about the same time Justice Silak was running for reelection, and she was opposed by now Justice Eismann.

The water rights issue became a very big part of that election and Justice Silak, who had authored the original opinion, lost the election.

The Supreme Court reversed the prior opinion. There was a lot of effort from environmental groups to pressure the Department of Justice to appeal the decision to the United States Supreme Court. We talked with the solicitor's office and encouraged them not to seek cert. Ultimately Justice decided not to seek cert. So there is no wilderness reserved water rights in Idaho.

CLIVE STRONG In 1968 our own Senator Church authored the Wild and Scenic Rivers Act. The Wild and Scenic River Act, unlike the Wilderness Act, had language in it stating that it expressly created a federal reserved water right, but only the minimum amount necessary to achieve the purposes for which a river is designated.

This case became important because the Salmon River, which was impacted by the Wilderness claims, was also designated under the Wild and Scenic Rivers Act. Likewise, portions of the Clearwater River are designated under the Wild and Scenic Rivers Act.

Potlatch Corporation, represented by Jeff Fereday, took an active role in arguing that, despite the language in the Wild and Scenic Rivers Act, Congress did not intend to create a reserved water right. We initially supported Potlatch's position in the District Court, but did not pursue the issue on appeal. The Supreme Court, in the companion case to the Wilderness decision, held that the Wild and Scenic Rivers Act did create a reserved water right.

Once we got those decisions back from the Supreme Court, the SRBA District Court directed the parties into mediation. And, basically from the time of the decision until about 2004 we spent negotiating a Wild and Scenic Rivers settlement.

Those were very contentious discussions. Merlyn Clark was the mediator. Our position was that the United States had not shown any basis for the quantity claimed.

Both parties were kind of at a standstill on the issue, because there really is no methodology for determining the minimum amount of flow necessary to protect the rivers. On the other hand, we couldn't deny there was a right. That was really the reason why we reached a settlement. There was enough uncertainty that we both sides recognized we needed to find a solution.

That solution was to quantify the right based upon exceedence curves. I believe we used 20 percent exceedence curves. But, we also provided that the rights would be subordinate to all existing rights and to a certain amount of future uses in the Salmon River and Clearwater Basin.

The settlement agreement, which was approved by the court in 2004, has a provision in it that sets out a process for tracking the amount of water that is available under the subordination provisions. And it's put into an accounting database so we can track how much water is available for future development.

When we were in a particularly tense negotiation session in Merlyn's office, the United States was taking a position I thought was unreasonable. I advised Merlyn I was ready to end the mediation and leave.

Merlyn had a bowl of candy on the table. I reached in and grabbed one. On the inside of the wrapper, it had a message, "never settle". I handed that to Merlyn and said, this is where we're at. I still have that wrapper. Ultimately, we were able to get past the subordination issue reach a settlement.

DAVID SHAW Some of the federal attorneys have been challenging to deal with on the non-Indian negotiations. Different attorneys. Peter Monson was involved in all of the Indian negotiations. And different Department of Justice attorneys have been involved in the other negotiations. And I think that made a big difference.

During the wild and scenic negotiations on the Salmon and Clearwater, we had a negotiation session in Utah, Salt Lake. And you know Clive is not very tall, and the federal attorney is a fairly tall fellow. And we were around a table that's just about as wide as this (indicating). And the discussion got heated enough that Clive and the other attorney were both on their feet and their noses were about 6 inches apart across a table like this (indicating). All my funny stories have to do with Clive.

So I think it seemed like in the case of the tribal negotiations, the attorneys were willing to make a decision and move ahead. And with the other negotiations, it's been difficult to get a decision from them. And it's hard to negotiate with somebody when you can't get them nailed down, so to speak.

DAVID SHAW We set about trying to quantify the in-stream flows for the wild and scenic rivers, starting with the Salmon River where, of course, there was lots of development not only on the main stem but on the tributaries. And that process went on for years, it seemed.

Some of the wild and scenics, like the Lochsa and the Selway, there was basically no development there. Those were easy.

We did the in-stream flows then for the Hells Canyon -- I think it's National Recreation Area. Whatever the designation was. But there were some in-stream flows there and minimum lake levels that were negotiated.

And currently we're working on the wild and scenic claims for the Owyhee that still are not resolved. There was litigation over the in-stream flows for the Deer Flat Refuge on the Snake River. Ultimately, our court said there are no in-stream flows, and that was resolved through litigation. The negotiations weren't going anywhere. And some of the private water users took that up, and the court agreed that there were none.

We did INEL as federal reserved water rights.

There's a little piece of Yellowstone that comes over into Idaho. We did those.

Anything else on the list? I think that pretty well covers the federal reserved water rights of any significance. Oh, there may be some from Mountain Home.

ROGER BURDICK The one that I found most interesting, based on my history-buff-dom, if that's a word – was PWR 107 which was an implied federal water right for water holes and springs on – out in the rangeland areas.

Originally, Judge Hurlbutt, I believe, had ruled there was no implied water right under public water – or – what was the name of it? PWR 107 and 108 are what they are, but they are – Public Water Reserve 107 – 1926. And that was a water reserve that was initiated because even though the states – the U.S. Government had given land and water rights to the States, there was still large groups of United States land in the arid areas. And they were finding that people were going out and fencing the water sources – the pot-holes, the springs, the creeks – and cutting other people off, thus interfering with the development of the West, it was felt, by monopolizing the water. So we've been trying to monopolize water from the very beginning. It goes on today. But having said that, they passed this law; and then it went through certain machinations. But the issue then became one of: What was the extent -- was there an implied water right?

The Idaho State Supreme Court reversed Hurlbutt and said, yes, there was an implied federal water right, pursuant to PWR 107. It came back during my watch -- the issue -- and it had been pending during Judge Wood's watch. And so we had the definitive hearing, and the opinion was put out and not appealed. The issues, basically, were: What's a spring? What's a water hole?

I, basically, said – plain language – a spring is a spring; I defined it by a definitional term. A water hole is a water hole, by a definitional term. Then the other issue was – obviously, the Federal Government wanted it to apply to tributaries and all streams, et cetera, because that would enlarge their implied water right. Ranchers in the State of Idaho wanted it combined to just those holes in the ground. We ruled that – as I remember, that it could be tributary to a stream; but the amount was only that which a single family could use, based upon PWR 107 being a portion of the homestead laws where a single family got X amount of land.

And so we gave a little bit of something to everyone. We reduced the federal definition of their water right but expanded what the State and the ranchers wanted. It was not appealed, which was very surprising, and continues to this day.

I loved it because of all of the research. It was a very controversial political issue; and, as a result, you had different Interior Secretaries giving different interpretations, based upon what President they worked for.

And so we went through, on a forty-plus-page opinion, and worked through all of those interpretations and came up with -- what was it? The final issue was, basically, that – withdrew surrounding springs and water holes, providing water sufficient for just a single-family use. It was an appurtenant implied federal reserved water right in the spring or water hole, giving rise to the land withdrawal, irrespective of whether or not the water flowing from the spring or water hole is tributary to a perennial running stream. The place of use for the water right is within the boundaries of the 48-acre section withdrawn. And water flowing from the spring or water hole outside the boundaries of that land does not create another land withdrawal or accompanying reserved water right. Otherwise, if it went off that forty-acre plot, the Federal Government could say that the entire stream was an implied water right.

ROGER BURDICK And this is a funny story, the Mountain Home Air Force Base case, a case you will never hear about: What happened with the Mountain Home Air Force Base case – and, again, it was an interesting historical case.

The Mountain Home Air Force Base, because of the Second World War, the Federal Government came in and said, "This is our land. It's a Federal Reserve." As a result, they had this huge Base. And, obviously, all of the water, et cetera, that was on there became the Federal Government's, based on taking the land back for the war. In the interim time, they had, then, condemned portions of state land to expand the Base throughout the decades. And so they, then, had wells on those condemned state lands. They wanted – their claim was that those were, again, federal reserved water rights and, therefore, they could use those to an unlimited capacity. And, quite frankly, the aquifer in the Mountain Home area is fairly fragile; and they could, basically – this is, again, some hyperbole – they could, in theory, dry up Mountain Home, Idaho, with a federal reserved water right.

Well, they came in. They brought in an adjutant lawyer who came in and had written a couple of Law Review articles, cited them to the Court about how, when you condemn state land, you get all of their water rights, et cetera, their federal implied water rights – or federal water – reserved water rights – not implied. And I ruled, no, that, in fact, you re-acquired this from the State of Idaho, not through the original mechanism of making a reservation but through the condemnation of the state law. And, as such, those water rights stay with the state, which was very surprising to the Air Force. I think it was very surprising to the State of Idaho. I think I was right.

But as we are putting the final touches on the opinion and faxing it out that night – Eric Wildman and I -- I turned to Eric and I said, "Eric, I'm not sure about this opinion. You know, these guys are putting cruise missiles through the windows of hotels in Baghdad; and they know where I live."

Lord, we had a good laugh about that.

And, of course, the Air Force appealed. And, all of the sudden, that case was withdrawn; and I was ordered by the Supreme Court to withdraw my opinion.

Who knows? I was still right.

They were the largest employer in the State of Idaho at the time.

Once land leaves the public domain, the United States cannot establish a federal reserved water right through the re-acquisition of the property. Significantly limited the scope of Federal Reserved Water Right Doctrine. The Air Force was only able to acquire water rights under state law. I don't think they wanted anybody to hear about it.

The Nez Perce negotiations

Burdick was keeping a close watch on the Nez Perce negotiations, which had been underway for several years by the time he began presiding at the SRBA.

DUANE MECHAM There were efforts underway in the early early 90s, maybe the late 80s, to initiate some negotiations. I was not involved actively in those because of other negotiations I had until 1995 when some of the other folks in those teams had gone to other jobs. Our solicitor at the time John Leshy asked me to take the lead attorney role for Interior; we still had Peter Monson very active. So I began working in 1995.

For all these negotiations, if there is a federal team appointed, the Interior Department appoints the team and the justice department appoints a representative, one of their attorneys to be on the team. So it is a federal team, but the Interior Department takes the lead.

I think the earlier rounds helped all the parties understand their respective positions and concerns. I think the Nez Perce Tribe better understood after those earlier rounds the nature of the concerns that irrigation districts hundreds of miles away had with their proposal, their claims I should say. That said, we entered into active litigation. Claims were filed in 1993 and the initial round of negotiation wrapped up in 1995; that didn't reach an agreement, so to keep the process moving we started actively litigating ...

If I remember correctly, it was actually Idaho Power, probably Jim Tucker, who – we were going to roll on this litigation, and Tucker said maybe its worth one more round and in this round maybe its worth having a court appointed mediator having protected discussions under court appointed mediation. The other parties and the federal government supported that. The tribes supported that. Not to put words in Clive's mouth but as I remember the state was willing to have a mediated round of negotiations but didn't want to totally stay the negotiation. A double track – which is not the easiest thing to do but in some instances what you have to do, to keep the pressure on.

Since sort of cutting my teeth on the Shoshone-Bannock I have a number of settlements over the years, and ended up being the chair of the negotiation team for the Nez Perce on the federal time. Regardless, every tribal community has negotiators bring to them a settlement, and it is always a compromise. That dynamic was at play with the Shoshone-Bannocks, they had actually a general election of the entire membership as I remember, and it very much was a dynamic for the Nez Perce, and they approached it in their own way with their tribal government. But they certainly were hearing about whether both the nature and degree of the compromises were appropriate given everything they've had to give up in other contexts over the decades. Every tribal community has to wrestle with that to some degree.

FRANCIS McGOVERN Normally I serve as a special master for judges to assist them in trying to resolve large cases. The parties met with me, I was interviewed by the parties, I was asked questions by the parties, and they agreed I should serve as mediator in the case.

I first met with the southeast Idaho constituents at Yellowstone and they invited me to fly with them in a plane from the headwaters of the Snake River. We stopped in Twin Falls, had a luncheon there, met with some of the other constituents, and flew on the plane if my memory serves me, to Portland – the length of the Snake River and on to the Pacific Ocean.

Subsequently I met with the Nez Perce Tribe and they had a helicopter that they had acquired to fly me up the tributaries of the Snake River, specifically the Salmon River, and its three forks. Then I spent a fair amount of time in Lapwai and went on the Nez Perce Reservation with members of the tribe.

Over the years of the mediation I drove throughout Idaho, Cottonwood to Lapwai and other cities, mainly in Boise. And we had a series of meetings with representatives of the attorney general and governor and departments in Idaho, governments associated with water rights – forestry, the tribe, environmental quality as well as a series of meetings with the various constituent groups both tribal and non-tribal to familiarize ourselves with the issue.

As the mediator my major concern is putting together a structure for the negotiation not only of the way in which the parties meet but also the structure of what the resolution might be. So my focus in the early stages of the mediation was to develop who should be at the table, how the table should be organized, what parties should be involved. . . .

Originally the issues were relatively limited to the flow of the salmon and the cleanliness of the water in the Snake River. It became apparent to me that the issues needed to be expanded, that the interest on the part of the parries really encompassed a large number of issues …

It involves picking the core negotiators, a much smaller group, narrowing down the issues, trying to resolve those issues, and then building out from those issues in concentric circles to all other interested parties over a period of time.

The difficulty we had with the SRBA was that there were so many interested parties that putting all of them at the table was simply unmanageable from a logistical perspective, and my feeling was that it would be virtually impossible to keep their level of interest and proceed to a successful conclusion if you had that many interests at the table at the same time. It turned out that in Idaho there was a relatively small number of very good lawyers who represented virtually all of those interests in one form or another. So

I decided that a better way to proceed would be to take those lawyers and let them be the core of the negotiations, divide them into committees, so that we could take the issues and come up with suggestions, and put the group together. And if the group could agree on approaches to resolving these issues, you could expand the universe of individuals who were interested, to see if they would buy into the approaches this core of lawyers had suggested as potential resolution. And then outward, further and further.

The mode that I suggested of this series of small and then larger circles was facilitated by the fact that I had been appointed by the court and there could be a protective order that would protect the confidentiality of the negotiations at each stage, so we could at each stage ... This was a risky process, because there always within the legal community are potential outliers who could be difficult to deal with. Generally speaking I prefer dealing with principals rather than lawyers but in this instance I felt that the lawyers knew each other well enough, would be bound by this confidentiality, would be faithful agents of the parties they represented and could effectively negotiate something we could share with others in a systematic way.

. . . I'm a great believer that the parties themselves should do the negotiation. That is to say, what we were talking about was reaching an agreement that would have legs in the long run. It does no good to reach a short-term solution that blows up very quickly. And so my feeling was, even though it took a very long period of time that the essence of the agreement had to come from the parties.

DANIEL HURLBUTT Well, one thing that was funny. It didn't really happen in court, but I remember there was a time when Francis McGovern, who I had appointed as a mediator for the Nez Perce rights, he was a professor of law at Duke University, and I remember he called just either the day of or the day before a status conference, when he was supposed to give a big report on the status of their negotiations, and he wasn't going to be able to make it, and he apologized profusely, and said, What can I do to make this right? And a joke, I said, Tickets to the Duke-North Carolina basketball game. I was just kidding him. He said, It's done.

It turns out he had two tickets to the Duke-North Carolina game, or had two season tickets to the Duke game. That was pretty funny. We've laughed about that many times since.

Hurlbutt went to the game.

It was great. Oh, yeah, Duke won, so he was happy. It was quite an experience.

DUANE MECHAM We first asked Francis to do a report on whether - engaged him on a limited question to report to the court whether a mediated round of negotiation was worth proceeding with and could bear fruit. I think it was in 1998 that he did that report and kicked off the next round of his involvement, and that's where I think Judge Wood came in.

I think the dynamics of those negotiations under McGovern – they were certainly very interesting.

The beauty of it was we didn't even recognize the beauty of it, because he did a couple of years a lot of shuttle diplomacy – understanding one party's positions, checking it out, checking on potential compromises ...

He did both (shuttle diplomacy and getting the parties in a room).

BARRY WOOD Judge Hurlbutt had used Francis McGovern over a period of years they had tried to introduce the subject in judicial circles to mediate a settlement. ...

There was a huge amount of filing, and Diana Delaney and others had moved it downstairs into the storage room. In the summer of 99 I was saying to Diana Delaney is anybody filing anything on the Nez Perce? Because as I recall Judge Hurlbutt had had it scheduled. We knew this hearing date in September or whatever was coming. Has anyone seen anything? Where's the filings on this? Getting a little concerned about it. Then all of a sudden, it's all downstairs, and it was a whole bunch of stuff. It was just a herculean effort. We got the filed out of the basement, read them, and heard the argument. The federal government in trust for the tribe wanted to bifurcate it – don't talk about quantity, just talk about the entitlement or right. Then after I issued a decision, that's when all of this came out about conflict. And right in the middle of that I had cancer surgery, in January of 2000. So it was an interesting period of my life.

That was a fascinating piece of the SRBA. I really wish it would have been decided on appeal, on the merits, rather than settled. Lots of different people took a lot of credit. To me it's a matter of getting it legally right.

DUANE MECHAM They were protected discussions. We had periodic updates, I'd say for the last two or three years for Judge Burdick, and we did our best to lay out what information we could. But – it was a situation where, especially the irrigation community, they didn't want to show their hand until they knew that all the parts were going to work together. I know that sounds general. But we were trying to resolve not just these Indian water right claims but also some very serious endangered species act requirements for the Bureau of Reclamation to provide flow augmentation from the various federal reservoirs in Idaho.

My perception, which I think made valid points they didn't want to resolve the issues on the tribal water right claims on Thursday just to turn around on Friday to deal with the ESA issues that are about the same thing. They didn't want any agreement they were willing to make public until they knew the tribes could accept it and the federal government could accept it.

DUANE MECHAM Francis wasn't there all the time and at a certain point the parties began working together without the need for a lot of active mediation or oversight. So theres some perception he wasn't there enough. In my sense he was.

We had some tough issues to resolve. My sense was he came in very effectively at the end to get us to that finish line.

DUANE MECHAM We announced the proposed settlement in the spring of 2004 which kicked off a round of approvals by each of the respective governments, and that led to the 2004 very last minute federal legislation approving the agreement.

REBECCA MILES I have worked for the Nez Perce Tribe for almost 15 years. I was born and raised here on the reservation. I currently serve as the Nez Perce Tribe executive director. It was before that I started working on the Snake River Basin Adjudication.

It was the Friday after my first week of being in the tribal council role and it was like an assignment list. Who wants to go down with the chairman to a meeting on a potential settlement? After that, I was entrenched in that. . . .

We had to make claims or we would have forfeited the water forever. There was no way around. The tribe probably never would have made claims, probably we would never have started this battle, so to speak. …

With ownership and quantifying: That's even how we view land. There was just such a difference in thought. In treaty times ownership of land was such a foreign concept – yeah, we belong to the land, we traveled in seasons, and this was a mild winter place down below in the valley, but to own land was a foreign concept. The same with water: What do you mean, you're quantifying water? How can you quantify water and say this is what you get? I cant even tell you what an uphill battle it was to explain the quantity of water that was in the terms. And explain acre feet to tribal members, what is an acre foot of water, all of that was so hard to explain. It was hard for me to understand at first.

DUANE MECHAM What can the executive branch support as a federal contribution? We were fortunate to work through Ann klee at the time; she had the ear of the secretary, she worked with OMB effectively, to get federal positions on what the federal contributions should be. So by the time that announcement was made, we were in agreement with the state and the tribe about what the federal contributions should be. That's not always the case, especially in other states.

It was a long list of things we had to do. And it was a lot of different things – forest practices issues, we agreed to transfer some operations at some federal hatcheries to them, federal responsibilities – we had to get that finalized. And the Snake River flow augmentation program had to be put in place.

What I did as federal chair at that point of the implementation team was to shift from Francis to a fellow named Ed Sheets. He was director of the Northwest Power & Conservation Council, the first director of the council, he had left that job in the mid 90s. I knew he was really good at facilitating process, and keeping things on track and getting things done in a multi-party situation.

PETER MONSON The thing I think that made it successful was that high level policymakers who made decisions were involved early on, and I'm speaking primarily of the federal government. Sometimes the federal negotiating process can be frustrating for outsiders to deal with. After a discussion, the federal negotiating team has to take it back to outsiders, the secretary of agriculture or interior, and they may be hard to get hold of or have differing views ... The federal negotiators might be out in the field int he region, or might be local to Idaho maybe or Oregon, but the decision makers are back in D.C. and it's hard to get their attention, much less develop strategy or positions ...

There were people such as Ann Klee in the Bush Administration, and in th Clinton administration, were motivated to get a settlement, we had marching orders to get a settlement and get it done. And that was needed, gave it a better chance of success than otherwise might have been the case.

FRANCIS McGOVERN Because of the complexity associate with the issues, it was necessary to bring in non-lawyer expertise to assist some of the committee. Some of it was straightforward, but some of it involve bringing in rather unique expertise the lawyers did not necessarily have. So we needed to enable the experts to talk with each other. Because my experience has been that generally speaking scientists agree on what is known but when theres something that's unknown they tend to make assumptions that are driven by the lawyers. So the idea was to have the expert denominate what was agreed to, what was known, and then explicitly indicate, we don't know about this, and we're assuming X.

CLIVE STRONG When we started the Nez Perce negotiation, we initially attempted to follow the same model used in the Shoshone-Bannock negotiations. But the Nez Perce reservation is located at the mouth of the Clearwater River as the Snake River exits into Washington. So their claims, which dated back to 1863, impacted every water user upstream.

When the tribe filed a claim on the Snake River for the entire flow you can imagine the consternation that occurred. People felt threatened. It was very clear early on there really wasn't much room for compromise. Obviously the state and water users couldn't agree to the in-stream flows. It would upset the economy. And, likewise the Tribe and the United States couldn't walk away from the claims otherwise they wouldn't feel like they had protected the treaty right.

The negotiations weren't going anywhere. We made the conclusion, "we" meaning the state, that this was going to be a situation where we had to establish the controlling law. So we filed a motion for summary judgment seeking to disallow all of the off-reservation in-stream flow claims. Steve Strack handled this litigation; he did an outstanding job in presenting the case. And, as we were litigating the motion, Idaho Power Company and the water users approached the tribe about to re-engaging in negotiations. The state initially stayed out of those negotiations, because we didn't see much opportunity or future for those negotiations.

Idaho Power Company and the water users had a different incentive for negotiating. The federal government had listed Salmon and Steelhead under the Endangered Species Act.

Idaho Power Company was in the process of relicensing the Hells Canyon Complex, and was concerned that the Endangered Species Act might require more water than it felt it could provide. And, likewise the water users were concerned the Bureau of Reclamation projects would be impacted by the Endangered Species Act because There was a push for flow augmentation out of the upper Snake River Basin. The water users feared that even if they won the litigation with the Tribe on the in-stream flow claims, they could still be subject to risk under the Endangered Species Act. So from both Idaho Power Company's and water users' perspective, they felt that they needed a solution not only to the water rights issue but also to the Endangered Species Act issue.

So they approached the SRBA District Court along with the Tribes and asked the court to enter an order requiring mediation. I believe that occurred in about 1998.

The state was reluctant to participate. We took the position that the state would only agree to negotiation if the litigation could go forward. We didn't have confidence that the mediation would be successful. We also conditioned state participation on an understanding that the state would not contribute to a financial settlement, and all existing water rights would have to be protected. In 1999, the District Court issued a decision granting the state's motion for summary judgment dismissing the Nez Perce off-reservation claims for Salmon, Clearwater and the Snake River.

The basis for rejection of those claims was the court's determination that when the Nez Perce Indian Reservation was created, the Tribe had disclaimed all rights to lands outside the reservation. In other words, the whole idea of the reservation was to release these lands for non-Indian development.

We argued the original reservation had been further diminished when it was opened up for non-Indian settlement. This meant that the reservation today only consists of lands held in trust by the United States for the benefit of the Nez Perce Tribe. Only about ten percent of the lands within the Indian reservation, are currently held in trust. The other lands are owned by non-Indians.

The implication of the decision was that there would be no reserved in-stream flow water rights for any of those lands outside the reservation or on any of the diminished lands. The decision obviously was alarming to the Tribe and the United States. The Tribe and the United States sought to disqualify Judge Wood who had assumed the role of SRBA judge after Judge Hurlbutt left.

The United States and the Tribe were incentivized by the decision to find a solution. The water users were incentivized by the ESA issue. And the power company was incentivized by the relicensing of Hells Canyon Dam and the ESA issues

Those incentives broke through the impasse we'd had on trying to find a solution. And, we ultimately put together a term sheet. Surprise, surprise. The term sheet consisted of a suite of measures that if implemented would resolve the conflict between the Tribe, the water users and the state.

In simple terms, the agreement consisted of three components. The tribal component, which quantified the water rights for tribal lands. And, that water right I believe is for 50,000 acre-feet out of the various streams that pass through the tribal lands. A trust fund was created for the tribe to develop on-reservation water supplies and water treatment plants.

The second component was called the Salmon/Clearwater component. The Tribe and the United States agreed to relinquish their claims to in-stream flows in exchange for the state creating, pursuant to state law, 203 in-stream flow water rights.

Those 203 in-stream flow water rights are intended to provide water for anadromous fish and other resident fish and wildlife.

A unique aspect of the settlement is the habitat trust fund. About \$38 million, \$25 million to the state and the balance to the tribe, is to be used to lease water and implement water projects to restore water in tributary streams. Although the Salmon/Clearwater are largely pristine areas, some of the tributary streams have been largely developed. So there's an ongoing effort to restore some of the flows in those streams.

Why would you do that? It's in order to avoid liability under the ESA.

We've been working on what is called a Section 6 Agreement. Section 6 refers to a section of the Endangered Species Act. Under that provision, what we are trying to do is develop a collaborative program that would benefit both the state and the Tribe in terms of protection of in-stream values in the Salmon and Clearwater.

The third component is what we call the Snake River Component. What that component does is provide for a 30-year biological opinion for the operation of the Upper Snake River BOR projects.

In other words, Reclamation will get incidental take coverage for its operations.

What Reclamation agreed to do, in exchange for incidental take coverage, was to provide up to 427,000 acre-feet of storage water from the Snake River Basin annually. That can be increased up to 487,000 acre-feet depending on the water supply.

All of that is done through the Water District 01 water bank pursuant to state law. It's a voluntary willing seller/willing buyer approach. In other words, the water users are compensated for the water they provide, and the United States gets the water it needs to address its concerns under the Endangered Species Act.

It's another example of how we avoided an impasse by expanding the scope of the negotiations. Once we added the Endangered Species Act into the settlement, there became a big enough problem that everybody had a vested interest in finding a solution., There was enough self interest on everybody's part to -- for everybody to give what they needed to get to settlement.

It's quite a remarkable agreement. I believe the total cost of that settlement was about $190 million. From the state's perspective, it allowed us to move forward and provide protection for our water users. It allowed us to continue to operate as we have in the past. And, it's consistent with state law.

The settlement did create a lot of consternation in the Clearwater Basin. There's a longstanding conflict between the non-Indian landowners and the Tribe over who regulates activities on lands within the exterior boundaries of the reservation. This diminishment issue was teed up in the adjudication and and could have been resolved once and for all.

As part of the settlement the parties agreed to not pursue the issue. So when we sought legislative approval of the agreement, there was strong opposition to the settlement. We ended up having a hearing in the Borah Ballroom at BSU, which was a very heated hearing.

FRANCIS McGOVERN For a mediator, having people realize when is the time for them to play their last card, to know when to hold them and know when to fold them as the song goes, is a real difficulties. As a mediator one hates to set artificial deadlines, because deadlines everyone knows are artificial don't work very well. ...

We made it very very complex. But by making it complex, we were able to create multiple narratives, where each of the constituents were able to tell a story that they had succeeded in this and they had prevented that.

REBECCA MILES Then some meetings started to turn, where we were able to talk about all the terms of the settlement.

And you had groups that are anti-tribe, they've been publicly anti-tribe, and all of a sudden their people in the background, whether they're at a store or whatever, they're saying, do not accept this settlement. And so we had tribal people listening to anti-Indian groups, that should register with you. Why do you think they are calling for you not to accept this settlement? We had people who wanted to see the tribe go away, they had jurisdictional issues, they don;t want to acknowledge the tribe exists, and they were all of a sudden becoming a lot of the tribal members' best friends. It was a crazy time. So we kept plugging forward.

DAVID SHAW The Nez Perce was also very different because they had very little interest in irrigated agriculture. That was the primary focus of both the Fort Hall and the Duck Valley Reservations. They do have some irrigation rights that were decreed, but mostly their interests were in stream for fisheries and other benefits. So that was again entirely different.

But that got rolled into the ESA, Endangered Species Act. Well, there was litigation over the salmon and flushing flows that NOAA Fisheries was looking for out of Idaho to help protect the salmon and steelhead in the Columbia River.

So those things got tangled together during the negotiations of the Nez Perce. And that agreement – I think that was adopted in 2005 – actually addressed both. It settled the ESA claims for water, as well as the Nez Perce claims, not only for water in the Snake

River, but their decree, so they were entitled to springs and fountains. So those had to be addressed.

And then also some irrigation claims that were fairly minor in the big picture. But still on some of the streams up there, they're significant. Surprisingly, north Idaho doesn't have a lot of streams like around the Boise basin, for example. So where there is water, it's significant that there are other uses that had to be protected.

Probably the experience with Fort Hall helped that little piece subplot, but it was still very different because not only was there a claim for the out-of-stream uses for irrigation, the Nez Perce also wanted to protect in-stream values. And on the Fort Hall that's a minor piece. It's hardly worth mentioning.

REBECCA MILES We flew to Boise. We met with governor Dirk Kempthorne at that time, and Secretary Gale Norton … all the other parties that were involved, water users, irrigators, people who have claimed water, who represented big organizations. So it was a unique type of meeting. For the most part, for a good portion of the negotiation, …

What happened after our public meeting – I didn't know my role. I was so confused. I had just got elected. How would they feel? And the tribe in general – settlements are not a good deal. Settlements are viewed as a sellout. Settlements are viewed as another taking of something from the tribe. This was the biggest decision the tribe was faced with – there has not been a bigger decision. And really we hope the tribe will never have to make a big decision like this again. That was a really tense time.

It was after that first public meeting I got involved.

That [old] treaty ever since has divided us.

DAVID SHAW The water user organizations? We've talked about the Committee of Nine. There's another group called the Federal In-Stream Flow Coalition. That was a marriage, if you will, of the Committee of Nine and the Idaho Water Users Association to be the public representatives during the Nez Perce negotiations.

And it turned out that Coalition continues today because of ongoing ESA issues. But certainly they played a significant role in getting the Nez Perce negotiations done and the ESA issues resolved in the -- I think it's called the Snake River agreement in 2005.

Idaho Power certainly was a major player throughout. It will be interesting in north Idaho if those kinds of coalitions form, because water use up there is so different than it is here. You know, later on the groundwater users, Idaho Groundwater Users Association, became involved. Those are the largest groups that I can think of.

The canal companies and irrigation districts certainly were not always collectively, but individually were major players.

DAVID TUTHILL When we look at New Mexico and Arizona and some of the tribal issues that have gone on for decades, we can be quite proud of the fact that ours actually did come to resolution, the federal part was funded for both the Shoshone Bannock and also the Duck Valley Tribe -- the Shoshone Paiute – and also the Nez Perce.

The Nez Perce was the most difficult to resolve and put together. It took the most time and was the last one to be resolved.

In developing that resolution -- the resolution went far beyond just within the boundaries of the Tribe.

It went to the whole issue of the anadromous fishery on the Snake and has led to a map of future processing for the state in a lot of areas that go far beyond the Nez Perce.

REBECCA MILES When we got into the terms of the settlement, just the opposite – why do they need so much water?

There were three types of claims of water we were guaranteed, there was land back to the reservation and all of those individually became a high issue. The first settlement, the water fisheries fund, it was $60.1 million, that was breach of trust by the united states for not protecting the springs and fountains that were guaranteed. That $60.1 million represented the damage. So basically illegally opening up the reservation, allowing it to be settled when the provisions in both treaties were that non-Indians could not come on the reservation without the approval of the tribe and the United States, well when gold was discovered they didn't protect that. So when that settlement happened, which was very fast and brutal.

To everyone else it was a lot of money; to our people it was like a slap in the face.

The second one was $23 million for water and sewer infrastructure. A lot of people were very angry about that. That was already the United State's trust responsibility; we gave them 13 million acres of and and they still haven't improved this. Everything was an issue.

The final settlement was the fisheries and habitat fund for the Salmon and Clearwater. That was also an issue: The United States is already responsible to protect the habitat of our fisheries in both of those drainages. And you know they were right. So there was that argument, and then also the water we claimed.

Some of these meetings went well into the night.

CLIVE STRONG One thing I've learned, it's important to go back and look at history. If you don't understand how you got to where you're at, you don't know what the problem is you're trying to solve.

The other thing is, it's important to have continuity in the players and a strong leadership. In the Nez Perce negotiations – again, just like in the Fort Hall negotiations, we had strong leadership from the water user community. Terry Uhling represented the Surface Water Coalition, a group of water users that had a collective interest to participate in the negotiations.

If I can say there was one thing that I wish I could have done differently in Nez Perce or we could have done differently, not me but we, is have more participation from the water users in the Clearwater Basin because that ultimately became a point of contention.

REBECCA MILES People would want to know how we got here. I would go back and do research. We would have former councilmen who were on years earlier when it first started. I went back and researched every resolution that had to do with this settlement, from the time we started making water claims. And I pulled every single name of a tribal councilman that was involved, and I listed every one of them for the public. People who were saying really bad things were some of the ex-councilmen that had actually been official negotiators of the settlement. And I pulled up every resolution, everybody who had been involved, every decision the tribe had made – and those were all public documents but they had never comprehensively been put together. And that really helped our meetings a lot: You're out here attacking you're out here saying things, let's put things in perspective. And so we did, and that really helped us move to opening terms of the settlement, and once we did that we really felt we were finally making progress. But now our work is really cut out for us, because the clock is ticking.

And you asked the question of did the tribal people get to vote on this? And no, they didn't. And that could have been a problem because there was even an effort to recall the tribal council, to try to get the tribal council to not be th4e onces voting on it. Do I think there's anything wrong with that? No. Do I think the tribal people should be more involved? Yeah. We probably will not make a bigger decision in 100 years.

REBECCA MILES The state of Idaho accepted the settlement and the government signed it into law. It was all eyes on the tribe.

I said, we need to bring in a third party who has no stake in this. So we did, we brought in four, and we went into executive session.

One of the folks we brought in was Professor Dennis Colson who was considered an expert on the Idaho constitution and we considered him an expert on Indian law. He came in and gave us several hours of his time and he just laid it out. Councilmen were able to ask anything, anything they wanted, what if we do this, why can't we go to World Court, and he just put it out there. Coming from that meeting, even though in your heart you want to vote no, your instincts are telling you that its not a good deal – the tribe didn't want to be here in the first place. But we're here. And this is what we're elected to do, is making tough decisions. …

Then the vote came down, and it came down 7-2. And we accepted it as a done deal. Its never been something we've been happy about. We had to accept it.

DUANE MECHAM The one pocket of resistance we experienced was not so much from what the resolution of the tribal water right claims but the resolution of what Reclamations' responsibilities would be for flow augmentation under the Endangered Species Act. Environmental groups that were challenging federal compliance with the dams since the beginning of the listings ...

Those environmental groups were very focused on making sure that Idaho would contribute water. And so they became concerned that the settlement would be too easy on the Idaho water user community. But their primary concern was that the local Idaho interest would go to Congress and get an ESA exemption written into the approving the agreement. That engendered its own round of discussions at the congressional level, with Interior and justice I think to some degree, involved where the state and local interests had to agree they were not going to seek this ESA exemption. With that understanding, the environmental groups weren't actively opposed.

PETER MONSON A lot of the Indian water rights decisions didn't reach adjudication decision because a settlement was reached by negotiation. Those settlements have become precedent in sort of an odd way. They're not binding. Participants in cases in other states look to the settlements in Idaho as a guidepost. Every settlement is different but they have elements in common.

DUANE MECHAM We were fortunate to have key policy folks involved both in the latter years of the Clinton Administration and under the Bush Administration. With Clinton it was Professor Robert Anderson at the University of Washington Law School, who in a previous life worked with the Nez Perce Tribe. And then Ann Klee, counselor to the secretary of interior. So we had immediate access throughout. This isn't always the case. But in this case it proved to be not only a benefit but also a necessity because of the far ranging issues and overlapping issues, endangered species issues.

BRUCE NEWCOMB The acquisition of the Bell Rapids water – I was very much involved in that. In fact, I had to go to the attorney general and ensure that I wasn't conflicted because my uncle had developed Bell Rapids, but he had since passed. But he had a grandson that still had an interest.

So I went to the attorney general's office and had them opine to whether or not I had a conflict. And they said I was far enough removed that I didn't, so I could negotiate with Greg Brown and Rosholt and all those guys. Clive and I negotiated on that, but I knew all those people.

. . .In the Nez Perce agreement we agreed to find a certain amount of water. Of course, we had the Bureau of Reclamation, and John Keys was a big part of this too.

And, so I was majority leader then. And, so we had the negotiations with Bell Rapids to acquire their water rights so we could provide flow augmentation water.

It was in-stream water, you know, a diversion right out of the river, and to develop 20,000 acres up on the bench. And so, you know, the high lift costs of bringing that water to the bench were getting such that they were vulnerable. And then we needed water that was actually real water that was in the river.

I think it was 26 million, but I'd have to go back and look. But it was good for all parties, you know. But you had to have Bureau of Reclamation buy into that. I remember we had to do some kind of a subordination with the Bureau, or they wanted to. And the solicitor came in with John Keys into my office. And John wanted to know – because we had to allow so much water to go down the river. And they wanted a fixed amount.

And I said, "We can only deliver that, you know, when we have the water. If we don't have the water, we can't do that."

And the solicitor said, "Well, we'll sue you then."

And I said, "John, I can't do that. I can do another one where if we have the water it will be given to you."

So I asked the solicitor to leave. And he says, "We can work this out, you know."

But he asked Golden Linford to leave too. He never trusted Golden for some reason.

BRUCE NEWCOMB . . . But anyway, we finally worked all that out. But we had all the right people in place. You had the Bell Rapids thing came together. And it was a long time. The hearings were right over here in Boise in the Student Union. And you had people from north Idaho that hate the Nez Perce tribe, you know, and didn't want the state doing anything. You had Helen Chenoweth that was there with her folks. They were very vitriolic.

In November 2000 U.S. Representative Helen Chenoweth-Hage, then nearing the end of her last term, released an opinion article reprinted in a number of Idaho newspapers, blasting the closed-door mediation process. "All Idahoans should be concerned about these negotiations," she wrote. "Not only are their vital water rights being affected, but the unintended consequences of some of the decisions could leave taxpayers holding a very large bill."

BRUCE NEWCOMB She was against it. She was leading a charge against the whole Nez Perce agreement. The interesting thing is, you know, it was five years I think in negotiations and putting it all together. And so anyway, I never asked for a roll call vote in the caucus – I didn't believe in that – except I would say "Now we're going to ask for a suspension of the rules so we can hear this bill today. So I need to know if anybody's going to object. If you are, tell me now. We could have a caucus on that." And in that case nobody said they would.

Yeah, the settlement. And it was a big deal. And so anyway, the majority leader gets up on the floor and asks in a sense to suspend the rules, Lenore Barrett, who was a clone of Helen Chenoweth's and chairman of local government committee, stood up and objected.

And I've got no shoes on, because I figure it's going to be a long debate. So anyway, I hammered the House. I said, "You, in my office now." So I'm running in my office with socks on my feet. I told Lenore, I said, "Do you like being chairman of the local government?"

She says, "Yeah."

I said, "You know, chairmen are part of leadership."

She says, "Yeah, I know that."

And I said, "So I'm going to give you a choice. You can go back out and withdraw your objection and still be chairman, or you can say you're going to object and we'll find a new chairman."

And she says, "Well, I like being chairman."

And I said, "Then it's your choice, Lenore. I'm going to give you the opportunity to make it right."

So she did, and we moved on.

CLIVE STRONG Each of these agreements, they're very complex and very time consuming. The Shoshone-Bannock agreement we started negotiating in 1985. We reached a settlement in 1990, and we entered the decree in 1995. So ten years to complete that process.

Likewise, with the Nez Perce, we started negotiations in 1993 and ultimately reached settlement in 2004. You'll see the same pattern with the Shoshone-Paiutes. These processes are complex. There's so many parties and moving pieces that it just takes time to kind of move the pieces around and put them in the right places to where you can reach a settlement.

In May 2003 Judge Burdick did send a letter to mediator McGovern saying he was "mulling the continued efficacy of the mediation" and looking toward shutting it down soon. Soon after, Burdick left for the Idaho Supreme Court. But his concerns were inherited by his successor, John Melanson, who in 2004 said he planned to order litigation to proceed if a settlement didn't materialize soon.

JOHN MELANSON I didn't have anything to do with the Nez Perce settlement, except it happened on my watch, and I got to sign-off on the order approving it. But, you know, that was an incredible thing to have that done. And the people involved in that should be proud of what they did, I think. And that's going to change management of particularly the Clearwater River for the future, I mean, for a long, long time.

. . . when I started, there had been a lull in the negotiations there. And we needed to get that set for trial. By that, I mean, I'm talking about the Nez Perce claims. And I can talk about the others in a second here.

So my thought was, and I think most judges will say this, this isn't anything magical. To get a case moving, you have to set it for trial. So that's what we did. And then the negotiations started up again. And it was getting pretty close to the deadline, I think, when they announced a settlement. And I was really pleased that they did that.

It wasn't going to be an impossible case to decide. There weren't huge technical issues. There were a lot of legal issues that we needed to deal with, the minimum stream flow, the off-reservation minimum stream flow claims, the springs and fountains claims, which I always felt were kind of interesting.

But those were all resolved. And I think in a good way for everyone, otherwise I wouldn't have signed off on it. But you know that there will still be things happening with that settlement. You know, there are, I think, annual buyouts on it. But I can't remember to many specifics on it right now. But I think that was a really positive thing.

So my role was to set it for trial. And, actually, you know, let the parties know, that if they didn't get it settled, I intended to try it.

The less visible tribal case in the SRBA, but also complex, involved the Shoshone-Paiutes, whose Duck Valley Indian Reservation straddled the Idaho-Nevada border.

The Duck Valley Reservation negotiations

CLIVE STRONG The Shoshone-Paiutes reside on the Duck Valley Indian Reservation. It's kind of a unique reservation in that it straddles the Nevada/Idaho border. Half the reservation is in Idaho, half is in Nevada.

This presented some real challenges because we were trying to resolve the tribal reserved rights for the Duck Valley Indian Reservation, but we didn't have the State of Nevada involved in our adjudication.

So early on we met with Nevada officials, and initially started a process in which Nevada was going to start an adjudication, and we were going to jointly negotiate one common agreement that would be incorporated into both adjudication decrees.

Ultimately that didn't work out. Nevada wasn't prepared to move at the pace we were prepared to move. So the United States had to file its claims.

PETER MONSON The Duck Valley, Shoshone-Paiute Tribe, was another unique situation because their reservation straddled the Idaho-Nevada boundaries, and that provided some unique situations.

The Nevada adjudication was more of an administrative process, and we participated in the Nevada administrative adjudication process for the purposes of quantifying the rights of the reservation in Nevada. ... We had to make sure our claims would all mesh together. One of the ways you quantify an Indian reserved water right is through the irrigation system plan, and so we had to account for water use and diversion in both Idaho and Nevada as part of the water use plan. That was something we had to make sure about.

DAVID SHAW In the case of the Shoshone-Paiutes on the Duck Valley Reservation, their consultant thought the Fort Hall Agreement was a terrible agreement. So it was not helpful there.

We negotiated for a number of years with the Shoshone-Paiutes. I started that while I was with the department and then continued to work on it as a consultant. I think, my own opinion, the Tribe's attorney was not reasonable in their expectations of what the Tribe was entitled to.

And as a result of – I don't know how many years we worked on that – there was just no opportunity for resolution. So we contacted the United States and asked if they'd be willing to accept an offer of judgment. And they said they would.

So we basically wrote a decree, the United States accepted, and the Tribe got snowballed. It was, I think, unfortunate because they could have done better, I believe, had their attorney not tried to be so aggressive.

And it's very different than Fort Hall. Fort Hall, we worked to the bitter end to get all the pieces in place to come up with something that everybody could agree to.

CLIVE STRONG Unlike the Nez Perce and Shoshone-Bannock, the Shoshone-Paiute Reservation is on the headwaters of the Owyhee. And so the impacts downstream for our water users were less. We didn't have upstream users to deal with. We just had to worry about the water supply coming down.

Once the claims were filed, we looked at them. There were only a few water users that were involved in that. One was Riddle Ranch owned by Pete Jackson. A very nice gentleman who worked collaboratively with us on this settlement. And, Simplot had some interest in it as well. We worked with these parties to make sure we had a solution that would not impact their water rights.

We didn't have to get into all the federal funding issues because that was going to happen more with regard to the claims in Nevada where most of the water supply is for the Shoshone-Paiute Reservation. Although it took about ten years, this was a relatively easier settlement because we just needed to protect our existing users.

PETER MONSON I think they came out all right, There were some difficulties between the Idaho side trying to get it agreed to by the tribes, but it all came together and I think it was a workable solution.

ROGER BURDICK As concerns notice, LU Ranches was a rancher who knew of the Adjudication, had gotten a report from the department, had kept it for a couple of years, and then when the -- they start – or when we – what was the procedural portion of that?

The issue was notice and whether or not there was a constitutional definition or constitutional due process in the notice requirements.

So they filed – they got notice that the department was denying all of the claims or some portion of the claims.

They waited a couple of years before they, then, came to the Court and – because they had already had – the time had already run for them to object to the department's objection. The only thing they could come in under was 60(b)(1), excusable neglect, surprise, inadvertence, mistake, to set aside the partial decrees that had been issued and say that the notice requirements were unconstitutional.

That was a big case, in that, if, in fact, we had found it was unconstitutional, we had to go back to the very beginning of the SRBA. And so I kind of sweated that case.

The court said, basically, "The issue wasn't the notice. You obviously had notice that the department objected. You obviously knew the SRBA was taking place. You obviously had a process to object. You just didn't." And then they declared that the notice provisions were constitutional, in addition.

Judge Roger Burdick was appointed to the Idaho Supreme Court in August 2003. Three months later he was replaced at the SRBA by another 5th District judge, John Melanson.

ROGER BURDICK The SRBA was a wonderful transition from being a trial judge, where you have a very busy docket – it's a very busy – lots of turn-over, lots of cases, lots of instant decisions – to kind of an appellate work. It was a great transition to this work. So when I took it over, I knew it was going to be hard, politically and intellectually; but I didn't realize it was more of an appellate-issue-type thing, also.

The 4th judge: John Melanson

JOHN MELANSON So I was about 32 when I got out of school, I guess. And then practiced law in Buhl, Idaho for about 13 years with Bob Weaver, who has since passed away, and Frank Dykas, who's an attorney here in town. And then after Bob died, and Frank moved to Boise, I was on my own there in Buhl, and practiced. And Mark Guerry joined me for a while, and I practiced with him for a short time. And then I became a magistrate judge in Lincoln County. I was appointed, I want to say, 1994. And then after that, I served as magistrate judge in Lincoln County for about six years.

The good thing about that was – well, I enjoyed living in Shoshone for one thing. But one of the good things about that position was that I got to travel a lot. I went to Hailey once a week to hear cases there, and Twin Falls once a week, and Gooding and Jerome, because I only had to be in Shoshone for one day a week, really, to hear cases. So they used me in other towns. So I got to know the attorneys, and the court clerks in all those counties, and the people working in the courthouses.

And then when a district court position became available in Minidoka County when Judge Hart retired, I applied there. And I was appointed as a district judge in Minidoka county. And there again, that was a small county, so I did travel quite a lot there.

I was a district judge for about eight years altogether. But during part of that time, I was presiding judge of the SRBA. I became presiding judge of the SRBA in 2004, and served until 2009, when I was appointed here at the Court of Appeals.

DAVID TUTHILL Judge Melanson is an intelligent, kind and thoughtful man who added depth and balance to the position. Again, he worked with Eric Wildman – those two teamed up.

Judge Melanson was wonderful to work with, very much enjoyed it, and he was able to successfully navigate some of the tough decisions.

JOHN MELANSON When Judge Burdick became Justice Burdick, he was the previous presiding judge of the SRBA. There was a vacancy. And Judge Wood would have done it. I think he was the likely successor, but he couldn't because – for a couple of reasons. I think he had a water right. But I think also, because his brother-in-law was Justice Eismann. So I think there was at least, maybe a perceived conflict there. So Judge Wood couldn't do it. And it had to a Fifth District Judge. I felt it did anyway because that's where the court was. It was a Twin Falls County.

It wasn't a matter of saying, oh, well, another judge in another county could do it, because the SRBA court staff was there in Twin Falls County, and those were the people that knew how to do the SRBA, basically. And including the case administrator. Diana Delaney, and two of the special masters were in Twin Falls then; one was here, in Boise, and their assistants, and they were all there in Twin Falls. So they really had to be there.

It wasn't seen, I think, as a position that you would necessarily seek out. I think there was some perceived difficulties with it. One, you had to do your own calendar, in addition to the SRBA. Also, the problem, at least that I thought about from the start, and it turned out not to be so right, was that there were two politically powerful groups involved; the Surface Water Users and the groundwater Users. And that any decision you make, potentially, could make one of those groups upset, angry. I don't know.

And so maybe from a political perspective, that wasn't the best job to have, but it turned out not to be so. And the reason is, I think, at least from my perspective, the members of both of those groups, I think, understood by then that judges were just making the best decision they could, given the facts, and the law, and that those things were bound anyway to go to the Supreme Court one way or another, and that's where the decision would be made. And so I didn't really run into that difficulty.

But back to the question. I decided after visiting the court, and speaking with Eric Wildman, who is now Judge Wildman, he was then the staff attorney for the court. After speaking with him, and the special masters, and seeing where the court was in terms of the number of cases left to process, the number of big decisions left to be made, the basin-wide issues that were undecided, you know, the time that it might take to complete it. And also, observing the fact that really, by then it was – I've used this expression before in connection with the court – by then it was a well oiled machine. It was functioning really well. And I thought, well, I could step into this, and do it, and rely on the excellent staff, and get it done. And so I volunteered, and was appointed by then Chief Justice Eisman to be the SRBA presiding judge.

And I think that part of my perception did turn out to be true. The court was really functioning well, and it continued, you know. And not because of anything I did, it was just already working well. I think the main contribution I made was to just set deadlines, and try to keep it moving.

JOHN MELANSON In fact, I did not even take a water law class at law school. And when I practiced law in Buhl, Bob Weaver, one of the partners in the firm, did the water law stuff. And so I really had a very limited exposure to it. I grew up in a farm community in Blackfoot. And I worked – I moved pipe a little bit, and bucked hay back in the day, back when you had to pick up hay bales, and put them on a flatbed. So I did that. So I knew a little bit about farming, and a little bit about irrigation. But not anything that would prepare me for a career in being a presiding judge in the SRBA.

I remember an incident, after I was appointed, I went o a water law seminar. I think it was one of the dividing waters groups, and I hadn't been appointed for very long. And one of the other participants asked me, well, I assume you have a background in water law.

And I replied in kind of a smart alecky way, "as if."

And that probably gave a bad impression. But it was true. I didn't have any background in water law at all. And that was one reason – well, I had to do two things then. I had to rely on the SRBA staff, and learn as much about it as I could, and as quickly as I could, and that's what I did.

JOHN MELANSON The regular docket in Minidoka County didn't require me to be there every day. So that was a good thing. And, in fact, even sometimes Judge Wood, who was the District Judge in Gooding County then, would help me out with my Minidoka County docket when it was necessary for me to be at he SRBA.

The thing is, you know, sort of a personal observation about that, I think maybe – I know we'll never do this again in Idaho. But if I had it to do over again, and if I had been in charge of anything, which I wasn't; I would have said, look, the SRBA judge should just be the SRBA judge. Because I always felt I was short-changing Minidoka County a little bit, because I was appointed to be the judge to be there, and then elected to be the judge to be there. And yet, I wasn't there very much.

The work got done. There is no question about that. We made sure of that. But I think – and I did talk to the county commissioners more than once about this, and brought the subject up with them. And said, hey, you know, the SRBA has to be done. Somebody has to do it. I'm sorry I can't be here more, but this is just how it has worked out.

So I, also, always have felt a little bit bad about that. But it worked out, you know, and we got it done. And now, Minidoka County has their own judge, who actually stays there. That's a good thing.

But to go back to your question. Typically, you know, the work at the SRBA, the grunt work, the hearings in the first instance are almost always conducted by the special masters. And they would be having hearings all the time, traveling around the state, just all over the state, having their hearings. And some of them were by telephone conference, some of them otherwise.

And so I would have cases on challenge.

Whenever a person – you see, the way it works is, a claimant of a water right files a claim with the Department of Water Resources and the SRBA. The department investigates, and makes the recommendations from the director's report. And then if a claimant objects to the recommendation, then the claimant has a hearing before the special master. And the special master makes a recommendation. And then if the claimant is dissatisfied with that, then the claimant can challenge that, then it comes to the SRBA Court.

And I don't recall that a huge amount of my time was taken up with challenges. We typically would, you know, decide those on the record, just like appeals, here at he Court of Appeals. So those usually could be handled with, you know, under my direction, by the staff attorney, and the law clerk that we had.

The cases that were more time consuming for me were the basin-wide issues. And those are the issues that the court dealt with in the first instance, and had the hearings on. And those were interesting, and more time consuming, from my point of view.

It's hard to describe a typical day, other than to say, that it could have involved any of those things. The work there was – we were busy, but not – I never felt overwhelmed. You know, it was just one of those things.

Judge Wood would – always talked about seeing surfers riding up on top of the wave. As long as you stayed on top, it was okay. That's how I felt, okay, staying after it, and staying busy with it, and that's what we did.

JOHN MELANSON I was lucky. I know that judges that went before me, particularly Judge Hurlbutt, had some real challenges just trying to start it up. He paved the way for all of us, and he dealt with the really difficult stuff. And then Judge Wood, and Judge Burdick dealt with procedural things, you know, that would come up.

I think the most difficult things for me, were the same things that were difficult in district court. The cases were intellectually challenging. They were, and still are. It involved a lot of reading, and a lot of thinking, and a lot of discussion with the law clerks, and the staff attorney. So, you know, by the time I was there, most of the real, I guess, visceral objection instead of just doing it in the first place, had passed. So we didn't have to deal with that, really. Every once in a while, we would run into that a little bit on our road trips, but not much. Not like they did in the beginning.

So, really, I think it was just the cases that – the case load, itself, wasn't challenging so much. It was just, you just had to keep after it. But the difficulty of the issues, themselves, were probably the biggest challenge.

JOHN MELANSON There were a lot of pro se litigants. And I think the reason there were, was, it was to be set up for pro se people. The claim forms were simple. People were able to fill those out without any real legal knowledge. Most people who have a water right know what it is, and what it comprises, and, you know, what property it goes to. And so they can do that part of it.

And really, I think, most of the hearings before the special masters that dealt with pro se litigants were pretty routinely conducted. And really, I don't recall having a lot of pro se challenges. So I can't say that there were more pro se litigants in the SRBA Court before the judge, than there were before judge, say, in regular district court.

It was sort of like the magistrate court versus the district court. You know, and the magistrates get he most pro se litigants, mostly because they have small claims cases, and traffic infractions. And then the district court hardly ever sees those folks, because they either live with the decision they get from magistrate court, or they appeal, and then get a lawyer. And so there weren't many pro se litigants.

The difference, you know, between the district bench and the SRBA bench, I think, was the fact that we were hearing most of the cases, essentially, on appeal. There were challenges of the special master's decision. So that made for kind of a smooth transition for me and to the Court of appeals, because I was used to reading briefs, and looking at the record, and pages, and pages of the record sometimes. But that's how we decided cases there.

JOHN MELANSON The rules are different, because there is a whole set of rules for the SRBA court. That's one of the things that the judges before me accomplished, Judge Hurlbutt, in particular, and Judge Wood, when he was a judge for a brief time, and then Justice Burdick. They really had the rules for the SRBA court pretty much put together before I got here.

So the rules were different. But the evidentiary standards were the same. The evidentiary standards would be familiar to anybody who practiced in district court, and really, most of the Rules of Civil Procedure applied as well. So I don't think there would be a big difference in that part of it.

JOHN MELANSON Technology played, and I think continues to play an important role in enforcement and investigation, you know, GIS mapping. And one of the things that I was really fascinated by when I first started, was that the department could use satellite and air photos to see where water was being applied to the land, because they could see where places were green. They appeared red on the map, but places were green that shouldn't be, unless they were being watered. And they could tell in that way whether water was being used there. And, you know, if there wasn't a water right that went to that land, then they would know that here was an unauthorized use there. So that was just in investigation, and enforcement. It was not really so much a part of the senior SRBA.

I remember when the GIS mapping started to really become useful during the time that I was there, and one of the things that came up because of it was – I think everyone involved, not just in the SRBA, but probably in real property law in general, began to see that here – if we used GIS mapping to describe real property, metes and bounds descriptions, for instance, there might be some discrepancies with the old way that it was done that was surveying. And so that sort of was a wrinkle that we just dealt with by, I think, the same way pretty much everyone has so far, and that's by saying, well, all these years we've used surveying. And we continue to do that, actually, although surveying it really takes more and more advantage of GIS mapping as time goes on. And those discrepancies are just going to have to be dealt with, if ever, not in the SRBA. And I remember having a discussion about that.

By then the SRBA Court's computer system, called iWaters, was revving up too full capacity.

JOHN MELANSON That's really , I think, a big advantage for the public. Anybody involved, who was interested at all, can look and see what has happened in just every case. And what is scheduled to happen in the future in the same cases, as well.

Increasingly too the court was using conference telephoning systems to expedite court proceedings.

JOHN MELANSON You know, I didn't use it much. The special masters did a lot, because they were hearing cases all over the state. And I think – I can't speak for them. I think they would tell you, it's useful as long as it works well. And everybody is on the phone that's not a cell phone, and they are not trying to talk to you while they are riding along in their pickup with their window open. It works okay for that. But not in cases where you have to take evidence in court, or testimony, and try to determine credibility.

And that's why – and this is one of the fun things that happened while I was there, video conferences became available. And it was going to be – and it was very expensive. But I think we split the costs. The court paid for part of it, and the SRBA – or the department paid for part of it.

The department was interested in having it not just for the SRBA, but because of their administrative hearings that they would hold around the state. So there was a set up at the SRBA courthouse, and also, there might have been one at the Twin Falls IDWR office. I know there was one up in Coeur d'Alene. And certainly, one in here, in Boise, I remember, because we used it. And that was just a real benefit to the court, and I think the litigants, that they wouldn't have to travel. In fact, I think some hearings have been held even where there was testimony, and evidence, that the set up we had allowed the parties to admit evidence.

And then there was like a fax machine that was part of the video conferencing set up. And so you could fax things instantaneously to all the other parties, and that worked really well. That was a big improvement over the audio, the telephone conferencing. And I think, I assume, it's being used still.

I remember when we were looking at it, we went over to the federal courthouse to see what they had and of course they had state of the art stuff. And one interesting thing was a camera that would automatically move and focus on the person who was talking. They still have that. And it's kind of an interesting thing. It doesn't make a lot of noise. It is hardly noticeable at all when it does it. Anyway, that was a big step forward for the court, I think, when the court and the department adopted that.

JOHN MELANSON Back in the day, when we used to travel around, and do informational meetings before basins would be open, you know, for claims taking, people would always ask, why do we have to do it? And I would always talk about that a little bit. Although at the time, I didn't think it was likely to happen. And I told them that, that, you know, I didn't want to – I wasn't trying to alarm anybody into thinking that the adjudication had to be done. The main reason was that the one that everybody states, and that's the Swan Falls Agreement. But, you know, there are practical reasons, as well, and that's one of them.

New federal water rights issues were arising in SRBA Court, some of the more prominent and far-reaching involving the Bureau of Reclamation.

DAVID TUTHILL The second fill issue, which is before the Supreme Court right now, is an issue that we're waiting for some guidance on from the supreme court. So that's an issue that's really been debated after my time. One of the issues that was done when Karl Dreher was director was when the bureau decided to purchase water from Bell Rapids, which is about 60,000 acre-feet per year, which was idled. So they bought this land, idled the land, and now it's a wind farm up on the south side of the river and allowed an additional 60,000 acre-feet to better augment the anadromous fishery.

So the Bureau of Reclamation has been a partner with Idaho in water management, but there's always a struggle – there's a tension between the state being directed by congress to manage water resources, and working with the federal agency which has built many of the dams and its role in managing water resources.

So this tension is an ongoing one, and the state – all of the states, as represented in Western States Water Council, are very careful to maintain the responsibility for water management while working with the federal government. That question is going to be ongoing past the SRBA.

The SRBA did determine the extent of the water rights, but the actual administration of the water, which the state is charged to do and is responsible to do, relative to the federal government interests in the water, will be an ongoing battle one would expect.

JOHN MELANSON And it's funny, you know, sometimes when you are a judge, you get good press, and sometimes not so good. In the SRBA, it seems like every decision you make is going to be – that there is going to be something in the newspaper about it.

And I remember when I first got here, and decided a couple things, there were some articles in the paper. I would joke that I would open the newspaper a little bit at a time, so I wouldn't get the bad news. But mostly, it was good news.

But I remember the Boise River had to do with the claims of the irrigation districts downstream. Their claims would have, essentially – I don't know – dewatered the Boise River of the part that goes through down here. And that would have been a negative thing, not only for aesthetic value, and the fishery, but also because there is a requirement of a certain amount of water to dilute the sewage effluent that comes out of the treatment plant, and recreation, too, was another factor. And I can't remember the merits of it, and I can't remember how it was decided. But it was decided in favor of leaving some water in the river.

And there was some good press over that. But I don't even think that got appealed. So that one wasn't really one that had much exposure at all. But it was one I remember.

NORM YOUNG At the time that the conjunctive management rules were adopted, and I think that was 1994, Higginson also adopted rules for administering Water District 34, conjunctive management rules for Water Direct 34. Karl Dreher picked up on that as the successive director and said, "Yes, this is the way this is going to work. There's going to be an overall statewide set of water administration rules." Conjunctive management rules being a subset of that, and then a set of rules for every basin or every source that's being administered separately would be a compartment in this overall package of rules.

So we set out to adopt the water management rules and didn't get that done.

All kinds of arguments were put out there. To the extent that groundwater is like reservoir water, does it really make any difference what diversion rate as long as you don't exceed the volume? If you're a groundwater user, that appeals to you. If you're a surface water user and you think that well next to the stream takes your water in a matter of hours, it makes a big difference to you.

Well, that was a hot enough topic that those umbrella rules never got adopted. So that's what faces the department now in terms of administering those individual water rights that have been very well defined by the SRBA. How do they now administer those versus each other?

ROGER BURDICK I also signed the Conjunctive Management Order, Basin-Wide Issue 5. I was very surprised. I thought that would take weeks of testimony, et cetera; but, by the time it came to me, people basically stipulated that, yeah, undergroundwater is connected to surface water in Idaho. It's certainly not like the Gila Springs Rule where you have to prove that the water is moving, as opposed to stationary. I just can't imagine how they proved that down in Arizona.

But I was surprised at how little that was controversial. I didn't give Idaho – or the Department of Water Resources – they wanted a remark, basically, of all of their rules and regulations; and I didn't give that to them which helped, I think, give flexibility to the concept.

DAVID TUTHILL One of my roles as the bureau chief was to address those issues that would come up and try to seek solutions with various parties. One of specific note is the basin-wide issue on conjunctive management or conjunctive administration.

Conjunctive administration

Just as far as terminology goes, the rules that we have are called "conjunctive management" rules. Some aspects of water administration call this relationship between groundwater and surface water as requiring "conjunctive administration" by the agency, whereas "conjunctive management" is the optimization of the two resources. So I'll speak to the conjunctive administration of the resource.

One of the expectations through the SRBA was that the SRBA would make some decisions relative to conjunctive administration. We recognize that to fully understand conjunctive administration would be a larger job than could be decided in the SRBA because every basin would need its own separate model; every groundwater diversion has a certain impact on a surface water right somewhere, but to determine that in the SRBA would be far beyond the capability – as we have learned since through modeling. For example, with ESPA – the Eastern Snake River Plain Aquifer – the modeling in that one aquifer has been very challenging and difficult and expensive. It has been successful, but just that one aquifer has been very challenging.

So we were seeking a solution for conjunctive administration through the SRBA that would be achievable and yet would address this question of conjunctive administration.

. . . The department conducted a number of meetings with the parties, the court, and really interested entities and over time developed a condition that would go in the general provisions which addressed this conjunctive administration.

Each basin has its own general provisions, but one issue that's common to all the general provisions is language that was developed through this negotiated process which identifies – which enumerates all the water rights for surface water, for example, that might not be delivered in association with other surface water rights – maybe non-tributary streams or streams that have been declared dry over the years.

The language identifies those water rights that might be delivered separately and then identifies those water rights that are from groundwater that should be delivered separately from the surface water rights, enumerates those, and then provides that all other water rights are considered to be connected and should be administered conjunctively.

So we went through that process, and out of the 158,000 water rights of which more than half are groundwater rights – significantly more than half.

The total count of groundwater rights found to be not connected is zero, but for each basin the general provision specifies this. So by this process we know that the groundwater rights are all connected.

The legal connection is there; the administrative and technical connection is not. So we came to an agreement that we could not get to the technical connection within the parameters of the SRBA. That was a major step for us, and in the end we all agreed with that, and that general provision was not challenged.

. . . A major step that we had to overcome was the extent of spatial determination in our water right recommendations.

By "spatial," I mean "location" because every water right has a location of point of diversion, a location of place of use. It's one thing to record it as a legal description, a 40-acre tract; it's another thing to see it on a map.

Back in '96 I was concerned about trying to resolve the adjudication without using GIS because the geographic information systems at the time were emerging as very powerful, and we could see the benefit of having GIS as a part of the adjudication.

The original database that had been developed for the SRBA was a DOS database, which worked just fine for the claims-taking. It kept track of all the claims and was fully adequate for that process.

But to evaluate the claims and make recommendations, we really did need GIS, yet it was a big hurdle.

I was musing about this, and I talked with a fellow by the name of Tony Morse – he was our GIS lead – on a hot summer day out in front of the building and said, "How do we do this, Tony?"

He said, "You start by developing a plan. You hire somebody to help you with a plan."

So we hired a local computer firm to do that. Ken Grover was the person assigned. We had $25,000 for this plan. He wrote a $50,000 plan for us – did a "Cracker Jack" job of developing a road map that we could use for initiating and for integrating GIS into our system.

So with that wonderful plan that he helped develop, we asked Karl for funding to make this happen.

Our computer person, Doug Werner, our database guy, was in the hall. I said, "Doug, we have to make this happen."

He said, "That's going to cost $1 million," and I said, "Well, okay."

So the next day Doug came up and he said, "That's going to cost $2 million," and it turned out to be $2 million. He was right.

Karl was successful in receiving funding from the legislature. We added – we used about $1 million for equipment, and about $1 million for contractors, and then added about $1 million of our own efforts – which was key – because we wouldn't have finished it without our own staff and our own staff learning how to do it. We were able to integrate GIS into the process where every irrigation right has a line around it, so we know exactly – not just the 40-acre tract, but the acres irrigated.

What this did was to take away so many objections because if we found 38 acres irrigated and the irrigator said, "Wait a minute. I have 45 acres irrigated," we would just simply take this map and share that with the claimant and say, "This is what we show. What acres are you irrigating that we're not showing?"

So instead of this being a contentious issue, GIS helped us hugely to resolve questions about spatial information. We were able to evaluate claims then spatially and integrate them in a basin. This provided the basis of what we have today which is a system where if you have a question about a water right, you can go to the website, enter the information, name, water right number or location and find information very quickly online (snapping fingers) and print a spatial map that shows the point of diversion and place of use online within two minutes.

PETER MONSON It was farsighted on the part of Idaho [management within the SRBA of groundwater]. Groundwater is much better understood now, and a lot of that is a consequence of including the groundwater in the adjudication. ... Those kinds of things are better understood now I think because they decided to adjudicate them.

ROGER BURDICK You know, A & B Irrigation -- their whole system is so complex – in terms of – they bring the water up. And then they use too much of it and store it, and then they wanted to re-acquire that as a second water right for their enlarged acreages. And they've been fighting that fight. I think we've had three or four A & Bs.

They haven't been very successful.

Limited the scope of application of the enlargement claims made pursuant to the Amnesty Statute, because that was brand new during that time period. It required that previously unauthorized enlargement rights claimed in the SRBA be subordinate to water rights that existed prior. Then it defined what constitutes groundwater and surface water for purposes of applying the mandatory permit and licensing requirements. I think, as I remember, in reading this, they said: Listen, this is either a recapture of drain or wastewater in which case we can get a new water right on -- or -- no. It is a recapture of our original water and, therefore, it can be applied to the enlarged area. The Supreme Court said, "No." If it is, in fact, a recapture of waste or drain water, you need a permit to get a water right; and, therefore, that would not apply. That would be subordinated to the existing waters. And, then, if it was groundwater, which they ruled it was, that also is subordinated. So they lost on both of their arguments in that regard.

Do you know how I figured it out? I thought that they said, okay, once we bring up a piece – a drop of water, we have the right to follow that water wherever it goes forever. And that didn't make any common sense either.

So – yeah. And then I happened to write another A & B – and I may have written two of them up here – the one about where they had to show that they were – where some of their wells have dried up, they have got to extend their piping, et cetera, to the wells that haven't before they can continue.

ERIC WILDMAN Basin 37, yes. The Wood River Valley, you know there's going to be a lot of objections and the basin is going to be real contentious. I tried to balance it out.

I can remember having a meeting with Dave Tuthill and Susan Hamlin up in Challis in a hamburger place, having dinner. Dave wanted to get all of the director's reports filed, and the goal was 2005. This might have been in 2001 or 2002. They were going to agents on contract to investigate the claims so they could get them all reported in by then.

That's great as far as getting the claims investigated and getting them reported. The problem is that there are so many claims and the litigants had to have meaningful time to review them, especially when you had like the United States who physically went through and reviewed every claim.

The statute specifies an objection period. That works fine if it's just one director's report that's coming out, but if you have 25 of them coming in all at once, that doesn't work.

So I had talked to Dave about does the department want to hold them and then just stagger the filing, or do they want to file them and make the court be the bad guy on staggering the objections periods.

Of course he wanted the court to be the bad guy on staggering the objection periods, and that's ultimately what we ended up doing. They didn't get them all filed by 2005, but they substantially did. Then we had to stagger the objection period out over a couple of years. But as part of that process, knowing when the director's reports were coming in and that the bulk of them would be in by '05, that's when I sat down and went through each basin and decided how I was going to assign to the special masters.

Groundwater and calls on delivery were beginning to become a major issue in Idaho generally, and would become even more intense in the years to come.

ERIC WILDMAN Without having the SRBA completed and having an inventory of all of the water rights, conjunctive management wouldn't be possible. Even though the state law provides for it and the department is required to do it, it simply couldn't be done without having all of the rights adjudicated. There's no inventory.

You look at what's going on in California now. They're not even regulating groundwater rights. They're having a water shortage over there. They're curtailing or cutting back surface rights, and what are the water users doing in response?

They're drilling wells. Of course drilling the wells just further impacts the surface supply.

So I think going back to when Musser made the call in the early '90s and we didn't have the rules of conjunctive management yet, but even with the rules of conjunctive management, without having a comprehensive inventory, we wouldn't be able to accomplish conjunctive administration. You know, Idaho really is at the vanguard of conjunctive management. I know Colorado does it, and they've had their rights adjudicated for years, and they have a little different system than we have in place, but a lot of other states, they acknowledge the legal relationship between the ground and surface water, but they're not really able to meaningfully address it. I know the litigation has definitely switched from the inventory in the SRBA to the conjunctive management. But I look at it like starting out on the SRBA when there's uncertainty over the adjudication statutes and some of the basic framework of the adjudication, it takes a little bit of time to get by those issues and get them decided, and then there's some certainty about the process. People know how things are going to operate. That's kind of how I look at conjunctive management.

We've had the first challenge to the conjunctive management rules in AFRD #2, and these are big issues. These are really issues of first impression. Other states aren't addressing conjunctive management. You can't really go to another state and look for case law on it. There's very little case law on it in Idaho. So most of these going up are issues of first impression.

I think once we work through all of the issues, and I'm in the process of working through it now, I think the process will move a little faster. You know, we hear about dissatisfaction over how long it takes to get through these issues, but again, they're issues of first impression. Once we work through them, there should be more certainty, and things should move more quickly.

CLIVE STRONG When I use the term conjunctive administration, what I'm referring to is administrating hydraulically connected groundwater and surface water under the prior appropriation doctrine.

Where this plays out most clearly is with regard to the spring flows in the Thousand Springs reach. The water that is coming out of the Eastern Snake Plan Aquifer comes out as a spring and then replenishes the surface water of the Snake River.

We have a similar phenomenon like that up in the American Falls Reservoir. And, as the development of the groundwater has occurred and the spring flows have declined, it has created a problem for people who rely upon the spring flows. It's probably worth describing how that occurred.

As I talked earlier, in the 1950s, because of technology, groundwater pumping became feasible. So we began depleting the spring flows. Prior to that time, if you go back into the early 1900s, the spring flows in the Thousand Springs reach were about 4,000 CFS.

By the 1950s, it had increased almost 6,800 CFS. And, that was because of recharge occurring to the aquifer as a result of the return flow from gravity irrigation. We essentially treated the Eastern Snake Plan Aquifer as a storage reservoir. It captured all of the return flow.

At the same time the pumping technology was occurring, some entrepreneurs discovered that the springs in the Thousand Springs area were ideal for fish farming. The water comes out at about 58 degrees temperature, which is perfect for raising trout. And as any good water user would do, they developed their water rights based upon the highest flow available on any particular day of the year. They essentially, similar to the hydropower situation, appropriated the entire flow.

Well, as these spring flows began to decline, the trout producers began to demand regulation of the groundwater pumping in order to protect their water rights.

Throughout the course of the adjudication, this issue has continued to escalate. We first saw it in 1992 when Twin Falls and North Side Canal Companies filed a petition – actually it was a complaint seeking to preclude any future issuance of water rights because of the concern that the spring flows were declining.

The case was settled based upon the director's agreement to conduct spring flow studies. Those were completed between 1993 and 1996. But, in 2001, as the spring flows continued to decline, there was clamoring for delivery calls. A delivery call is when a senior water right owner says you're materially injuring my water right, and therefore, you should be curtailed.

I was asked, along with Karl Dreher, to mediate between the groundwater users and surface water users. We entered into some interim agreements that were designed to develop a longer term solution.

Although we had a lot of good discussions, we weren't successful because the state of the law was too uncertain. Given that lack of certainty, we just could not find common ground.

In 2005, Clear Spring Foods and Blue Lakes Hatcheries made delivery calls. As those delivery calls were being decided, and there was a determination that material injury was occurring to them, it created another huge political consternation. There are about a million acres of land irrigated with groundwater. And, we were talking about curtailing a large portion of those acres. The economic impact to the economy was in the hundreds of millions of dollars; while the benefit to the fish producers was in the hundreds of thousands of dollars.

Speaker Newcomb held what we call the Hall of Mirrors meeting,* in 2004, when it looked like we were headed toward curtailment. An agreement was reached that forestalled curtailment while the parties attempted to develop a long-term solution.

BRUCE NEWCOMB I don't remember the year. I just can remember, because I remember Dan Popkey being out there trying to look through the windows, you know, to see what was going on. But we kept the press out. And I'd say we had close to 50 people. You know, Clear Springs, Kay Hardy, Clear Lakes, and all the groundwater users. Randy was there. Lawyers, I think all the water lawyers were there.

And so what we were trying to do is just get a -- because it was kind of a fire storm. And so just to kind of calm the waters so we could have a year to kind of work things out.

First of all, overload the courts and then have huge economic negative effects, you know, because you'd shut down everybody. And then you wouldn't get a resolution that would be timely, you know. And so we negotiated. And I think it took us two days. I'm trying to remember.

But they were long, tedious days. And we finally got an agreement.

And so, you know, getting an agreement finally came down to getting an agreement with Larry Cope and Kay Hardy. So we got it. And then she goes down to Phoenix, Arizona, to a wedding and changes her mind.

---

* Formally the Joe E. Williams Building, located across State Street from the Statehouse in downtown Boise.

And so I learned two things there. One is when you get an agreement, you need to have a document that everybody signs before they leave, because I come from the old school that if people give their word, they give their word, you know, but that's beginning to change.

And so basically, I had to go back to Larry Cope and get him to give up a little more. And he did.

Basically, we had put a moratorium on any calls and give us time to work this out for a year, and then all bets were off. And so it was a good thing, you know, because subsequent to that Clive came up with legislation that would help alleviate some of the concerns, and then mitigation plans were put together and stuff. And the weather changed. So that is what that was all about.

It was really funny because Bert Stevenson he would get mad. He sat on my right, and he was the chairman of the Resource Committee in the House. I had to set him at ease one time and take him outside out in the hall and said, "Bert you're going to blow this whole thing. You got to keep your mouth shut and keep your temper under control."

I mean it surprised me, because I had never seen him in that mode, because his mentor was Mack Neibaur, and Mack was kind of mine too. But Mack was always calm, collected. But Bert, he had a side to him that if you stick him in the side too many times he's going to show up, you know. But that really surprised me because I had never seen him in that mode before.

The weather was hot and the stakes were high. And the mitigation, you know, was – and, you know, out there by Minidoka they were pretty vulnerable. But no more than the guys that are sitting out there in Jerome, you know, but it was just above the bench, you know. And Wendell. And everybody had a lot at stake.

CLIVE STRONG Despite the state bringing money to the table, it still wasn't enough to solve the problem. So, we had the 2005 delivery call. Once the director found material injury and the Supreme Court affirmed, the handwriting was on the wall -- something had to be done to solve the problem.

The real fundamental principle of water law came to the forefront. That is – water flows to money. Because of the disproportionate impact of curtailment versus the benefit to the spring users, it became obvious to the groundwater users they needed to acquire some of the hatchery water rights.

The first transaction we did was the acquisition of the Pristine Springs Hatchery. That occurred in 2008. The Pristine Springs Hatchery is situated right below the Perrine Bridge next to the Blue Lakes Hatchery.

The director determined that the Blue Lakes Hatchery was entitled to 10 cfs of direct flow. In order to deliver that 10 cfs, it was going to require the curtailment of more than 100,000 acres of land. So, the decision was made to buy one of the hatcheries and deliver water from that hatchery to the other. SeaPac was willing to sell the Pristine Springs Hatchery for $26 million. We funded the transaction through a joint effort. The groundwater users needed ten CFS, so they contributed $11 million to the settlement.

The City of Twin Falls, which diverts out of the same complex, was confronted with a water quality problem. It was contemplating building a water treatment plant because of arsenic problems in the groundwater. The treatment plant was going to cost the City of Twin Falls in excess of $30 million to build.

So we offered to sell the remaining first-use natural flow water to the City, which it could use to mix with its culinary water supply to meet the arsenic water quality standard. The City agreed to pay $10 million for the water. From the City's standpoint it avoided a $25 million cost by acquiring the water.

The remaining $5 million came from the state, which ended up owning the hatchery and the second use water rights. The state then leased the Pristine Springs hatchery back to SeaPac, which operated the hatchery with the reduced water supply.

The outcome was to essentially that readjusted the water supply at sustainable levels. The Twin Falls *Times News* applauded the deal as an example of enlightened self-interest.

CLIVE STRONG That became a template for the next big settlement. Once the Clear Springs decision was issued by the Idaho Supreme Court, the groundwater users entered into an agreement to purchase the hatcheries owned by the Hardy family, which consisted of Blue Lakes, Rim View, and Clear Springs.

The reason that was important is the Clear Lakes hatchery is adjacent to the Clear Springs hatchery. So the groundwater users, by acquiring Clear Lakes Hatchery, were able to make direct delivery of water to satisfy the Clear Springs delivery call, just as happened with the Pristine Springs purchase.

Clear Springs Foods actually owns other hatcheries that had the potential to make a delivery call. These call were resolved by the groundwater uses transferring ownership of the Clear Lakes hatchery to Clear Springs foods. So Clear Springs got an alternative water supply to make up for lost production at its other hatcheries.

The Rim View Hatchery, which was excess to the groundwater users needs, is leased to Clear Springs Foods. So the groundwater users are recouping part of their purchase price.

JOHN MELANSON And then I think the cases involving conjunctive management were really interesting to me.

You know, everybody acknowledges that the rivers are connected to the groundwater. And some people even understand how. I don't. Except I acknowledge that they are connected, and that – but I think it can be really different, depending on the underground geology, how use of water in one place can affect use of water in another. And then, of course, you know, the use of groundwater in one place can, likewise affect use of groundwater in the other. And those cases were always really interesting to me, just the science of it, and the expert testimony on it.

ROGER BURDICK Number one, in the large portion of them, we have sustained the SRBA, the District Judge, in those cases. So I think that shows, number one, the quality of what's coming out of there, based on their staff and the experience of that staff and Judge Wildman's expertise in the area. I mean, I don't want to be simplistic because, obviously, this is not; but it always boils down to whose ox is getting gored, priority versus economic development.

All of these water calls go to that. I think we've been very consistent. The Constitution says "priority." What can you do with that? We tried in American Falls – American Falls II, was it, that Trout wrote? – to put in some amount of reasonable language of reasonableness – that kind of balanced the economic development and priority. I think, Justice Schroeder, when he was watermaster for – or master for IDWR on that series of cases tried mightily to do some of that. But priority always has to come out at some point.

The other issue is that we had connected sources, anyway, in all of our Decrees. All of the Partial Decrees in the Sub-Basins made use of the connections, anyway. I mean, that they were – oh, what was the language? I can't remember. So I think we were using the issue of the connectiveness of surface water and groundwater in Partial Decrees in 29 – in Sub-Basin 29 and other Sub-Basins – yeah, "connected" – "connected water source," I think, is the word.

I think everybody understands, to some extent, it is all connected; and, as a result, the conjunctive management issues are issues of science, trying to find the connections, rather than issues of law that apply to all water in Idaho.

So I think that's where we are now. It's an issue of science. Science and tracking and knowing where the water goes underground so that we can apply the law to it. I don't like to be simple about these things, but sometimes you have to be.

SRBA goes on the road

JOHN MELANSON I mentioned those little road trips that we would take as the basins were, you know, beginning to take claims. And those were meant to inform the people about what an adjudication was, and why they should file their claims, and just to try to provide a comfort level for them. And, you know, I can't say that it did that sometimes. I always felt like the guy from the government saying, hey, I'm here to help. And, of course, people roll your eyes then. And I think all of us maybe felt that to a little extent.

There was one meeting we had up in Howe. And Howe is a little tiny town up in the Pahsimeroi Valley. And there is a grange hall, and a bar. There might be two bars up there. I can't remember. But we went there. And it was a meeting in the evening, because we would usually hit two or three places in a day. And this one was the last one of the day.

And so the bar was already busy when we got there. And we had heard that there was a guy that was really opposed to the adjudication, and he was going to come over. And at sometimes, you know – and I know previously that there would even be law enforcement people present, but we didn't have anybody with us.

And I remember – and I'm trying to think who was there. I think Candice McHugh might have been there from the department, back when she was working with the department. And I can't think of who else. Eric and I were there, of course. But it never materialized. But we thought, oh, man, we're in trouble now. Because we're out here, on our own. It's starting to get dark. And it was just a tiny meeting. I think maybe 10 or 12 people showed up. And, actually, the meeting went pretty well. It turned out that he guy that had talked about disturbance, was there. But he sat there with his hands folded, and didn't do anything, no disturbance.

We had one up, I think, it was up in Council, where there was an angry person there. That we didn't have one closer to where she lived. And I can't remember. I mean, nothing ever came of it. She just seemed really upset.

But the one that really comes to mind, as far as it being more like the old times, before I got there mostly, was when we had informational meeting up in north Idaho. And this isn't even part of the SRBA. It was part of the north Idaho adjudications, because the SRBA Court was handling those as well. And just before I left, we went up for a meeting, and we had one up in St. Maries, and we had one in Wallace. And the people there, I think – and I probably can speak to this a little bit. But some of the folks there were opposed to the adjudication, I think, because of the concerns that they had, and perhaps, still have about the tribal claims.

And the meetings were orderly. But I think the concern that the people had was really probable. And so it wasn't the most comfortable informational meeting I've ever attended, but we got it done. And the people's questions, I think, they were heartfelt, and legitimate. And we answered them, at least from their point of view, we answered them as well as we could.

But, you know, there were times I know previously before I got here, when they even had to have law enforcement present at the meetings, because people were so angry about it.

And, you know, as far as any problems, or outbursts, or anger at the hearings, themselves, I just never had any problems with that at the SRBA. You are far more likely to run into those in small cases in magistrate court.

ERIC WILDMAN Then we have a public informational meeting where the court shows up. They can meet the judge. The staff attorney can answer some procedural questions and go over how the court process works. More importantly, they can also meet with IDWR agents and go over where their areas, potential areas of disagreement may be or if there's errors in the preliminary director's report, things that they can potentially resolve up front. But people can see the process, meet the staff, see that the judge doesn't have horns. I think by having those public information meetings, it does defuse some of the tension. I was at that meeting in May, Idaho, and I think after we got to meet with people and answer questions and have the opportunity to correct misinformation, I think that helps considerably. ...

I've enjoyed when we've moved into specific basins or we're dealing with issues where we've had the court view the premises. We traveled over to Reynolds Creek and Sinker Creek over in Basin 57. We traveled over to Big Lost over in Basin 34. There's always a lot of characters. You know, it's open to whoever. We set the ground rules and whoever wants to show up can show up, but you're always going to have somebody trying to get their point across, and you've kind of got to remind them of what the ground rules are.

When we were in Basin 34, we had one of the water users complaining that he wasn't getting his full amount of water. This is when I was out there with Judge Wood. We're midway on this ditch, Judge Wood says, "Well, where is your point of diversion?" He points probably about a mile and a half down the road and said, "Well, it's a mile and a half down there." As you know, your water quantity is measured at your point of diversion, not at your place of use. For some reason, that just sticks in my mind.

The public information meeting in May, Idaho, was another one that stuck in my mind. I think it was because Dave Tuthill had prepped us that there were people that wanted to opt out of the adjudication, and it was kind of a dreary day when we pulled into May. There was a bar across the street from the Grange Hall that we were in. There were people pulling back the curtains and looking out the window and pointing. I didn't know what to expect, but it all turned out well.

Of course, there was the time we were in Salmon for a hearing. I was working for Judge Burdick at the time. We were in Salmon for hearings and getting ready to go on the bench and Burdick forgot his shirt. He had to send Virginia down to the store and pick him up a shirt.

We had one of the public information meetings, and I believe that one was in Salmon at thc Elk's Club. We were just getting into Salmon, and there was some water users up there that weren't very happy to see us. Of course, the Elk's Lodge there's a bar right adjacent to it, so people were going into the bars and getting drinks and then coming back in. That one was fine, too, but that one was interesting.

I think I really did enjoy traveling around to the different counties and using the different courthouses. It was all real interesting and a good experience.

ROGER BURDICK I was at a Water Users Conference once where I think they brought Special Masters Bilyeu and Booth and Judge Wildman – I don't remember if it was while he was Presiding Judge or the Staff Attorney – but where I think he described how they had to deal with the issue of whether an assault claim could be filed in the SRBA because somebody got in a fight over a water issue.

JOHN MELANSON I know a couple of times we went up the Payette, up to Council. And we went up to White Bird. We had a meeting at White Bird, one at Riggins, and Grangeville. And in each of these, you know, the people would come with their questions about whether, you know, about filing, and what it meant, and, you know, just all good legitimate questions.

And I remember one time, the local watermaster was there. I can't – his last name was Bosco. He was Jim Bosco. He said, just call me "Bosco." He's a very colorful and fun guy. And he really wanted to show us the reservoir. So we loaded in four-wheel drives. And this was in between meetings. We had a meeting in, I want to say, Cascade, and a meeting in New Meadows. We had a couple of hours in between there. He took us to this reservoir, and showed us how he controlled the water coming out of the dam there. That was really interesting. And then we went down to town, and had lunch with him, and a couple of people from the staff.

BRUCE NEWCOMB Ultimately my swansong was House Bill 800, which we got through the House. But in the Senate is when I knew I should start thinking about retiring because people would say to Clive and I, you know, "I think this is the right thing to do, but if I vote this way, I can't get reelected," you know, because Idaho Power – the metaphor I used is I looked across the rotunda to the Senate and I saw all these black flies. And it looked like there was a dead cow over there. And I so I walked over there, and they were all lobbyists that were hired by Idaho Power to kill House Bill 800.

. . . Well, it was, you know, basically, the whole thing about the Snake River Plain Aquifer in its natural state before the flood irrigation occurred, you know, when they opened up the Egin Bench and that country, and they had Bureau of Reclamation canals they kept full of water all year long in the wintertime and stuff, that became the artificial recharge.

So the levels from 1951, which was its natural state, to where they were – and I can't remember the peak, 1970-something, I think, was the peak of Snake River Plain Aquifer. And then we started to mine it a little bit.

Then it seemed to me to make sense, and lots of other people, and Clive, too, is, you know, we should have a recharge program so that when you have that water that's just flood water, you know, you have a way to divert that and put it into the Snake River Plain Aquifer so you can recharge it like you used to do with Egin Bench.

So we had John Peavey come. We had John Evans come. I think Karl came. I think we had a whole history of the whole thing. And so, you know, and in the Senate you had Dean Cameron that never knew, you know, the whole history and all the angst that went through this. So that was one of the real purposes was to educate the legislators that were there as I left to what the history was.

It was to do the recharge and, you know, to divert the water and get it. And, you know, even though it was flood water, Idaho Power didn't want us doing that. And then there was the resistance to some people, you know, the contaminants that might go with that. And where are the sites that you put it in and how the delivery system you get there.

[The opposition] was mostly Idaho Power – well, because they wanted to own the river. That was what it's all about, is they wanted to own the river. And whether there was flood water or not, they wanted to end it. And so that was their big fight.

. . . I mean they hired everybody to kill that bill, and they got it killed, you know. And then the governor's office had Jim Yost. And he was always in Idaho Power's pocket, you know, from the get-go.

He was the resource guy for the governor's office, for Dirk Kempthorne and later – I think he came in originally – well, he was with Butch, and then Butch put him over in the Northwest Regional Power Council. But he was always, you know, there. And so he would say things like, "Oh, I kicked your ass on House Bill 800."

And I said, "Yeah, you and Cox's Army." I said, "If I had the money that was put into that," I said, "I would have kicked your ass.

You never would have seen the light of day." Pardon my language. I still get angry about that.

JOHN MELANSON I always thought we had an excellent relationship with IDWR. It's kind of unique, because IDWR, as I mentioned, investigated the claims, and then presented their report. And the court relied on the reports. It was sort of like IDWR being the court's expert witness in a sense. But there was also, of course, the obligation to remain, you know, unbiased and impartial.

But on a personal level, I always felt that we had a great relationship with the director. During the time I was there, Karl Dreher was the Director, and then David Tuthill. I didn't get to know Director Spackman very well at all, because he came on not long before I came to the Court of Appeals. But it was always – and not just the director. You know, the attorneys working for the department, we got to know them a little bit.

We traveled with them some, because whenever a basin was – I can't remember the terminology – but they were going to begin claims taking in a basin, we would go, and usually, sometimes the Director would go with us, and often an attorney or two from the staff, and maybe one of the technical people. And we would go and have informational meetings in these little towns. And so we would get to go to lunch and diner with them, and get to know them a little bit. And that was one of the things I really enjoyed about the job.

I think Director Dreher and Director Tuthill were just really good people. And it was a pleasure to get to know them, and the attorneys. You know, one of the things I always said when I would go to seminars when I was the presiding judge, I couldn't say much, you know, because of the ethical rules we have, of course, we couldn't discus the case at all, and any of the merits of any of the cases. But I would always praise the attorneys, not just the IDWR attorneys, but the attorneys who represented litigants.

It was a pleasure to be a judge there, because it was like having experts in the field be the ones that were presenting the case to you. And that's a lot different from the way it can be sometimes in regular district court. I really, really enjoyed that. And I really enjoyed getting to know those attorneys, too. That was one of the best parts of being the SRBA Judge.

Performance metrics 2007-14

In January 2007, with the arrival of the new state administration of C.L. "Butch" Otter, David Tuthill was named interim director of the Idaho Department of Water Resources, replacing Karl Dreher.

Finishing the recommendations

DAVID TUTHILL We completed our recommendations in the SRBA early in 2007 – our last basins were recommended. I was appointed as interim director in January of 2007 and director in April of 2007.

Thus by the time I became director we had almost totally completed our initial recommendations. Many of the basins had been fully decreed, some had not been, but that initial big work to create director's reports and make recommendations had been completed. Then most of the work was being supportive of our legal staff where the big burden goes from the agency with the legal staff supporting to the legal staff with the agency support.

So I had the background of having gone through that process. When I became director, I had the challenge of the calls for 2007. That was a very interesting time. We had an excellent Deputy Attorney General staff consisting of Phil Rassier, Garrick Baxter, Chris Bromley, Nick Spencer and Andrea Courtney – they assisted tremendously in the response to the calls. We also had an excellent technical staff, led by Don Shaff and Carter Fritschle from adjudication, Michael Ciscell from GIS, Hal Anderson from Technical Services, and many others.

The groundwater users barely survived – barely cobbled together enough mitigation in 2007 to avoid a call. They were saved at the last minute by the dairymen; provided enough water to avoid actual curtailment. So that year was challenging but very interesting, but I think the director's job ever since the initial calls – which were probably back in 2005, I think, under Karl – has been to ensure that the mitigation provided by the groundwater users was sufficient to prevent curtailment.

It's an unfortunate position to be in, in a state where we have 1.8 million acre-feet on average unappropriated natural flow passing over Milner Dam. So we have opportunities for better management in the future for Idaho, I believe, but right now we're in the position of having to address those calls on a year-by-year basis.

We're in the position right now in Idaho, I think, of evolving to a more intensely managed process of our water – of which we are blessed with great supplies – to avoid these annual calls, of the spectre of annual calls, but that's where the department has been in this last ten years or so.

In 2009, after about six years at the SRBA, John Melanson was appointed by Governor C.L. "Butch" Otter to the Idaho Court of Appeals. His successor was the long-time staff counsel at the adjudication court, Eric Wildman.

The 5th judge: Eric Wildman

BARRY WOOD He was my first law clerk. It was the first job out of law school that he had. I was just becoming a district judge. Roger Burdick had a law clerk down in Twin named Stephanie Fawcett, and Stephanie had gone to law school with Eric. And so it was in the middle of the year, a nontraditional time to hire law clerks, and Judge Burdick was telling me how smart and good Stephanie was, so I said to Stephanie, do you know anybody that's good that would be looking for work? She said yeah, there's this guy in my law school class that's now doing hard rock mining down in Utah, and surveying for this mining company. She got me in touch with Eric, and Eric came on up. He was in the process of waiting for federal funding for a federal job. He decided he liked being my law clerk, and he was my law clerk for two and half years or so. [Then] he went into private practice for a while.

ERIC WILDMAN When I got out of law school, I clerked for Judge Wood. In fact, I was going to take a job with the department of Energy in Hanford, but they kept postponing the start date. So in the interim, I figured I better start looking for something law related.

So through Judge Burdick, who was a district judge at the time, through his law clerk who I went to school with, she contacted me. I was working, doing some mineral exploration for a company that I worked for before law school, and she asked me if I was interested in coming down and interviewing for a law clerk position. I said sure.

So I went down and interviewed with Judge Wood, told him that I was waiting on this other job, and it would probably be four months down the road, but that I would clerk for him in the interim. I started clerking for him and liked it. When the other job came ready, I just decided to stay. I clerked for Judge Wood for over two years.

Then after clerking, I worked with Tom Arkoosh in private practice in Gooding and did a little bit of everything. I was on the Federal CJA panel, did a lot of criminal law, but also some water law.

Then when Judge Hurlbutt retired from the SRBA, Judge Wood was the Administrative District Judge, and so he had to step in and help until they found a replacement. He encouraged me to apply for a staff attorney position, because when I started clerking for Judge Wood, he had just started as a district judge from a magistrate judge. There was a big backlog when he started, and we worked really well together.

So he encouraged me to apply for it. I told him I would make a one-year commitment. I took a year leave of absence from working with Tom. I really liked working at the SRBA. I enjoyed the history and the issues that were involved. It was a really good experience. I was familiar with the case because I did have a few SRBA cases in private practice.

When Judge Wood's brother-in-law, Justice Eismann, was elected to the Supreme Court, the Supreme Court took him off of the SRBA. Part of the enticement to getting other judges to step up to the plate was me sticking around. So I had the opportunity to work with Judge Burdick who took over after Judge Wood. Then when Judge Burdick was appointed to the Supreme Court, Judge Melanson took it over. I worked with him for five years.

When Judge Melanson was appointed to the Court of Appeals, I thought, well, maybe I'll put in and give it a shot because I felt like if I could get appointed to the bench, I knew the SRBA case well enough and I knew I could complete it. There wasn't a lot of interest from other judges in presiding over the case. Even with Judge Burdick and Judge Melanson, it took a little bit of convincing to get them to preside over the case.

So I was appointed at the end of 2009, and here we are, 2014. My goal has been to complete the SRBA by the end of August of this year. If it's not completed in its entirety, there may be a few straggler cases, but other than that, it should be done.

August 25th there's going to be a ceremonial signing of the final unified decree. I do qualify that as ceremonial because there are no guarantees that all of the claims will be processed.

The Supreme Court expressed an interest in having a ceremony. It is a huge accomplishment given the size of the adjudication and the relatively short amount of time that it's taken to complete. It's still a long time, but when you compare it with other states and the size of this adjudication, we've done really well in moving the case to completion.

But there was interest in having a ceremonial signing and a celebration, and the Supreme Court wanted to get a keynote speaker. To set this up, they needed to have some type of time line as to when the case could be completed, which is very difficult for me to predict. I have a case up on appeal to the Supreme Court still that I need to deal with when it gets back down. I also have no control over what litigants file. We're still getting late claims ...

DAVID TUTHILL Then the right choice was Eric Wildman. He had done so much for the adjudication in writing decisions, and he was really in the right position.

Sometimes in history the right thing happens at the right time, and for him to be appointed as the district judge was the right thing – and, of course, he has done a wonderful job in the position. He's totally well suited for the job and has the right experience.

So we've been blessed by five excellent judges.

DAVID TUTHILL Some of the water right issues came to the director that were challenging and difficult – most were handled at the bureau level – but, as the nature of how these things go, some are handled at higher levels. A great deal of time and effort was spent on those. They were very contentious.

In general, the Wood River Valley had very complex water rights. More than 100 lawsuits were filed – before the SRBA even started – up in the Wood River Valley.

. . . the Frost decree in that basin, for example, was the decree; and if it decreed a stream as a dry stream, that was a dry stream unless there had been some change.

The earlier decrees provide an example of some of the contentiousness in the basin and some of the complexity of the water rights.

So, as a consequence, the recommendations in that basin were made last because we had the most experience at that point and could use our best tools, and best talents and techniques then. As it turned out, the staff did a very good job of making recommendations.

In fact, there was a county commissioner in the Gooding area who was critical of the department activities. His name was Jerry Nance, and he was an excellent county commissioner in that area.

He came to me after the initial hearings in the Wood River Valley and said, "I have an apology to make. You-all did a much better job than I had thought." It was very nice of him to say that.

The staff did an excellent job – not only in that basin, but in the other basins – and what we came to find was that of the 20 percent of rights or so that were objected to in each basin, that most had been accurately recommended by the department, and it was a matter of working with the claimants to show that the recommendation was correct.

Who owns the storage water rights at the Bureau of Reclamation reservoirs Water users claims they owned it; the Untied States claimed they did. In a 2007 decision, the Idaho Supreme Court concluded that the United States had legal title but the water users have a beneficial title – suggesting the water is being held for the benefit of the water users.

Determining who has storage

CHARLES McDEVITT I don't think the Boise Project has any rights. I think the rights are held by the Federal Government and by the irrigation districts that make up the Boise Project Board of Control.

The Boise Project Board of Control is simply an operational, administrative entity that was created by contract by six – I think it is five or six irrigation companies, in agreement with the Bureau of Reclamation, which was then ratified by Congress. So it's a unique creature. But I don't think it has any water rights. The worrisome thing about that Supreme Court opinion of which you speak is that – I don't know – that was Pioneer – I think that was the Pioneer case – is the Court held that the beneficiary interest was held by the Bureau of Reclamation, but the beneficial interest is in the irrigation district. So that would hold it in trust, so to speak, for the irrigators who are the true owners. That statement bothers me a little bit. If the true owners of those water rights are these individuals, I think they are entitled to a beneficial interest. But if they're the owners, I see, down the road, some significant litigation between them and the districts.

DAVID SHAW Most of my work for the attorney general's office has been on federal reserve water right negotiations. That's continued. I've worked for them on the Shoshone-Paiutes for the Duck Valley. That kind of was a transition, because I think we had started on those while I was with the department, and then I continued. I've continued to work on Fort Hall. I worked on the wild and scenic. I worked on the Nez Perce.

Nez Perce is interesting, because I worked for the Federal In-Stream Flow Coalition on matters on the Snake River and I worked for attorney general's office on matters on the Salmon and Clearwater. So that was an interesting experience.

Generally, the parties were aligned and the coalition carried the weight, so to speak, on the Snake River stuff and the attorney general's office on the Salmon and Clearwater. I continue to work on Owyhee and on Fort Hall. Still trying to clean that up.

CLIVE STRONG A fortuitous thing for us was continuity on the federal side of the litigation. It's very unusual to have government employees stay through these type of long cases. But on the federal side, Peter Monson was there at the beginning. I can remember a meeting in Washington, D.C. It would have been around 1987 or 1988. Jim Jones and I, met with Myles Flint, who was the head of the natural resource section at that time. Peter Monson was in the meeting and just a junior attorney like me. He ultimately became the lead attorney for the federal government, so we were contemporaries throughout this process.

It really helped having continuity. Even though we were adversaries, we developed trust in one another, which allowed us to have candid conversations that might not otherwise have been possible in the traditional adversary relationship.

DAVID TUTHILL So what we had, as an advantage over other sister states, is three branches of government working together in concert – and not every step was exactly applauded by the other branches but, in general, we moved forward together.

ERIC WILDMAN We don't really have a full-on water court, so to speak, but when I was appointed, the Supreme Court also assigned me to hear all the administrative appeals from the Department of Water Resources.

As we kind of wind down the SRBA and move into conjunctive management, there's still some interrelation of the issues. And I think having one judge preside over an adjudication and focus primarily on just the adjudication, I think the Supreme Court felt it was also important to have one judge preside over the delivery calls or the administrative appeals. Otherwise, the administrative appeals would end up before any one of the district judges in the state. You're not really getting a body of law or law of the case that's coming out of one court.

There's multiple final orders that come out of a delivery call, and there's a potential for filing and seeking a review in more than one county.

Essentially, what you would have is piecemeal appeals involving the same delivery call in different counties. If you had the final order on the delivery call and then you had a final order on the mitigation plan and you had two different judges deciding it, the administrative record is the same for both of them. It simply didn't make sense to not have just one judge hear them. So that's what I'm doing, in addition to the adjudications.

I was going to say one other thing that I said I would get back to it and I didn't get back to it, and that was dealing with the deferrable, domestic, and stockwater claims when we were talking about the steering committee.

You know, in 1988 the state and the United States stipulated to provide for the deferral of small D&S claims as defined by statute. It was important for the United States to stipulate so we would not run afoul of the McCarran Amendment. But at some point we recognized that if we were going to defer them outside the final unified decree, we would have to have a process for that, and there was a stipulation that addressed about the process.

Well, what the steering committee did was also recommended -- and the court implemented it back in January – that any of the further domestic and stockwater claims that were filed would use that alternative process. The court, I'll still hear them, but the notice process and everything is outside the standard SRBA process. It's a publication notice. It's a different process, but we've implemented that now starting the first of the year in conjunction with the orders closing out the basins.

I was going to say also, with respect to those orders closing out the basins, we kind of staggered them and set them up with the goal of trying to end the adjudication this summer.

Another look at trust water

CLIVE STRONG We probably should come back and talk about trust water.

When the Swan Falls Agreement was put together, the parties had a conceptual idea of the trust. Nobody, however, thought about about the practical aspects of implementing the trust. With the exception of Idaho Code Section 42-203(b)(2), there was virtually no attention given to the implementation of the trust. It's ironic. If you look at the Swan Falls Agreement, you will only see a single reference to the trust in one sentence of the agreement. This, I suspect, was because of the relief that was felt after the settlement was signed, and the focus on moving forward with the adjudication. When Idaho Power Company filed its claims in the adjudication without reference to any subordination or the trust, I became concerned.

I remembered the history of the agreement and felt that the claims were inconsistent with the agreement. I had a number of unsuccessful discussion, with the company.

So as we moved forward in the adjudication I brought the issue forward to the governors.

As with most controversial issues its easier to set them aside. So the issue languished until we got to the stage of the adjudication where the company's water rights had to be reported to the court.

That occurred, I believe that in late 2006. The director was due to issue his director's report in Basin 02, which is the Milner to Murphy reach. I advised Attorney General Wasden that we needed to do something to memorialize the trust.

We were in the process of transitioning from Governor Kempthorne, who was moving on to become Secretary of Interior. Governor Risch was in an interim role, and Governor Otter had just been elected Governor. It was a difficult time to get a decision.

Ultimately the attorney general decided to file a change of ownership for the hydropower rights that were the subject of the Swan Falls Agreement.

CLIVE STRONG When we signed the Swan Falls Agreement back in 1984, the company insisted on signing the 1180 Contract, the 1180 Contract being the one that was being challenged constitutionally.

The dilemma that we ran into was the 1180 Contract was negotiated in 1983 and `84, and so it had dates in it that were different than the dates in the Swan Falls Agreement.

While I use the term Swan Falls Agreement, that's really a misnomer. The Swan Falls Agreement was really more an agreement to agree. It isn't what you would classically think of as a contract. It was rather a suite of measures that, if implemented, would ultimately resolve the conflict between the state and the company.

So we had to implement both legislatively – legislative matters and administratively had to administer a state water plan and had to get congressional approval and we had to get court approval. It was ultimately getting all of those things in place that really resolved the Swan Falls conflict.

But the decrees were really the last element to cement that down. So what we had to do was reconcile the differences between the 1180 Contract and the provisions of the Swan Falls Settlement.

And the way we ultimately did that – the company's – in the 1180 Contract and in the Swan Falls Agreement, they talked about subordinating to uses existing at the time. From a water law perspective, uses are hard to evaluate, because we do everything based on priority date. And we don't keep data about when uses occur, when the use started. We were having a difficult time trying to figure out how to reflect with clarity, for administration purposes, how those rights would be reflected.

Ultimately what we agreed to do was to say that all water rights that are with a priority date before October 25, 1984, enjoy the benefit of full subordination. That was important because there were a lot of what we call beneficial use claims.

In Idaho before 1971, I believe it was, you weren't required to have a water right. You could establish [a right] just simply by putting it to beneficial use. At the time we were doing this agreement, we didn't have all the water rights adjudicated. That's what the SRBA was going to do. So to identify that and be able to more forward, we selected that priority date. Everybody with the priority date prior to October 25, 1984, they get full subordination. Water rights with the priority dates after October 25, 1984, are then trust water rights with an exception. Because the company agreed to subordinate to some applications and permits that existed – that had priority dates prior to October 25, `84, but hadn't been put to use, we had to figure out a way to describe those.

And we ultimately hit upon an approach in which we went through and reviewed essentially all water rights after 1971. We were pretty confident anything before 1971 was going to get the benefit of full subordination and get decreed in the adjudication.

We hired consultants and went through all of the claims from 1971 to the present and had to look at the extent of beneficial use of each one of those water rights in order to identify the class of water users that while they might have a priority date prior to October 25, 1984, they didn't – under the Swan Falls Agreement, the use had to occur before, I believe it was, July 1, 1985. We had to figure out all of the rights that fit into that class so we could determine whether they got the benefit of full subordination.

And there was another smaller class of rights that might have priority dates junior to October 25, 1984, but had had beneficial use before that that we had to also sort out. And we ended up developing a graphic depiction of that might be helpful if I just make this a part of the record so people can see it. It sorts out graphically, and that was the only way we could finally get an understanding on how to classify all the water rights.

But coming back to your question, how did the decrees reflect that, we have conditions in each of the decrees. And the power company's water rights are decreed at the 3,900/5,600 CFS level with priority dates based upon the original rights of Swan Falls. They only have water rights at Swan Falls. Because the way the Swan Falls Agreement works is if we're maintaining that 3,900/5,600 at the Murphy gauge, then all of the hydropower rights that are affected by the Swan Falls Agreement are deemed to be satisfied upstream.

CLIVE STRONG The company immediately responded by filing an action against Governor Otter and Attorney General Wasden asserting it would never have agreed to give control of its water rights over to the state. We entered into some very intense litigation with the company.

So, again, we were back to the same kind of dark days we had in `83 and `84 with the company. We moved forward with a motion for summary judgment in the SRBA District Court. In 2008 Judge Melanson issued a decision – I believe it was about April of 2008 – finding that in fact the company's water rights above the 3,900 CFS flow at the Murphy gage were held in trust by the state. That included all of the company's water rights for its facilities upstream from Murphy and downstream from Milner Dam. Michael Orr's work on this case was nothing short of brilliant.

Once that decision was rendered, it opened the opportunity for new discussions with the power company. And, we entered into what is called the 2009 Framework Reaffirming the Swan Falls Agreement.

In that framework, the company agreed the hydropower water rights were held in trust by the State of Idaho. We were able to get decrees entered in the SRBA District Court confirming the trust. And, we were able to get water rights approved by the SRBA District Court confirming the minimum flows at the Murphy gage.

The trust water rights also expressly identify the rights that are entitled to full and partial subordination. The decrees make it clear that all decreed and licensed water rights with a priority date earlier than October 25, 1984, the date of the Swan Falls Agreement, are protected. They enjoy full subordination. So even if the minimum flow falls below 3,900 or 5,600, those rights are not subject to curtailment. It's only water rights diverting trust water that are subject to curtailment if the flow of the Snake River falls below the Murphy minimum flow.

Trust water is that water within the "trust water right area" made available for appropriation as a result of the Swan Falls settlement. It's that area hydraulically connected to the Snake River upstream from the Murphy gauge. So if you think of a map of Idaho, it extends essentially from the Murphy gauge all the way up to the Rexburg area. Water rights that have a priority date junior to October 25, 1984 within that area, with a few exceptions, are subject to curtailment if the flow of the Snake River falls below the Murphy minimum flow.

We were looking at the possibility of having to open up literally tens of thousands of water rights to go back and put those subordination provisions into the partial decrees. By using this priority date of 10/25/84, we basically said any water right before that gets the benefit of full subordination. We memorialized the full subordination provision in the hydropower decree itself, so we didn't have to go back and put conditions on all the previously decreed water rights.

The only partial decrees we had to go in and put conditions on were the ones identified as actually diverting trust water. Each one of the trust water rights has a provision acknowledging it's a trust water right held in the name of the individual and is subject to curtailment if the actual flow of the river falls below the decreed minimum flow at Murphy.

JOHN MELANSON We had, at least during the time that I was there, and I think for the most part, through the whole adjudication, the support of the legislature. I think the legislature recognized that we had to do this. Not only was there the law in place, that said we had to do it, there were practical reasons, maybe more than I just talked about, to get it done. And the sooner the better.

And so we had the support of the legislature. And by that, I mean, not only their financial support, which is hugely important, but also, I think their – I don't know, their moral support. I don't know if that's the right word. They were behind the adjudication. And I think there may be exceptions. But the ones that – the members of the legislature I know, seem to me to be behind it. And there was the support of the court, itself. That was a big part of this. That the Supreme Court had to do this when it was filed.

And I think there was a recognition by all of the presiding judges that it just had to – we had to keep moving it forward. Part of that was a concern that at some point, everybody was going to lose patience. And I'm speaking now of 27 years after it was filed.

And I think – Well, I know when I started, that I felt an obligation to tell the legislature how long it would take to finish it. And I missed the mark a little bit. I really thought I could finish it in fiscal 2012. And that's when I assumed I would still be there when it was done.

And so, you know, I was wrong. And I guess the lesson I take away from that is, don't be too optimistic when you are dealing with the legislature. I don't think they thought I was – that I was dishonest. I just think they thought I was optimistic about when we could get it done.

I never felt any animosity at all there. You know, when I went to the – once a year when the presiding judge goes to the JFAC meeting with the director of the department, I always felt I was among friends there. So that was a good thing.

Anyway, I've always felt bad that I told them 2012, and it turned out to be a little later than that.

But the good news is, is that we are getting it done, and not too much later than I said.

So we had the support of the legislature, support of the courts. And really, I think for the most part, we had the support of the people involved. I think people did see the need to get it done. There are exceptions that are obvious in that group. But I think from their perception, I think they had their reasons.

It's hard to describe all – that whole group. You know, I think there were some people, particularly in areas where they were dealing with tribal claims, there was some distrust here. And it probably went both ways. So people didn't want o file their claims in the SRBA knowing there could be tribal objections to those claims.

The same with the federal government. You know, people having claims bordering federally managed property, like the Forest Service, or BLM, or even had water right claims on federally managed property, say, for stockwatering, there was some distrust here. And I think they didn't want to file their claims, because they knew then that here could be some objections from the federal government.

And I think again, too, there were people that knew that – and this may actually be the largest of the folks who opposed it. I don't know. Who were, I think, content with the status quo. That even though that they knew there was maybe some doubt about what their actual water right was. That they knew that their neighbors had those same doubts. And they had gotten along so far, and they wanted to keep things as they were.

And there probably are as many reasons for the people not wanting to proceed with it, as there were people who objected to it. But mostly, I think people who are involved did support it. So we had the legislature, the courts, and the litigants, themselves. And I think that's what made a difference here.

ERIC WILDMAN In '09 we started scanning all of the documents in every case. You pull up a register of actions off our website. All the documents are there. There's a hot link to them. Litigants can, or anybody can access the documents, and we have that at no charge.

I know having documents available to the water users not only made life a lot easier for the water users and the litigants, but it's also made it a lot easier for the court because the clerks used to spend a significant amount of their time chasing files and making copies for people. Now it's just the click of a mouse. So I think that's a real significant development that's made the court a lot more accessible.

Winding down the SRBA

ERIC WILDMAN In fact, in 2011 we first started initiating proceedings on winding down the SRBA. Among other things, I wanted to get going on proceedings on the form and content of the final unified decree. The form and content issue of a final unified decree is always controversial and subject to objections. I was just going by experience from other states regarding a final unified decree. There was never any consensus, and there was a lot of litigation over what it should look like.

I initiated the proceedings and designated it as a basin-wide issue. Whoever wanted to come into the case had the opportunity. Then I set up a steering committee. Again, whoever wanted to be on the steering committee could be on the steering committee. I charged the committee with making recommendations as to the form and content of the final decree, as well as what processes should we take to start winding down the case.

I appointed Special Master Booth as the chair of the committee. The committee met several times, and they couldn't come to a consensus on everything. I expected they would not, but in their report they indicated where they couldn't come to an agreement. Then based on that report, I went through and accepted parts and rejected parts and came up with a proposed final unified decree. I then issued an order and let parties challenge my order.

They did come in and challenge it. We had hearings on the challenges. Following the hearings, I made some changes to my proposal. Then if any party was in disagreement, they could still appeal from my decision, but there were no appeals.

So at this juncture, the position is that the form and content of the final unified decree is settled. It's final. So when we finish all of the remaining partial decrees and the final unified decree is entered, there shouldn't be anything to appeal from unless somebody is appealing from an individual partial decree and their appeal is timely. I really wanted to start early on this process. When I started with the SRBA in 1999, I started keeping a notebook of things that I felt should be addressed in the final unified decree. We had put savings language in all the partial decrees that referenced that the partial decrees would be subject to a final unified decree, whatever form that final decree should take.

So I knew there was going to be certain information that wasn't addressed in either a general provision or a partial decree that we would need to address in the final unified decree. For example, we have from the early days, consent decrees. We have the stipulation and order that deals with the deferrable domestic and stockwater rights. These things need to be tied together and addressed in a final unified decree.

The other thing that the steering committee recommended was that the court start closing basins to additional late claims. We implemented a process starting shortly after 2011 where, pursuant to docket sheet notice, the court would issue a notice of intent to close the basin to further late claims by a date certain. Attached to that order were lists of water right numbers that were of record with the department for which no claims had been filed. Parties had an opportunity to review those water right claim numbers and file a late claim.

THEODORE BOOTH The form of the final unified decree has been litigated and established. Essentially, there were two components to that that I remember. One, it was designated as a basin-wide issue: What is the form and content of the final unified decree? Two, there was a steering committee that the judge assigned me as the chairman of the steering committee.

In reality, the leader and the heavy lifting was done by Clive Strong and Chris Bromley in that process. They were the ones that came in with the drafts and, frankly, the credit goes to those two. That's not to say there weren't – there were a lot of good lawyers and participants in that process: David Negri from the federal government, and Dana Hofstetter was there and Candice McHugh. I can't remember everybody that was involved, but certainly we would sit around a big table and we would hash out these various issues. So that steering committee process, I think, worked real well because even though it was a basin-wide issue, this parallel steering committee process wasn't in an adversarial, you know, it was more of a settlement moderated type of environment.

ROGER BURDICK I was on the little steering committee for the development of the Final Unified Decree that Judge Wildman put together, and that was – one of the most discussed topics was how to incorporate that into the Final Unified Decree. You know, honest to gosh, I don't even remember that.

CARTER FRITSCHLE [Biggest challenge to completing the adjudication] I would have to say it has been the late claims. While many of them are welcome because they are needed to fully describe the water use on a particular parcel of land, and we definitely want to make sure all legal existing water uses continue, some of them have been more along the lines of claims for "super water rights" that include uses that have not even been developed yet, or priority dates that are completely unrealistic. Sorting through the late claims, and trying to fit some of them into the "puzzle" of water rights has been a strain on IDWR's very limited resources as the SRBA has been moving to completion.

CLIVE STRONG When you say, now is your last opportunity, there's always somebody that comes out of the woodwork. It amazes me that after more than 20 years we still have people saying, oh, I just remembered my late claim I need to file.

So I think it was about 2011 we approached the court and said, if we're going to get to a final decree, we have got to be able to stop taking claims. We need to put an end to this.

Again, through the process of developing the final unified decree, we agreed upon a process where we would enter orders closing the basins. There were four successive orders that as we finished out late claim taking in each of the basins, we would close out those basins. We're at the point where no more claims are to be accepted. But, we still find people trying to file claims.

And in terms of issues, you would have thought that all of the issues had been aired out. But we're actually now dealing with one that is called the refill claim.

That was an issue that we felt was resolved five or six years ago and now is still an active and live issue we're working on.

ERIC WILDMAN When I started, I was always looking towards the end and trying to work backwards. In 2011 that's why we wanted to start the proceedings on the final unified decree, because I've always tried to push things as fast as I could, recognizing that it still takes time to process these things. Because of the size of the adjudication, you have special notice processes that take longer and the like.

But for all of the pre-commencement water rights, unless they were ones that were excluded by statute, or the deferrable D&S claims, which I'll talk about in a second, there is finality. We have a full inventory of all of those water rights.

Of paramount importance is the fact that the department also has been diligent about ensuring that the transfer processes are kept up with so that we're not back to square one. We can follow the pedigree of the water right, and it will trace all the way back to the partial decree issued in the SRBA.

So even though water rights are always changing and switching hands and being transferred, it's not going to affect that inventory. That's been a problem in a lot of other states. You know, if you're not keeping track, after you complete the adjudication, if you're not keeping track of the transfers that happen subsequent to it, then you lose that inventory. Because we will have a full inventory, there is certainty in the water rights. There never was the certainty in the water rights when you had beneficial use claims, posted notice, licenses, and old decrees. It's very difficult for a water right user to know how their water right compares to the tabulation of other water rights on the system. Now since a lot of the water, particularly on the Eastern Snake Plain Aquifer, is fully appropriated and there's moratoriums in place, if somebody wants a water right, they have to go get it from somebody else. Or when you're dealing with delivery calls, if there's certainty in water rights, it at least makes it easier to come up with mitigation plans or solutions to the delivery calls, buying out water rights if need be or what have you. But until there was this full inventory of water rights, it made that process much more difficult.

JOHN MELANSON I haven't really dealt with other states as much as, say, Judge Wildman has. He's been involved with Dividing the Waters for many years now. And Dividing the Waters is a group of people from water rights, people from other states, and adjudication people, who get together and discuss best practices, and so forth. And I wasn't that involved with that.

But I think what happened in other states who haven't been as successful, is the funding wasn't consistent for the adjudications to take place. Also, they tried to do it piecemeal. You know, we jumped in.

The Snake River Basin is huge. It's more than 80 percent of the surface area of the state. And so we tackled it all at once. And then shortly after that, decided, well, this has to include groundwater, too, because it's all interconnected. So not only did we have our surface water, but all the groundwater, as well. So it was a monstrous project.

I do have a lot of respect for Judge Hurlbutt. I just can't imagine starting that from scratch, and jumping in there, and doing it.

But to the point of the question. Other states would perhaps look at that, and say, well, you know, the Snake River Basin is kind of big. Let's take the tributary. Let's do the Salmon River first, which would be big enough, or the Clearwater. Let's take a tributary, and do them one at a time, and then maybe do the groundwater separately. So you can see how that would take a long, long time.

Although it would maybe be cheaper – not in the long run, but involve a little less money upfront to do. I don't know.

And then also, we had piecemeal funding, where the legislature would, in these other states, sort of lose interest in getting the adjudication done. I don't know if that's right. And that's probably not. I don't want to attribute that to the legislature so much as, perhaps, they didn't have the money available. That might be more in line with what, actually, happened. And so the adjudication would stop.

And I just can't imagine doing it that way.

Because you have the expertise. You know, you have the judge who knows a little bit about water law. You have the special masters, who are experienced a lot about water law. You have attorneys participating in the adjudication, essentially, water law experts. You have the court staff who are dealing with water law. And then you shut it down. And you say, not only are we shutting it down, we don't know when we're going to start it again. Those people get different jobs. And when you start it again, you really are starting from square one. So that can't work. And I think those are the main differences.

So I would think if we were to do it again, we do it he same way. And say, we're going to tackle this. And we're going to pay for it every year. And we're going to stick with it until it's finished. And that, to me, is the way to do it.

Of course, I'm not – I don't have to pay for it. And, you know, I think that's one of the things, the sense I had in going to those JFAC meetings every year, is that those people had a limited amount of money, and a whole bunch of people who needed it for different causes. And the SRBA was just one of them, you know. But fortunately, they came through every year.

DUANE MECHAM Its important for the tribes to bring their priorities to these settlements. The priorities the tribes brought was, look, we know the Hells Canyon Dam isn't going to go away soon, but in our aboriginal area we still have the Clearwater and the Salmon rivers that are key habitat areas for the fish that are important to us, and are undammed, that are viable habitat areas. And you see this reflected in the term sheet.

A lot of that direction as I recall did come from Francis.

ERIC WILDMAN I know all of the special masters and judges that are involved in western adjudications and water disputes throughout the United States. In talking to them, Idaho has been a good model for an adjudication. I mean, they always look to Idaho as the poster child – maybe I shouldn't use that term – but for processing an adjudication.

It's just when this thing gets completed, and it will be completed, it will be great to have been a part of it. You know, I like to hope that I contributed to getting it completed in a timely manner. I know some people would argue that it's taken longer than it was originally anticipated, but I think in the overall scope of things we've done a pretty good job.

DAVID TUTHILL I had planned in my career to leave in 2008 and go into the private sector. I had expected Karl Dreher to continue on. That didn't happen, so I applied for and was appointed as director.

I very much enjoyed the job. It was a tremendous job. I enjoyed working for the governor more than I had expected. That was one surprise to me. It turned out to be a wonderful job.

So I enjoyed it, but in 2009 we had a good water year. I had a good successor in Gary Spackman. My father and grandfather were businessmen, and I wanted be a businessman. I wanted to join the private sector, and I'm glad I did that at the time. It has been an interesting challenge since then, and I enjoy every day just like I did with the department.

. . . When I left, I would say we were in great hands with Gary Spackman and with the legal staff that we had. Phil Rassier had been a wonderful counselor for the director for more than 30 years. He retired the year after I left, and I still work with Phil every week. He's part of our team, and it has been wonderful to have him involved. Garrick Baxter has been a great replacement for Phil and carries that effort forward very well. Gary Spackman is the best person, in my view, to be director. I'm very pleased that he was eventually appointed as director. So the department administrative staff is very solid, very well trained.

JOHN MELANSON I like what I'm doing now. I like the people I'm working with. I've got an excellent staff. And the other judges here are just a joy to be with. They really are. But I've always said, the SRBA was the best job I ever had. And sometimes, I truly am sorry I didn't stay to finish it. I really enjoyed working with the people there.

I'm glad Judge Wildman is doing it now. And of all the people who could have followed me, and taken over, he was the one to do it. But I miss it.

DAVID TUTHILL One of the major outcomes of the SRBA has been more certainty in water rights – more certainty in the fact that groundwater is connected to surface water, more certainty in what the extent of the water rights are, and now they're quantified and established. Still, the uncertain portion is Mother Nature. As long as Mother Nature is kind and provides water in the river, then delivery calls don't have to be made.

We saw a good example this year where early on it looked like Mother Nature was not going to be kind, and the director sent out letters to many saying that they had a potential of being curtailed because the groundwater users don't have enough mitigation in a short water year really to prevent curtailment.

They have enough mitigation in a normal year or a year that's a little bit short, but if the year is very short, the only solution that we know of right now – that I know of right now is curtailment. I don't think they will be able to avoid a curtailment unless they do something different in the future.

What can they do? That gives rise to some of the opportunities that they have for ensuring that they can survive calls in the future – and that's another story.

CLIVE STRONG At the end of the day, we expect to have determined in this case about 159,000 water rights. The dilemma that you have once you have that number of water rights is how do you put them together in a way that they're usable for future generations, that you can use them as your baseline and you can keep them updated.

So as we began to close in on the end of the adjudication, it's not like a normal order you can write out a few lines and say it's here by ordered. You have got to be able to bring all of these partial decrees – when I talk about water rights, each one has a partial decree. You have to bring them all together to show how they relate to one another.

The SRBA District Court under Judge Wildman set up this basin-wide issue. He gave direction to Special Master Ted Booth to convene a party of the willing to sit down and try to fashion what the final decree would look like. And, frankly, we were kind of creating it out of whole cloth, because there really isn't any other examples to follow.

But it's kind of going back to the old steering committee process. We got a large group of affected interests that sat around a table. And over the course of four to six months, we were able to actually sit down and craft out a proposed final order.

The way it's set up, it's a short order – I can't remember the exact number of pages. Something less than 25. But, then it incorporates, by reference, attachments. We'll have – one attachment that defines the scope of the adjudication. Another will contain all the partial decrees in one place. Another will show which claims were disallowed. It's important to know which ones are no longer valid, because we're going to have to clean up the IDWR database.

Another attachment will contain all of the federal reserved water right agreements. There is an attachment that contains the order on how to claim deferred *de minimis* domestic and stockwater rights. The final unified decree really becomes kind of, shall we say, book that brings all of the critical documents together in one place.

It's quite remarkable that we were able to with virtually no dissension fashion the final unified decree. We expect the final unified decree to be in the neighborhood of 250,000 pages.

One of the things that we did, and I think it was a very important, was involve the county clerks and recorders. A majority of the Idaho counties will be affected by the decree.

So we reached out through Special Master Booth to the clerks and recorders with the help of the Association of Counties and involved them in the process

We're going to end up having probably two copies of decree, one the court will maintain and one IDWR will maintain. But, we're going to make an electronic decree. So it will be accessible to the public.

Technology has played a very important role in the SRBA, and this is a place where I think it will be invaluable. Inevitably in water cases there will be conflicts that arise. What we hope to have created is a baseline that will avoid revisiting the past. Once the decree is entered, all water rights within the basin will be determined. And, if you don't have a water right listed in the decree, it no longer exists.

CLIVE STRONG If the policy objective is to sustain the spring flows at the levels they are today, which is about 5,200 CFS, then we have to do something to offset the depletions that are occurring.

This brings us back around to the Swan Falls Agreement. As a result of the Swan Falls settlement, the state policy is to sustain the flow of 3,900 CFS at the Murphy gage. And, this year we're beginning to approach that number.

Since the state policy is also to allow depletions above Milner to reduce the flow to zero, we we need to begin to regulate to the ESPA to sustain flows in the Thousand Springs reach.

That means a couple of things. One, we need an active aquifer recharge program, which we're working on. We need to continue to look for opportunities for conversions. And, we need to deal with the trust water rights. We have an opportunity to do some long-term planning now that we have the cornerstone laid.

LAIRD NOH My impression is that one of the great good fortunes that we have in Idaho particularly in this area is that we for so long have had organized water districts, we have had a very strong water bar, very good leadership, and I think the Idaho Water Users Association has been a wonderful tool. . . . I think the ability for people to think rationally and reasonably and reach agreements was very much facilitated by the water users association.

JOHN MELANSON there are a couple of reasons it took a long time. And one, was that the department could only investigate the claims so fast. They only had the personnel to do it. And I don't mean this at all, and I hope nobody would ever think that I mean this as a criticism of the department. They could only do with what they could do with money and assets that they had. And I think they did an amazing job of getting it done, and getting those claims investigated.

I think, too, another factor that contributed to the delay a little bit, was the same thing that contributes to delay in every court case. And that is, that sometimes the parties need to take time to get ready for their trial. And sometimes they request continuances. And, you know, at some point, the court has to say, no. But as long as you see the parties working toward getting ready, and/or working towards settlement at the same time, you try to accommodate, if you can. So I think those things were a factor.

You know, really , one of the things I was thinking about, thinking about this interview was, you know, the question could be asked: How could it have been done sooner? And I think you could do it really fast, if you wanted to put just billions of dollars into it up front. You know, and say, in this imaginary world with unlimited amounts of money, we're going to have, instead of three special masters, we're going to have 30. And instead of one presiding judge, we'll have ten.

And we'll pay for all of it at once, and get it done right away. Well, we just couldn't do that. So I think we did the best we could. And by "we," I'm talking about the State of Idaho, not just the court. We did the best we could with what we had.

NORM YOUNG There's a number of, perhaps, booby traps involved in the way the adjudication plays out.

Again, as the agreement was put together and the subsequent legislation, the idea of the unauthorized developments both outside of the critical groundwater areas and within the critical groundwater areas, different statutes. The one for those outside of the critical area was found unconstitutional and redrafted and readopted. The one for within the critical groundwater areas is still on the books.

And it has a requirement that two years after the adjudication is final, whatever that means, that the department, the director, must determine that the expanded uses are not -- that there's a plan to cover water for the expanded uses or they've got to terminate use. Interesting.

[And] the idea that if you did not file and you don't get your right adjudicated, you don't have a right anymore. How many of those are going to jump up after August 25 and what can be done about it? I hope there's not any, but if there are any, I hope there's something worked out so that it can be resolved.

CLIVE STRONG Oftentimes there are things left unresolved.

That's what happened with the Swan Falls Agreement. It's not that there's been a change in the Swan Falls Agreement, all the key elements and principles that were set forth in the framework and the

Swan Falls Agreement itself are being implemented. It's just, how do you memorialize that?

From my perspective, this effort of memorializing the agreement was extremely critical. If you look back in history, the whole Swan Falls conflict was as a result of the failure to document what the understandings that were reached.

It's natural to expect that parties' recollections and interests will change over time. And so the biggest thing I think that has come out of the adjudication vis-a-vis the Swan Falls settlement is a memorialization of the understanding reached in enforceable decrees.

It has led to a very positive relationship with the company. We're working together collaboratively to address the growing demands on water supply and how to maintain a water supply sufficient for hydropower generation and other water needs of Idahoans?

ERIC WILDMAN We have acknowledged that this is a compulsory lawsuit. They have to come in. Not everybody wants to be here. Obviously, not everybody can afford counsel. Judge Hurlbutt set up the process with a lot of user-friendly "check-the-box" standardized pleading forms.

In the Coeur d'Alene, we're keeping the forms the same but adding one additional form. We acknowledge that we're going to have a lot of pro se litigants. So if we make it easier for the litigants, it's also easier for the court. We have check-the-box pleadings and real user-friendly forms. It definitely makes it easier for pro se litigants, as well as counsel.

I know from being on the Supreme Court's Technology Committee where the state is in the process of switching its case management software, the trend is now, not just in adjudications, but the trend in regular district court is that there is a lot of unrepresented litigants. And because of the new technology that you have available with the case management and pull-down menus, there's a lot available to assist unrepresented litigants with filling out pleadings and filing and providing guidance as to how to process a lawsuit. But we've tried to make the SRBA as user-friendly as possible.

Also acknowledge that the courthouse is here in Twin Falls and the geographic area of the SRBA covers 87 percent of the state. So it's very difficult to require litigants that are up in Lewiston to appear down in Twin Falls for hearings. So we've been very liberal with telephone participation, and we've had, for about five years now, video teleconferencing.

We're just about wrapped up so we're not doing it now, but the court has historically traveled around to different counties and conducted business in the various courthouses. I think that was one thing that was popular with the legislature. They wanted the court to be out and have a presence in the different counties.

DANIEL HURLBUTT [Other states have been watching closely:] I'm aware of it because I think it was very shortly after I started talking with John Thorson, the Special Master in the Gila River Adjudication in Arizona, the two of us concluded that it might be beneficial to set up an annual, semi-annual meeting, or biannual meeting of judges and masters handling cases in the west, just to confer and compare notes. And we did set up a project called Dividing the Waters, which was sort of an educational meeting of judges and Special Masters in the west, and we met every – basically every 18 months in different states, and had a pretty rigorous two or three-day program, which included field trips to look at water sources, water facilities, areas of problems.

That project was funded variously by the Ford Foundation, the Hewlett Packard Foundation. Normally would receive participation from 50, 60 judges and Masters around the west. I think about two and a half or three years ago the Dividing the Waters project was unified under the auspices of the – what is the name – National Judicial College, which is situated at University of Nevada Reno, and now is run with them and funded through them.

So it's still an ongoing process. John Thorson and I were the founders. John Thorson is still somewhat involved, as is Justice Hobbs, who will be at the August meeting that is to honor the finalization of the SRBA. So that's ongoing. That has generated articles and books and continuing conferences on water law. In fact, I participated in one at the National Judicial College that includes some federal judges who are now facing water issues in various areas, even in states like Georgia, Florida.

So yeah, I'm very aware that it's served as, I don't know modeled, but it's certainly been looked at by other states, jurisdictions, and the federal courts, in terms of how you handle complex water litigation, and maybe bring it to fruition.

PETER MONSON I started out as a young attorney on the SRBA and I was hoping to stick it out to the very end.

For me it was a career case, a very rewarding case.

Reflections on an adjudication

DAVID TUTHILL People in Idaho wonder how it could take so long to adjudicate all these water rights, but those of us that have been with the other western states are just marveled by how things worked right for us.

. . . We benchmarked every year with the Western State Adjudication Conference – that we held twice in Idaho during my tenure. We had the privilege of really being the primary mentors on how to adjudicate water rights in the state. We had the most success of any of the states, and "little Idaho" was proud to demonstrate what we had done. We provided input for the other states and suggestions – and learned from the other states, to some extent, but for the most part, we were in the lead technically, administratively, and judicially.

Frankly – it sounds most boastful, but that was the truth of it – and we're still recognized as the state that is a leader in adjudication.

ERIC WILDMAN Judge Hurlbutt really gets the credit for how he set it up. There's a lot of different ways you can set up an adjudication. I'm familiar with other states and how they've set them up. Some of them do them administratively. The ones that do them through the courts have done them a little bit differently than what we've done here in Idaho.

But the way it was set up, it was broken down into manageable chunks. There was a good process in place. I should say that it wasn't without some of the difficulties that other adjudications had.

In the early '90s, we had the challenge to the constitutionality of the adjudication statutes which put it on hold for a while.

I think one of the things that's been real beneficial is the support from all of the three branches of government. I think everyone acknowledged the importance of it and wanted to get it done. There wasn't always that sentiment early in the '90s because there was a lot of litigation over the adjudication statutes. When you're litigating those initial issues, it seems like you're not making progress because you're not processing claims while you're litigating these other issues.

I think after we got past that hump in the mid-nineties and started moving towards getting the claims processed, and they could see that we were making progress, I think attitudes changed. You're always going to have some challenges to your statutes or your processes, but I think one thing that I've always tried to do, and the judges that I've worked under, is try to move them through the process as fast as possible. I have to get my decisions out within the 30-day time period, and so try to get everything moving as fast as possible to get it through the system.

Because of the size of the case, there's always going to be procedural issues and jurisdictional issues and that type of thing. We've just tried to move through them as fast as possible. From my perspective, there's kind of always been a light at the end of the tunnel, but I've known it's going to take us a little while to get there, but I never really felt like there was something that was going to unravel the progress.

VERN CASE I farm about 110 acres, and I have 50 head of black Angus cows. I grow corn and hay and sometimes some wheat or barley. Most of my ground is flood irrigated; in the last year I've pumped in through sprinklers and wheel lines on 17 acres. I bought my first 40 in 1971, I think it was, and about 20 years later I bought my folks' 70 acres.

I've been a director of the irrigation district for 34 years, and had lots of experience with water rights even before the Snake River Basin Adjudication. I was one of the Nez Perce negotiations well before the SRBA started.

I think the SRBA was a good thing. It was long overdue. We're just now, in the upper Boise Basin above Lucky Peak, starting with monitoring the water rights above the dam, putting them into priority dates.

CARTER FRITSCHLE I have to give a lot of the credit to the individual water users in Idaho. For the most part, they did not want to have their rights “re-adjudicated”. But, once the process started, the water users were willing to work with their neighbors, the court and IDWR to resolve conflicts, and have their water rights described as they had been historically developed and used. Of course there were exceptions, but most just wanted to come out of the adjudication with water rights that were fair to everyone involved, and accurately described the water use.

CLIVE STRONG One of the unexpected benefits of the adjudication was the opportunity for the tribes and the State to develop a stronger intergovernmental relationship.

ROGER BURDICK The other issue that I think is – that a lot of people forget, especially after the first eight or nine years – we couldn't be where we are without the lawyers of Idaho being about half-way reasonable, in terms of getting direction from the Court or from the Supreme Court, applying that in good faith, applying it to their clients, giving up where they need to, not where they don't have to, and coming to resolution on so many thousands of cases.

You know, a lot of people think that the lawyers have just used this as a Full Employment Act. Quite frankly, I don't think we succeed at all without a cadre of – and you would know better than I the lawyers that are the top cadre that have been with it from the beginning – without them wanting to get it finished, also in their clients' best interests.

JEFF RAYBOULD I think things have gone on pretty well as they always have. I'm sure there are isolated instances where as individual water rights went through the adjudication process perhaps those rights changed a little to match whats happening on the ground versus what the original claims said was happening. But all the rights I'm associated with are administered much the same way as they were prior to the start of the adjudication.

I think as we're finishing this adjudication its real milestone in the history of the state of Idaho.

JIM JONES Not everything proceeded as I thought it would. But I think, you know, from an overall standpoint I think it's worked out really well.

I think, you know, people look at it from other states and say, "How did they get so much done in so little time?"I mean when we embarked on the process, I think we were thinking ten years and $10 million or something like that. It's been substantially more in both regards. But still, a lot smoother, as you will, than the experience in other states. Some states started long before us and still haven't been able to get as much accomplished. So I think it's been, you know, a worthy project. And I think it's worked out fine.

VINCE ALBERDI It was a wonderful process; what we've done is outstanding compared to what other states have been able to do.

DAVID SHAW Major accomplishments: I think those need to be listed because there are some.

The federal reserve water rights determination is huge. Not many states have been able to accomplish that. The outcome of the adjudication up in Washington finally got done, and that took years. Montana is still struggling with their federal reserve water rights that are still at issue. The Klamath, Arizona, New Mexico, Utah. And Idaho's are pretty well done. We've still got some loose ends on Fort Hall. I don't see that they're going to be contentious. I've been wrong before. The wild and scenic claims on the Owyhee. But for the most part, they're done. And that's a huge accomplishment.

For the most part, the water rights have been defined. And that by itself is – I don't know how many thousands there are. You may have a better idea, but that in itself is a major accomplishment.

And you know, the state should be happy that that's been successful. I know it wasn't done in ten years like was originally proposed. But it's done, nonetheless.

The interim administration has been successful once it got kicked off and approved. So the new information that was available because of the adjudication could be put in place on the ground, and that's been important, I think.

Another thing you have here is "Were the goals achieved?" I guess on a scale of zero to ten, I'd say we're at a seven. Zero being nothing got done, ten being everything perfect. I guess you could have a minus ten, because some really bad things could happen that didn't. But zero to ten, I think we're a seven.

And the disappointments, I guess, would be we didn't get the information in the decrees the department really needs to administer water rights. And that's evident by the litigation now over the surface water call, the Rangen call, the other spring users' call.

When we set out to do the adjudication, it was my expectation, and I think the department's expectation, there would be instructions in the decree for the Director to do conjunctive administration, to do whatever he needed to do to instruct the watermasters to distribute the water.

And that part didn't happen. And that goes back to some of the conflicts with the judge, because he was not willing to put those things in the decree.

The records are not being kept current. You can go out today – I'm sure you've experienced this – and find rights that have been decreed that are no longer current. The ownership's changed, the address has changed, they've been split, they've been – who knows. And I'm not sure how you solve

What I always said was if you could make the title insurance companies ensure water rights, that would get taken care of. That's not going to happen in my lifetime. Maybe it will yours. And it's mostly the smaller water rights.

The people who are irrigating, for example, or if there's a bank involved, those people understand the value of the water, and they'll do their due diligence to be sure the water rights are in place and everything's correct before they go forward. But it's 10-acre tracts and the domestic rights and those sorts of things.

And we never were able to devise a means – the statute says you have to update the information, but it doesn't get done. I think those probably are the two biggest concerns that I have, that we didn't close the loop, we didn't quite get it all done the way we hoped it would be done.

JOHN ROSHOLT The court? I think it was always well managed. I was pleased that the legislature had the fortitude and perseverance to stay with them as to the appropriations.

Because early on, you know, the promise was, no more than 10 years and a couple of million dollars per year. Now we're in the, what, 25th year, more than that, 27th year. But we're still doing better than, by comparison, Wind River in Wyoming and Aquavella in Washington.

Part of the reason you keep going, you keep hunting these things is so you avert what happened in the Klamath, in Oregon. Because I think had they had an adjudication and had the fed rights defined and adjudicated, they wouldn't have had the debacle they had as to fish versus irrigation over there.

KARL DREHER No other state in the history of the western United States has completed such a large adjudication.

And, the fact that it almost failed, that it almost succumbed to legislative negativism, but didn't and succeeded; the fact that the Nez Perce settlement got done and funded in Congress – it was a series of remarkable events.

DUANE MECHAM I'm very active in our neighboring state of Montana, in the Flathead and Salish-Kootenai, which has a lot of similarities to the Nez Perce situation, with some added complications. I've had occasion over the last six months where folks opposed to what we're trying to do in the Salish-Kootenai settlement misrepresenting what we did in the Nez Perce settlement, saying the Nez Perce and the United Stats gave up on all these claims, that the state rolled over the tribe and was successful in thwarting this attempt to get water secured ...

My rejoinder to that has been, including to some folks at the Montana legislature has been, it is technically true that at the end of the day the Nez Perce tribe did not receive a single off-reservation federal or Indian reserved water right. But that's hardly the end of the story.

And here's where I would credit the state of Idaho for bringing in some proposals that allowed, in the priorities of the tribes, protections of those flows, and flow augmentations, to be accomplished through other means but in ways that benefits not just the tribe but also the state as a sovereign that understands the salmon runs are important to the state, and not just to the tribe.

ERIC WILDMAN I think now, though, when we're getting into these other adjudications, the Coeur d'Alene, and if we do the Palouse and the Clark Fork, we're not reinventing the wheel, and we've fleshed out all of these issues. The same law that's applied in the SRBA is going to apply up there. We're using the same processes. We're not really going into uncharted territory like with the SRBA.

So I don't think the importance of which basins you're going to start with is as significant. We don't really need test basins in the other adjudications. The order that the rights are being reported out now are for other reasons than testing legal issues.

BRUCE NEWCOMB I think make sure that your Department of Water Resources is independent. Find somebody who is astute in the attorney general's office and groom them for the long term, and make sure they're dedicated to that from the beginning to the end, you know, and that they're insulated from political pressure.

And so I think that's really essential. You know, and this state isn't done. We're starting on north Idaho now. And there's a lot of different deals up there, not the least of which is the State of Washington, you know. And so we're not done yet. But as far as Snake River Basin, we're coming to the end.

DEAN STEVENSON The adjudication brought water issues to the forefront. What is a water right? What does my water right mean? I now understand that it is the state's water and I just have a right to use it. Some people still don't really understand that. But, before the adjudication people did not necessarily see the resource was finite. People did not really understand water measurement and what constitutes an actual water right. We all learned quantities.

Water adjudication is not concluded in Idaho. In some ways, it has only just begun.

The Swan Falls Framework recognized that the "key to effective management of the Snake River lies in a comprehensive determination of the nature, extent and priority of all of the outstanding claims to water rights." Although the adjudication has been a long and, at time, contentious process, the final unified decree provides the foundation for the state to complete the journey it embarked upon when it signed the Swan Falls Agreement – effective state management of the waters of the Snake River. The question remains: Does Idaho have the foresight and political will to control its own destiny by taking this next step?

Chronology

1976-85	**Swan Falls**
1974	Idaho Power files application with PUC for Pioneer Coal fired plant
1976	PUC denies IPC's application
	State Water Plan Approved by IWRB
1977	June 22, 1976 Memo from Tom Nelson to Jim Bruce
	Matthew Mullaney on behalf of a number of ratepayers and conservation interests
	file complaint with PUC against IPC for failure to protect water rights
	Idaho Power files Swan Falls I case
1978	Idaho Legislature seeks to amend state water plan
	Idaho Water Board sues legislation
	District Court rules in both Swan Falls cases
1979	___
1980	___
1981	___
1982	Idaho Supreme Court reverses District Court's Swan Falls decision
1983	Subordination battle in Idaho Legislature
	Idaho Power files 7,500 lawsuit
	Senate Bill 1180 approved
1984	Subordination battle in Idaho Legislature continues

	Martin Family Trust Lawsuit challenges 1180 Contract
	Swan Falls Framework signed in July
	Swan Falls Agreement signed on October 25th
	Technical Committee formed to develop hydrologic
and	economic studies
1985	Swan Falls Settlement approved by Legislature
	USFS opposes Swan Falls Agreement
1985-93	**Launching an adjudication**
1985	General Adjudication authorized
	Legislature directed negotiation of federal reserved water rights in response to request from Shoshone-Bannock Tribes (HCR 16)
	Negotiations began with Shoshone-Bannock Tribes
1986	Idaho Code 42-203B(2) rewritten as a result of IDWR proposed rules regarding trust water area
	Idaho adjudication statute rewritten to ensure McCarran Amendment jurisdiction (Ad hoc committee including Shoshone-Bannock attorney developed amendments)
	State agreed to delay adjudication in favor of negotiations
1987	Congress directs FERC to approve Swan Falls Agreement (December 29th)
	June 17th, Petition to commence adjudication filed with Fifth Judicial District Court and requires entire Snake River Basin be included
	Petition to commence adjudication granted on November 19th
1988	First round service of process begins
	Idaho Supreme Court affirms geographic scope of adjudication (115 Idaho 1)
	United States files a petition for writ of mandate precluding IDWR from collecting filing fees
1989	Cert denied in Boise-Kuna Irrig. District v. United States (geographic scope)

		September 1, 1989 Shoshone-Bannock term sheet agreed to by parties
		SRBA Court approves deferral of *de minimis* domestic and stockwater rights (42-1401A(5) and (12)).
	1990	1990 Fort Hall Indian Water Rights Agreement signed
	1991	Idaho Legislature ratifies 1990 Fort Hall Agreement
	1992	IDWR files three test basin director's reports
		Northside and Twin Falls Canal Companies file complaint seeking to stop IDWR from processing applications – led to conjunctive management studies in 1993
	1993	United States Supreme Court reverses filing fees decision (508 U.S. 1)
		United States files approximately 50,000 claims
1992-95		**Writing new rules**
	1992	Role of director becomes an issue in test basins
	1993	Negotiations begin with Nez Perce Tribe
	1994	SRBA District Court strikes down enlargement and expansion statutes (Basin-Wide Issue 1)
		Adjudication Statutes rewritten to change role of director
		New statutes enacted to address expansion and accomplished transfers
		Legislative Council reviews SRBA and issues report in 1995
		December 7, SRBA finds adjudication statute amendments unconstitutional
		December 14, Professor Colson testifies that SRBA district court is seriously flawed and that legislature has power to amend adjudication statute
		Musser v. Higginson, 125 Idaho 392 – held a writ of mandate could be issued directing Director to deliver water

1995 Idaho Supreme Court reverses SRBA district court upholding most of the adjudication amendments, 128 Idaho 748

1995-99 Basin wide (Idaho Supreme Court issues 14 decisions)

1995 Idaho Supreme Court held SRBA not required to consider public trust doctrine

Idaho Supreme Court denied declaratory judgment action challenging conjunctive management rules

1990 Fort Hall Agreement Approved by SRBA District Court

1996 Idaho Supreme Court finds that Fort Hall Water Users do not have standing to challenge 1990 Fort Hall Agreement

Idaho Supreme Court upholds enlargement and accomplished transfer statutes, Fremont Madison v. v. IGWA

1997 Idaho Supreme Court holds that excess flows are not a water right, A&B v. ICL

State v. Hagerman Water Right Owners – Idaho Supreme Court recognizes doctrine of partial forfeiture

Idaho v. Hagerman Water Right Owners – Idaho Supreme Court rejects private attorney general theory award of attorney fees (130 Idaho 718)

1998 Idaho Supreme Court holds that decree may include general provisions, Idaho v. ICL, 131 Idaho 329

Idaho Supreme Court holds that PWR 107 water rights for United States, United States v. Idaho, 131 Idaho 468

SRBA District court holds United States is entitled to federal reserved water right for Sawtooth National Recreation Area and Wild and Scenic River

SRBA District Court orders mediation of Nez Perce claims

1999 Idaho Supreme Court affirms district court that Multiple Use Sustained Yield Act did not create

	reserved water right, United States v. City of Challis, 133 Idaho 525
	SRBA District Court grants summary judgment dismissing Nez Perce Off Reservation claims
2000-07	**Picking up speed 11 Idaho Supreme Court Decisions**
2000	Wilderness and Hells Canyon reserved water right decision from Idaho Supreme Court
	Wild and Scenic Rivers Idaho Supreme Court decision, Potlach Corp. v. United States
	Idaho v. United States, no reserved water right for Sawtooth National Recreation Area
	SRBA District Court dismisses Organic Act Channel Maintenance Claims with Prejudice
	United States seeks disqualification of Judge Barry Wood
	Roger Burdick becomes SRBA Judge
2001	Deer Flat Wildlife Refuge claim denied by Idaho Supreme Court 135 Idaho 655
	SRBA orders mediation in HCNR and Wild and Scenic River subcases
	Mediation of surface groundwater conflict
2002	United States v. Idaho, Idaho Supreme Court denies motion to disqualify Judge Wood
2003	Idaho Supreme Court upholds constitutionality of SRBA notice procedures, LU Ranching v. United States
	Wild and Scenic Rivers Agreement
	Hells Canyon National Recreation Area Agreement
2004	Snake River Water Rights Agreement
	Hells Canyon National Recreation Area Agreement approved by SRBA Court
	Wild and Scenic Rivers Agreement Approved by SRBA Court
2006	Idaho Supreme Court held United States is legal owner and spaceholders are beneficial owners of storage rights, United States v. Pioneer

	Attorney General Wasden files change of ownership for mid Snake hydropower water rights in late December
	Order approving Shoshone Paiute Consent Decree
2007	Idaho Power files complaint against State of Idaho seeking declaratory and injunctive relief affirming title to hydropower water rights (Basin-Wide 13)
	AFRD #2 Decision
2007-14	**Toward the finish**
2008	SRBA District Court issues Memorandum Decision and Order finding State of Idaho holds hydropower water rights in trust
	Pristine Springs Purchase
2009	Framework Reaffirming Swan Falls Agreement approved by Idaho Legislature
2011	First of four orders closing basins to claims taking
	SRBA issues order granting partial summary judgment on incorporation of subordination provisions on trust water rights
	Blue Lakes Purchase
2012	Water District 02 formed
2013	Blackfoot Management and Equitable Adjustment Agreement
	Final Unified Decree approved (Basin-Wide 16)
	Final Order closing all basins to claims taking
2014	Murphy Monitor Plan recommended for approval
	Murphy Minimum flows approaching 3,900 cfs

Editor's note

This book was envisioned as a conversation around a large table, as many of the key participants in the generation-long Snake River Basin Adjudication held forth on what happened and why and what it all mean.

The idea was to collect many of the people centrally involved in the Snake River Basin Adjudication, and let them tell their story – and through the telling, illuminate how the adjudication came to be.

These people did just that. They did something even more remarkable: Spending many hours talking about the law and lawsuits, politics and legislative battles, water and farming and irrigation, and managed to emerge with a story that left nearly all feeling optimistic and accomplished.

This oral history would not have happened without their generous participation, and the cooperation in fact was remarkable (just one person we approached declined to join in). The result is an unusual collective insight into not just a massive legal case but an immense project that will have a powerful effect on the state of Idaho for many years to come.

We would like to thank all of the people involved, who also include the people who interviewed them, and who transcribed the interviews.

Specifically, we would also like to thank M&M Court Reporting, which reduced rates on transcripts; Lori A. Pulsifer, RDR, CRR (Owner) and QnA Court Reporting, LLC, which provided two free transcripts; Barker Rosholt, which donated of part of the transcript cost; Rigby, Thatcher, Andrus, Rigby, Kam & Moeller, Chartered, which donated part of transcript cost; Racine Olson Nye Budge & Bailey, which provided a $100 donation for transcripts; and

Associated Reporting and Video Inc., which reduced its trascription rate. Sandra Thiel at the Idaho Department of Water Resources developed two of the maps in this book specifically for this project, and on short notice. Thanks!

Ann Vonde, who works with Clive, contributed a great deal of help in editing and organizing the mass of material.

And so did Linda Watkins at Ridenbaugh Press.

Candice McHugh organized a lot of work and coordinated the extensive work of the Idaho State Bar's Water Law Section.

And especially: Clive Strong deserves a whole lot of the credit for putting this project together, bringing people and groups together and organizing the end result. It wouldn't have happened without his persistence and many, many hours of work on everything from basic planning to organizing quotes to catching typos.

Randy Stapilus
August 2014

Printed in Dunstable, United Kingdom

91223987R00170